• Nairobi

KENYA

MT. KILIMANJARO
— CHAC
sha Moshi

GANYIKA

Lushoto
USAMBARA
MOUNTAINS
• Korogwe

Tanga
PEMBA
ISLAND

ZANZIBAR

ZANZIBAR
ISLAND
Zanzibar Town

MSASANI BAY
Dar es Salaam

Bagamoyo

Morogoro

Pugu

Kilwa

INDIAN
OCEAN

Lindi

Nachingwea

Mtwara

MOZAMBIQUE

TANZANIA

N

MOROCCO   Algiers
ALGERIA

ATLANTIC
OCEAN

AFRICA

THIOPIA

SOMALIA

Kampala • Nairobi
CONGO
• Kinshasa
ZAMBIA

ANGOLA
Lusaka

S.W.
AFRICA

SOUTH
AFRICA

Cape Town

Dar es
Salaam
TANZANIA

MOZAMBIQUE
MALAWI

Salisbury
RHODESIA

INDIAN
OCEAN

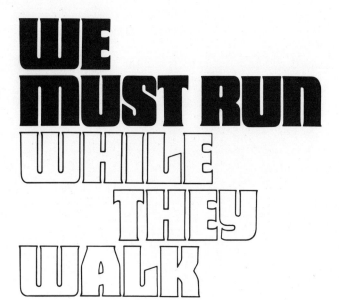

WE MUST RUN WHILE THEY WALK

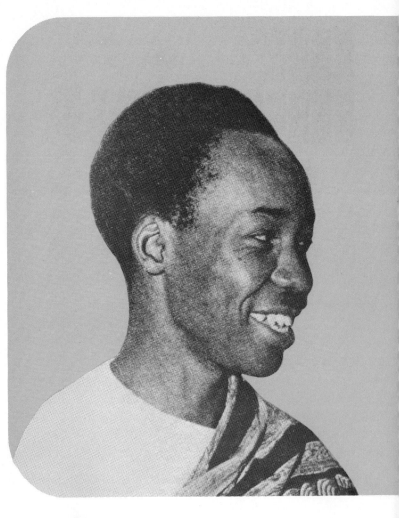

RANDOM HOUSE | *New York*

WE MUST RUN WHILE THEY WALK

A PORTRAIT OF AFRICA'S JULIUS NYERERE

William Edgett Smith

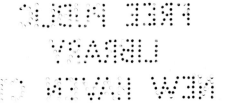

For my mother and father

ACKNOWLEDGMENTS

I SHOULD LIKE TO THANK President Nyerere for permission to quote from several of his essays and speeches that are included in his books *Freedom and Unity* and *Freedom and Socialism*, published by the Oxford University Press. More important to the writing of this book, however, were the many interviews that the President kindly granted me over a period of several years. He is in no sense responsible for the book's conclusions; yet it could not have been written without his unfailing courtesy and patience. I should also like to thank all the other persons, some named and some unnamed, who helped so much.

W. E. S.

New York, June 1971

WE MUST RUN WHILE THEY WALK

JULIUS NYERERE is forever reminding his countrymen that they cannot go to the moon. "Our tools are as old as Mohammed, we live in houses from the time of Moses," he may cry, as he once did to a group of Chagga tribesmen, who grow coffee on the slopes of Mount Kilimanjaro. "The Americans are going to the moon! The Russians are going to the moon! *We* can't go to the moon!" Or he may lament gently, "While the Americans and the Russians are going to the moon, we Africans are dancing," or shout angrily, "Our friends are using their brains while ours sleep and grow fungus, they are sending rockets into outer space while we are eating wild roots!" One might have supposed that the thirteen million citizens of the United Republic of Tanzania scarcely needed to be reminded of these facts, but Nyerere, who is known to his countrymen as *Mwalimu,* the teacher, carps on them relentlessly nonetheless. "I should have been a preacher in a pulpit instead of the President of a republic," he once remarked to a friend, and indeed his talks upcountry, where he travels as much as half the time, are less like political speeches than stern lectures or even haranguing sermons: he never seems to tell his listeners exactly what they want to hear. "Look," he once shouted, in his staccato Swahili, to the peasant farmers of a new tobacco settlement, "in the United States they get twenty-four hundred pounds of tobacco to the acre. And here you get six hundred. But over in Urambo, not

3

many miles from here, they are already getting fifteen hundred pounds to the acre. This is something we can do! It's not like going to the moon. We can't go to the moon! But *this we can do . . .*"

Nyerere has been preoccupied with such comparisons since long before his country became independent in 1961. At that time it was known as Tanganyika, the name it had borne for forty-one years as a British mandate and later trusteeship territory. In April 1964 Tanganyika formed a union with the tiny offshore island republic of Zanzibar, and the new nation became known a few months later as the United Republic of Tanzania. Thereafter the term Tanganyika referred to the mainland portion of the United Republic.

"The problem was overwhelming," Nyerere remarked one day in early 1964, a short time after an army mutiny had nearly destroyed his government, "and I still see it. You do not just say 'independence.' It must mean many other things. And it is not good if the people become over-interested. The problem becomes *formidable* if they see it too quickly. Do you see? It's 1964 for everybody in the world, *including* the Masai," those tall, lean, spear-carrying warriors of the East African plains, "and the pressure for all to live in 1964, including the Masai, is fantastic. People tell me, 'The Masai are completely happy.' I tell them, 'It's not a question of whether they are happy. That's a philosophical question. I'm not trying to make them *happy*!' But"—chopping his words hard—"there is a difference between clean water and dirty water. My problem is to get that woman clean water. My problem is to get her a healthy child. Happy! I'm not involving

4

myself in that." He gave a sort of ironic shudder. "I don't know if my own family right here in State House is any happier than the Masai. The question-is, What kind of water are the Masai drinking in 1964?"

He was sitting on the veranda of State House in Dar es Salaam looking down across a yellow-green lawn toward the glistening turquoise Indian Ocean, a slight, wiry man with a high forehead and a toothbrush mustache. In those years he still looked far more like an earnest graduate student than a *baba wa taifa*, the father of a nation. He wore khaki slacks, a bright sport shirt and leather sandals. "In the twelfth century," he continued, "this problem perhaps would not have been formidable. But today the standard of living in the United States of America is part of Tanganyika. Sometimes I wish I could put Tanganyika on another planet. Then we could give it a hundred years to catch up. But we can't do that, we can't isolate ourselves. The Masai *know* that these things are possible— milk for children, clean water, good houses: these things are objective, desirable, necessary. But the Masai don't easily accept the disciplines required. Clean water requires piping. That pond must be drained. Work! But it requires knowledge, technical know-how. Germany was virtually razed, and Japan, but they had the necessary attitudes and skills for reconstruction. So I have to build these attitudes. But I can't wait. I can't wait to train Masai vets and doctors. So I have to borrow skills. But borrowing is difficult because"—very slowly again— "certain attitudes of resistance have been created. That same fellow who wants clean water piped to his village would say, 'Hey! Why are you getting an Englishman to

5

do it?' And if I tell him, 'Because there isn't a Masai engineer,' he will ask"—mock astonishment—" 'Why not?' " At which Nyerere burst out laughing, apparently as much at the stubbornness of the Masai as at the ridiculousness of the situation. "You see?"

ONE COOL APRIL MORNING in 1966, in the season that passes for autumn in Dar es Salaam, Nyerere set off for a four-day tour of one of mainland Tanzania's seventeen regions, Tabora, which lies deep in the interior along the ancient trade and slave route that once ran from Bagamoyo, on the coast opposite Zanzibar Island, to Lake Victoria and Lake Tanganyika. His grey Mercedes-Benz sedan arrived at the airport at seven-forty-five, preceded by a single police car with flashing blue light, and Nyerere, waving his ebony hand stick, jumped out and began to shake hands and trade quips with the handful of government officials who had come to see him off. His hair had turned quite grey in the preceding two or three years. He was wearing a collarless, coat-style shirt and matching trousers of a Japanese drip-dry fabric. Such uniforms had come to be known as "Tanzanian suits," since practically every man of influence in Dar es Salaam had followed the President's lead and begun to wear them. Many Europeans and Americans in East Africa, already uneasy about Nyerere's growing friendship with China, had seized on the introduction of the uniforms as yet another indication that Nyerere was "going Chinese." The Tanzanians, exceedingly sensitive to such talk, were going to great pains to point out that Nyerere had first seen such a suit on Zanzibar and admired it for its simplicity, and that Chinese Premier Chou En-lai

6

himself, during his state visit to Tanzania, had remarked that the suit was not heavy enough for the Chinese climate.

Nyerere also wore an Arab cap from Zanzibar, a *kofia*, and it was this novelty that caught his colleagues' fancy. "Ah, you like it?" he said to the chief justice. "Perhaps you would like one? No?" Then he climbed into the government's twin-engine Aero Commander, taking the seat beside his British pilot. He was followed by his Minister of State, Bhoke Munanka, his aide-de-camp and two young security men. A moment later the little plane took off and immediately disappeared into lush green bush country, thereby revealing a fact generally obscured by the pleasures and intrigues of life in the capital: that the wilderness of Tanganyika begins at the far end of the Dar es Salaam runway.

THE FIRST DAY. Amid signs of KARIBU BABA WA TAIFA (Welcome, Father of the Nation), Nyerere was spirited off to Tabora's new community hall for a lunch of chicken, Indian pasties, tea and cakes. Then, in the hot midday sun, he handed out one hundred and eight literacy certificates to adults who had learned to read and write during the preceding year. One young mother, who set her baby at the President's feet as she accepted her certificate and bowed, was so flustered that she forgot the infant until after she had returned to her seat. Later, on the veranda of the regional commissioner's house, Nyerere chatted with the local elders of the Tanganyika African National Union (TANU), the political party of mainland Tanzania. "Why do you wear that?" one elder chided him. "It's a Zanzibar cap." "No," said Nyerere, "it's a Tanzanian cap," and they all laughed, because the concept of Tanzanian union

7

still seemed unreal. Hashim Mbita, the President's young press secretary, said the cap was an expensive one, worth 80 shillings at least. "You seem to know a lot about them," Nyerere said. "Have you been making them on the side?" For a while they argued about the merits of the bride-price tradition, which involves the payment of cows or other wealth by the prospective bridegroom to the father of the bride. One elder defended the practice and added slyly, "Besides, I have four daughters." "But *I*, brother," Nyerere shot back, "have two daughters and five sons, so I must pay." The talk turned to a recent rash of cattle thefts, and Bhoke Munanka, a huge, good-natured man who serves sometimes as the butt of the President's jokes, spoke at length of the various methods of marking cattle illegally. "He is an expert," Nyerere said. A moment later, in great good spirits, he told in Swahili a long story about his childhood—"about the hairs of a goat's head," Hashim whispered—and, whatever he said, it caused the men to howl with laughter.

In the afternoon, the party drove forty-eight miles south to the Moravian leprosarium at Sikonge, where Nyerere dedicated a new clinic. The patients gave him a drum, and he responded by buying a second one. On the dusty road back to Tabora, Hashim, who had spent his childhood in a nearby village, spoke of how the rural life was changing. "We used to think the European was selfish because he looked out only for himself," he said. "We would say scornfully, 'He behaves like a European.' If a man had three or four hundred goats, he would slaughter one at the weekend, and everybody would be welcome. It was a terrible insult to have someone leave your house hungry. But now the people are so dependent on the cash economy, they buy for themselves only. If a guest arrives after a meal is over, there is nothing left for him."

THE SECOND DAY.   North of Tabora on the Mwanza road, thirty women waved as Nyerere drove past. "This is Kazima," Hashim said. "We will stop here on the return. *Mwalimu* always stops here." At Isikizya, Nyerere urged the tobacco farmers to increase their yields per acre, inspected a new baling station, and called for his Polaroid camera so he could take a picture of four women carrying water jugs. "This is a first-class picture," he said. "Not bad for an amateur, eh?" The women were too shy to reply. At Nzega, he cut a red ribbon to open a new cattle dip, but the cattle were frightened and refused to pass through it. "Too many people," Nyerere said. "Give them way." At the Maria Nyerere Maternity Clinic, named in honor of his wife, Nyerere was presented with a trayful of gifts, and the party sat down to tea. Here, as at Tabora, a gigantic woman, the local chairman of the national women's organization, stood before his table, urging him to eat more chicken and cornbread, and waving her handkerchief as a fan. She pointed through the window at an old mud hut, and Nyerere smiled. "She is explaining," he told a visitor, "why she seated me here. She wanted me to see the old clinic we inherited from the Empire. Also, she says she can now read and write her name. In colonial times she knew nothing, she says, she had to use her thumb print for her name." The new clinic had been built under the national self-help program, Nyerere said, under which villagers donated a day's work a week to a community task; the clinic had cost $8,600 for materials, but was said to be worth at least twice as much. "One of the troubles we had with self-help in the beginning was that, when a building like this was finished,

9

there might be no one to run it. But under our five-year plan, a midwife will be provided."

At Bukene, Nyerere thanked the people for their work but warned them, "There is a Swahili saying, 'A brewer whose brew is praised is likely to dilute it.' Don't do that. If you do that, you will bring shame to us." Then he made his main point: "Nzega district has a higher cattle population than any other district in the country. Cattle is our wealth, and you must use your wealth. Every year you must sell some cattle to get money for your children's schooling, and for better houses. Look at the Chagga. The Chagga have gotten rich on their coffee. You must use your cattle to make you rich too."

In late afternoon, as Hashim had predicted, Nyerere stopped to see the women of Kazima. Mostly widows, with a few children and grandchildren, they had moved to this open land a few years earlier from Tabora, six miles away, after Nyerere had urged people to leave the towns and go out and cultivate the soil. The women served boiled peanuts and corn to the President, and then they told him their troubles. Their rice had dried up for lack of rain, they said, but they had earned 300 shillings on their tomatoes. "If you had grown three times as many, you'd have made nine hundred shillings," Nyerere said, and one woman replied, "It is true, *Babu*, it was our folly." She complained bitterly about the red tape involved in getting water from the nearby dam; vouchers were now required, she said. Nyerere wheeled around to the area commissioner, the official in charge of that part of Tabora region, who replied, a bit defensively, "It is to prevent unauthorized people from spoiling the water." Nyerere told the women not to worry; he had a plan for piping water from the dam to the village, and he would tell them about it soon. As he prepared to leave, the women sang for him: *"Nyerere has called the people to go to the country, he wants to see those who took hold of the soil,"* followed by a local tribal song, which Hashim translated: *"The child of the lion is a lion/ You have finished the night / Now put on the fire and cook."*

THE THIRD DAY. "Look at me," Nyerere said to a group of children. "If you weren't so shy, this picture would be beautiful." Instead it was fuzzy. "Ah," said Nyerere, in mock dismay, "the camera let me down." Then he tried a picture of a young farmer, his wife and suckling baby, but the Polaroid was out of film. The aide-de-camp ran for more. "I'm trying my best for the 1970 elections, you are my witnesses," Nyerere said. When a farmer boasted that he had made 82,000 shillings—almost $12,000—on his tobacco the previous year, Nyerere expressed surprise. "That's twenty thousand shillings more than *my* salary," he said. "I should move to Urambo. I'd save my hair from turning grey."

To a foreign visitor he shouted, "Look at this hoe, this *jembe*." He was pointing to a single-stroke hoe with a three-foot handle, the basic farming tool in Tanzania. "You see? No matter how hard a man works, even if he works twenty-four hours a day, he cannot achieve very much." Later, at the Urambo Farmer Training Center, he discussed the oxen plough as an alternative to the *jembe*. "I'm sure the oxen plough is the answer," he told the British principal. "I'm a very big oxen-plough man."

When Nyerere asked a farmer how much tobacco he had grown the year before, the man shrugged and said he didn't know. "Aha," said Nyerere jubilantly, "maybe you don't want to say, for fear we will assess the personal tax."

11

The man laughed timidly. As Nyerere toured a small tobacco field recently planted by the local TANU youth
league chapter, the Tabora Member of Parliament, an Indian, criticized the youth league's effort as uneconomic.
"What do you mean?" demanded Nyerere. "We're getting
into the third year of our five-year plan, and Tabora hasn't
planned *any*thing yet, but you criticize those who have
started something. Why is that?"

On the regional commissioner's veranda that evening,
Nyerere listened on his portable radio to the British Broad-
casting Corporation's short-wave news broadcast, followed
by a panel discussion on the political situation in Rhodesia.
When one panel member suggested that African members
of the Commonwealth might "secede" if Britain did not
adopt a more active policy, Nyerere burst out laughing.
"Secede!" he said. "They think we are still part of the
Empire."

THE FOURTH DAY.   For two hours Nyerere presided over
a Tabora town meeting. The questions, all of which dealt
with local problems, were delivered with surprising gusto
and at considerable length. Nyerere answered each question
slowly, reasoning as he talked, but his voice changed constantly; one moment it was shrill and animated, then
whispering, then fast and imploring, then sputtering with
laughter.

Exactly who, he was asked, should be required to pay
the business tax to the local council? Nyerere gave some
examples. "A woman who makes *vitumbua*"—rice fritters
—"and sells them in her home so she can buy soap and
matches, she should not be required to pay the tax. A man
who sells cigarettes or textiles in his truck, that's different.

12

He should pay the tax, I would say, not because his business is mobile, but because it renders a profit."

What about people who sold milk and coffee? Should they be licensed? "Milk can be dangerous if it is not treated hygienically," Nyerere said. "Therefore those who sell it should be known, and it is easier to know them if they have licenses. As for coffee, I think your council should include it in the same category as work done by womenfolk at home. There is not much profit in it unless it is sold on a very large scale." An argument broke out over whether milk merchants should be taxed if they sold only from their own homes. "I recommend that they be licensed," Nyerere said. "But it is up to the council."

"The council prays," said a TANU elder in a flowing white *kanzu*, "that industries be established in Tabora, such as a shoe factory, a leather factory and a tobacco factory." Nyerere referred the first two examples to the M.P.s from Tabora, and dwelt at length on the third. "I once asked a leader of the tobacco industry why a tobacco factory was not going to be built at Tabora or at Iringa, where tobacco is grown in abundance, and why Morogoro was selected as the site of a factory instead. I wanted him to convince me. The answer I got was this. At present, tobacco is grown mainly in two areas, Tabora and Iringa. Iringa has a small factory already, but it is not large enough to take in all the tobacco grown in Tanzania. We could expand it. But the problem is transport. Tobacco from Tabora to Iringa must be loaded and unloaded twice before it would reach Iringa. You see? If Tabora were to have the factory, it would be the same. So Morogoro was selected. The tobacco from both Tabora and Iringa can

13

go straight to Morogoro without being unloaded. Secondly, there is the problem of moisture. There is more moisture at Tabora than at Iringa or Morogoro. So Tabora was dropped.

"And thirdly, there should be a focal point where all our tobacco would be auctioned. For example, in Salisbury there is a place where all Rhodesian tobacco is auctioned, and buyers from all over the world go there and buy the tobacco. Morogoro will be a suitable place for our tobacco auction. Buyers will be able to go to Morogoro to buy our tobacco and then return to Dar es Salaam the same day. I do not think they would like to go from place to place in our country just to buy small amounts of tobacco. In the future, when the crop is larger, we will surely have a factory at Tabora. But meanwhile, the factory at Morogoro will be built, and we will expand it four times until it can take forty million pounds of tobacco a year."

By the time the meeting was over, it was very hot. "This is what I am trying to do," Nyerere explained to a foreign visitor. "The other day, at Urambo, you saw the old style, where I would talk for an hour or two. This way is much better. It gives me a chance to hear *them*.

"Tabora is a second home to me," he continued. "I spent six years here as a schoolboy, and three as a teacher. But Tabora is a problem. We are on the old slave route here, you know. The people are the sons of slave sellers. They like to argue too much."

ONE EVENING THAT WEEK, Nyerere stood on the regional commissioner's veranda chatting with townspeople who had come to see him, including a young man and woman whom he greeted warmly, and an old woman who seemed to be

14

very worried. As the visitors and the TANU elders began to drift away, Nyerere sat down and switched to English.

The man and woman, he said, he had known in Tabora fifteen years before. "I used to teach them English in the evenings. Once, during Ramadan, they all stayed home. I was very angry. I said—I shouldn't have gotten so angry —I said, 'If you don't come, all right, I have other things to do.' " He laughed. And the old woman? "This was her problem. She is a poor woman, I don't know how old—sixty, at least. But her mother is still alive. Her problem is to support her mother and herself. She was very keen to get hold of me. I told her yesterday morning, 'Come to the regional commissioner's house in the evening.' But she was afraid she might get lost in the confusion. So she went with us to Sikonge and back, and today to Nzega and back. Well, at Bukene, her town, we forgot to deal with the problem while we were there, so I didn't have a chance to tell her what we have done. I asked the area commissioner if he could find her a job that would cover her needs, and he said yes, it was possible."

He was asked if he would repeat in English the story he had told the elders about the goat's hair. "Ah, that," he said, with a despairing laugh. "I don't think that story can be told in English. But, very well, I will try.

"When I was about ten, my father sent me one day to accompany his first wife—one of my stepmothers—to another village, eight or ten miles away, where one of her relatives had died. As we were about to leave this village, to return home, she was given a goat by her relatives. Well, since I was a boy, it was my function to lead the goat by a rope. But the goat refused to budge. And as I was struggling with it, one of her relatives said, 'Don't worry, I'll make

15

it easy for you.' Well! He took some hairs from my head and some hairs from the goat's head, and mixed them with some roots, and chewed them together, and fed them to the goat. He said, 'The goat will follow you now,' and the goat followed me, all the way home." He laughed with glee. "Yes, very tame. It followed me like a dog."

He was asked if he felt it was difficult for an African leader to bridge the gap between tribal life and the modern world. "I don't believe it is as hard as one might think," he said. "I was twelve when I went away to school. In tribal society, a boy gets to be practically an undergraduate by the age of twelve. Yes! You know a lot of life at twelve. You know as much as there is to know of open society. You're kept apart from the elders' secrets, of course. But you know a lot. When I go home now, my people are always surprised at how much I know of tribal life.

"In a sense, if you have become satisfied with one form of life, the question is, How do you make the jump? Almost by what the Christian calls revelation. If you have lived one life and have matured in that life, it is very difficult to make such a leap from Hinduism to Christianity—even, I think, from Protestantism to Catholicism. My confirmation in tribal life was never wiped out. As a boy of twelve, I already had beliefs I had accepted. I had to be convinced before I could accept a different kind of faith, a faith in a defined God.

"The Christian rejects tribal ideas. Yet he has less reason to do so than many others, because he too believes in things that cannot be explained scientifically. All I know is, the goat followed. The maximum I can say is: I don't know.

16

"The tribe of this man"—he pointed to Hashim Mbita—"had a vaccination against snakebite for ages past. You could *see* the Nyamwezi be bitten, and not fall down. If anybody had said to me, 'Other tribes fall down from snakebite, but not the Nyamwezi,' I would have said, 'Rubbish!' But that would have been based on ignorance. In any case, I'm tolerant of the beliefs of my own people, and of science, too."

By that time it was dark, and all but two or three of the elders had gone. Nyerere was asked if he would describe his impressions of China, which he had visited the previous year.

"Well," he said, "I wish the Cold War were not a complicating factor here. I wish we could just speak simple facts. If you take me to see General Motors, I will marvel. If you take me to London, I will say, 'How wonderful.' Last year I visited Holland, a small country but a very advanced country, and"—his voice high in wonder—"they are spending hundreds of millions of pounds to *push back the sea!* Well! All I can say is: 'Wonderful!' But it is irrelevant to what we can do in Tanzania. The assembly plants in America and Europe are irrelevant. Oh, the time will come—but not yet.

"That water, that little dam you saw today. That cost fifteen hundred pounds. That we can do. And if we could make dams like that everywhere, and give everybody water, it would be a revolution.

"China is different. China is a backward country trying to pull itself up. But it is two steps ahead of us. No— three steps in some places, two in others, *one* in others. You can see the steps, and you say, 'Boy! Why didn't we think

17

of that? We should do that!' I should send many people to see these things. But it has nothing to do with the Cold War. It is a question of what we are capable of.

"I've been telling my own people, 'We've got to change, we must mechanize, we must have better tools.' But what are better tools? Not the combine harvester. If I were given enough combine harvesters for every family in Tanzania, what would I do with them? No mechanics, no spare parts . . ." A shudder at the thought. "It would be a very serious problem—unless, of course, I sell them for hard cash. But we still have to give the people better tools, tools they can handle, and can pay for. Americans, when they speak of better tools, are talking about something quite different. We are using hoes. If two million farmers in Tanzania could jump from the hoe to the oxen plough, it would be a revolution. It would double our living standard, triple our product! This is the kind of thing China is doing. An ancient people, dealing with the difficulties of feeding seven hundred million people. The *stage* of their development is relevant to us. I wish I could state this as true, observed fact, and nothing more. But when I say, 'From China we can learn,' they say we are going Red."

He remained silent for a moment. "But also," he said slowly, "there is a problem of attitude. I don't know quite how to put this. There is a difference between Eastern and Western countries, and between poor and rich countries. Let me try to illustrate this. We have a medical school in Dar es Salaam. The other day the students went on strike. They wanted better conditions. Some are doing medical studies, and others are in the health-inspection course. They all wanted better conditions. And, in addition, the medical students didn't want to eat together with the health-inspec-

18

tion students. Yes! I said—I was joking, of course—'What is this, Alabama in Dar es Salaam? They want separate facilities!'

"Well, all but two students went on strike. Of those two, we discovered, one had returned from studying in Russia, and the other from East Germany. Now, I suspect —I may be wrong—but I suspect they didn't go on strike for two reasons. In the first place, they may have compared the facilities we were offering with those in East Germany and Russia, and decided ours didn't compare too badly. But it was also, I suspect, a difference in attitude. The West"—he broke off and remained silent for a moment— "is just too individualistic. All the textbooks of Western countries talk about rights, rights, rights, and no duties. The Charter of the United Nations is a charter of rights. Very good. This is very good. You couldn't state it better. Schools, churches talk about rights all the time. And duty is usually defined as 'obey the law.' The minimum! And a large number of crooks *do* obey the law.

"In the Eastern countries, there has been a reaction to this. A reaction, I think, that works like a pendulum; to strike a balance, you must swing each way. When human society has exaggerated something very much, I think the opposite must be established before a balance can be reached. And the Eastern countries have something Africa needs: a stress on duty. The West looks at this as privation of freedom. They would say, 'Duty! They regiment the people.' Yet I feel that for our type of world, where it is so easy for a man to make himself comfortable at the expense of the many—especially those in power and those with an education—we must look at the other side of the coin. One of the biggest dangers now is corruption at the

19

top. This is the *silent* scramble for Africa. Make yourself rich as quickly as possible! And if that is questioned, you are questioning the people's freedom.

"One thing I have in common with the West is Christianity. I am Christian. I think it curious that we should learn these things from the East. Christianity is a revolutionary creed, but something went wrong somewhere. Africa, I know, I know, if we don't learn anything else from the East, we must learn to despise private property a little. But the big scramble for personal wealth in Africa is not going to help. There is not enough wealth on this continent. It will all be at the top, and the people will be left with nothing."

"Those who receive this privilege of education have a duty to return the sacrifice which others have made. They are like the man who has been given all the food available in a starving village in order that he might have the strength to bring supplies back from a distant place. If he takes this food and does not bring help to his brothers, he is a traitor."

"YOU HAVE TAKEN ME to that big German house and I have had a good sleep there," Nyerere told a crowd in December 1962, soon after he was sworn in as President of Tanganyika. "I eat well so I may forget about doing work. But it is your job to come to me and urge me to work with you. Don't complain. Just come and remind me to work."

State House is not, strictly speaking, an old German house. The Government House of German colonial times had been destroyed by Royal Naval gunfire in 1914. The present structure, a pleasant ramble of whitewashed Moorish walls and corridors surrounded by palms, frangipanis and bougainvillaea, was built by the British after World War I. It served as the official residence of the British governors during the forty-one years of mandate and trusteeship. Nyerere never liked the place, and referred to it privately as "my prison." "He never wanted to live there, never," his brother Joseph has said. "People would say,

'There's the big Government House, where we've always seen the governor. Now we want to see our own man there.' He would say, 'So what? I don't actually have to live there.' " But he endured it for three and a half years. It has remained his office and official residence, but since 1966 he has lived elsewhere.

A visitor to State House is often surprised to find it so peaceful. A Thomson's gazelle and a peacock wander aimlessly on the lawn. A dhow, arriving on the monsoon from the Arabian peninsula, can be seen gliding along the horizon toward the narrow mouth of Dar es Salaam harbor. A servant, in a white suit, walks noiselessly down an open corridor carrying two mangoes.

In Nyerere's second-floor office, the same stillness prevails. A ringing telephone rarely interrupts him during appointments; his closest colleagues, including Second Vice-President Rashidi Kawawa—who is known in State House shorthand as "the V.P. Two"—are more likely to drop by to see him. The First Vice-President, Sheikh Abeid Karume, lives on Zanzibar but sometimes flies over to Dar es Salaam for weekly Cabinet meetings. In former times, Nyerere maintained private telephone lines to the offices of the other East African Presidents, Jomo Kenyatta of Kenya and Milton Obote of Uganda (who was overthrown in an army coup in January 1971), but these were canceled a few years ago to save money. At the time of the Rhodesian unilateral declaration of independence, in November 1965, Nyerere often conferred by telephone with his friend Kenneth Kaunda, the President of Zambia; but the only connection available at that time—a reminder of Africa's vulnerability—ran from Dar es Salaam to Lusaka, the Zambian capital, by way of London and Salisbury, the capital of Rhodesia. A direct line was later installed. Even today, if Nyerere should wish to telephone another neighbor, the President of Burundi, his call would pass through London and Brussels.

"HE JOKES ABOUT EVERYTHING," Joseph Namata, who served as Nyerere's principal secretary for three years, once said. "He never shouted at me, but he can shout if he is angry. He may say, 'Why did you *do* this? You can't do such a thing!' Once, a regional commissioner locked up a European for a fortnight, and we didn't know about it until we received a complaint from an ambassador. The President called the regional commissioner to Dar es Salaam —yes, a great distance, more than four hundred miles— and ordered the European released immediately. The regional commissioner is no longer a regional commissioner. But that happened months later—so you could not connect the incident with him."

During his mornings at State House, Nyerere reads a stack of reports and memorandums, which he initials "J. K.," for Julius Kambarage, his first and middle names. Most of his staff members address him as "*Mzee*" (literally, "old man"), although a few say "*Mwalimu.*" Soon after independence, Nyerere declared that he didn't wish to be called "Dr. Nyerere" or "Your Excellency," and he periodically reissues directives reminding his countrymen that his official title, to be used only in "very formal references," is "The President of the United Republic of Tanzania, *Mwalimu* Julius K. Nyerere," and that his wife should never be referred to as "Lady," or any of her assistants as a "lady-in-waiting." "A worshiping secretary had begun to refer to Maria as 'Lady Nyerere,' " a family friend has

23

said. "Well, he wasn't having any of that. He said, 'She *is* the First Lady. But she is Mrs. Nyerere.' "

One of his most famous sermons (later published in his book *Freedom and Unity*) was a blistering letter to his colleagues asking their help in "stamping out the disease of pomposity." "The growing tendency to confuse dignity with sheer pomposity must be checked," he wrote in 1963, "or it will destroy the dignity of the Republic . . . Nothing could be more disrespectful to our National Anthem than to treat it as a popular song hit, to be plugged the moment any member of the government appears on the scene. Yet we sing it on the most unsuitable and unlikely occasions, and if some unfortunate passerby does not happen to notice us, we take offense and start shouting about 'insults to the Republic' . . . It is not customary in other countries to play their National Anthem without warning just because some government official happens to have landed at an airstrip on a visit to his mother-in-law . . . It is the same with police escorts. Hitherto, whenever I have questioned the value of all this very undemocratic pomposity, I have been assured that the people like it. But this is highly doubtful. Do they really love being shouted at to get off the road because the President or a minister or a regional commissioner is taking an afternoon drive? We should stop deceiving ourselves. This sort of pomposity has nothing to do with the people, for it is the very reverse of democratic. We must stop it!"

NYERERE'S FRIENDS believe his instinctive dislike of living in State House was reinforced by the army mutiny of January 1964, during which the President was forced to flee from the official residence and go into hiding. In any case,

two years later he built a seafront home at Msasani Bay,
a few miles north of Dar es Salaam. For security reasons,
the area around the house was cleared of trees, and a fence
and guardhouse were built; and for a while it appeared that
Nyerere might change his mind and never move in. "We
insisted he should have guards at Msasani," Joseph Namata
has recalled. "The barbed wire and the lights, we put those
in. Well! He refused the house! He said, 'This is my private
house, I'm not afraid, why don't you leave me at peace in
the house?' And at first he refused to occupy it. Finally
he changed his mind because his wife persuaded him, not
because we in government prevailed upon him. All the furni-
ture in it is his own. I had bought a radiogram [a radio and
record player] from public funds, as I would do for State
House, to entertain our visitors. He refused to take it, so
I sent it back to the shop. He wanted this house to be pure."

In the same manner, Nyerere has tried to protect the
privacy of his family life. His wife Maria is a shy, handsome woman who has borne seven children and has stoically
endured her husband's public career. "I know, I know, he
doesn't belong to me," she has occasionally complained to
friends, "he belongs to Tanzania." She rejoiced in the move
to Msasani Bay and soon was saying, "We are living a
family life again." Her friends regard her as a woman of
strong will, a devout Catholic who, when Julius returned
from three years of study at Edinburgh, delayed their
long-planned wedding until she was certain that he had not
changed. They also recall that it was she who persuaded her
husband to flee from State House on the morning of the
mutiny, just as she later convinced him that they should
move to Msasani, even if the house were not to be as private
a refuge as he would have liked.

"He doesn't want to dictate to anybody, not even to his wife and children," a family friend has observed, "but he has a certain way. Well, the other night, for instance, his wife—she's a cinema fan—took the children to a film, Elvis Presley or Cliff Richard or somebody. Julius said afterward, 'You know, one time years ago when I was in the States, a radio interviewer said to me, "Mr. Nyerere, do you like rock and roll?" I said, "Well . . . it's not exactly like African rhythms, I suppose I enjoy it, I don't know how to do it myself." Then he asked, "How about Elvis Presley?" So I replied, "What *about* Elvis Presley? What *is* Elvis Presley?" Well! That was the end of the interview. And the interviewer said to me afterward, "You know, by that reply of yours, you have made many friends and many enemies." '

"Well," the family friend continued, "he recited this in front of his wife, as a cue to her. Then he said to her, 'If Elvis Presley comes here, he can stay over *there*'—he shuddered, like this—'I don't want him too close. I don't think I'd have too much to say to him.' "

In october 1966, a few months after Nyerere's trip to Tabora, a group of four hundred students, most of them from the Dar es Salaam University College, marched to State House. They were protesting against a new law which required that they spend two years in the National Service, and be paid roughly 40 percent of what they would earn as university graduates in civilian life. They were especially angry at Vice-President Rashidi Kawawa, the minister in charge of the National Service program, and carried signs bearing such messages as To Hell With Kawawa and

His SCHEME and—the ultimate insult—LIFE DURING CO-
LONIAL DAYS WAS BETTER.

At the steps of State House, they were met by Nyerere,
Kawawa and most members of the Cabinet, and their spokesman proceeded to deliver their "ultimatum" in a high-
pitched twang. The government, he declared, was trying to
throw "the burden of financing this extensive scheme on the
shoulders of young and helpless students," and he offered a
compromise: "Either we be paid our full rights of earning,
or else all those in the high-income brackets should also be
in that category which could be interpreted as a form of
sacrifice rather than a form of exploitation." In other
words, if university graduates were expected to spend two
years in the National Service at 40 percent of their civilian pay, government officials should make sacrifices too.
"Therefore, Your Excellency, unless the terms of reference
and the attitude of our leaders toward students change, we
shall not accept National Service in spirit. Let our bodies
go, but our souls will remain outside the scheme"—wild applause—"and the battle between the political elite and the
educated elite will perpetually continue. Thank you."

Nyerere began to speak in a calm, almost perfunctory
manner. "I did, I have understood your protest. It is not
really addressed to the Second Vice-President, it is addressed to the government, we have got your message. I
understand it, I want to see if I can explain a little, I want
to be absolutely clear that what we have said to your leaders
has got to you.

"This matter did not start yesterday. It is the intention of the government that National Service should not
merely be for ex-primary [school graduates] or for unem-

27

ployeds; it is *national* service. It should include secondary [school graduates], and university graduates, and all others. We asked, 'At what point in the life of a youth, at what particular point, do we ask him to enter National Service? Do we take him before he finishes his education, or after?'

"So we decided *no*"—his voice was cracking a bit now —"you don't cut his education, you don't interfere with it, you wait until he has completed his education. We made that decision. I think it was an extremely considerate decision on the part of government. Very considerate. Very considerate. But it had some definite implications. If you wait until a student has finished his education, his training as a teacher, then he has certain expectations. If he is trained to be a teacher, his salary will be—what is it? Seven hundred and sixteen pounds a year? Ah, seven hundred and sixteen plus seventy-six. This is his salary, seven hundred and ninety-two pounds. This teacher, he has in mind: 'At the end of my education, I get seven hundred and ninety-two pounds.' This is his expectation. So. If you wait until he completes his training as a teacher, you have allowed him to think, 'Seven hundred and ninety-two pounds is my right.' As your spokesman said, 'my full right.' " He rolled the *r*. "My full rrrright.

"We made other mistakes. We said, 'Treat them differently. Count as National Service the work they do as teachers or doctors or engineers. A student has been trained as a teacher; very well, let him go into the classroom. If he is a doctor, let him go to the ward, let him go to Muhimbili hospital, count that as National Service.'

"Obviously, if we had taken you people and said, 'OK,

don't let them finish their education yet, let them complete their National Service first,' then you would not be talking to us, or to the Vice-President, asking him to resign. You would not be talking about forty percent. Forty percent of what? You would have no salaries. I mean, really the easiest way to get out of this damned forty-percent rubbish is to ask you people to do National Service before you go to university. That's all.

"Now, I explained this forty-percent business ages ago. Since then we have changed it. We've changed the damned thing. We have said, 'We guarantee a minimum wage—the government minimum wage in Dar es Salaam; no National Service person will be getting less than one hundred and eight pounds a year.' In terms of the teacher, you knock off one hundred and eight pounds from the seven hundred and ninety-two pounds, and then take forty percent of the rest, and you add that together, and I am told this comes to three hundred and eighty-one pounds. Did you also say, Mr. Vice-President, 'Free housing'? And were you also saying, 'No direct taxation'? Were you really saying this? That on an income of three hundred and eighty-one pounds, no taxation? This is rubbish, when we are talking about National Service. The nation says to its youth, 'We want your service.' And the youth does not then turn to the nation and say, 'For how much?' The youth simply says, 'Where? What to do?' This is the meaning of National Service."

Calmly, again: "Now, I've accepted your ultimatum. And I can assure you I'm going to force nobody. You are right, your bodies would be there, your spirit wouldn't be there, you are right. I take *nobody* into the National Ser-

29

vice whose spirit is not in it. Nobody! Absolutely nobody!"
Hesitant applause.

"It's not a prison, you know. I'm not going to get anybody there who thinks it is a prison camp, no one! But
nevertheless it will remain compulsory for everybody who
is going to enter government service. So you make your
choice. I'm not going to spend public money to educate
anybody who says, 'National Service is prison camp.' No"
—very quietly now—"I won't have this. I have accepted
your ultimatum."

After a long pause he began again, chopping out every
word in fury. "You are right when you talk about salaries.
Our salaries are too high. You want me to cut them?"
Fairly strong applause. "Two years? I'm not talking about
two years. I'm not building this country for *two years*. I'm
willing to slash salaries. Do you want me to start with my
salary? Yes! I'll slash mine." Cries of "No!" could be
heard. "I'll slash the damned salaries in this country. Mine,
I slash by twenty percent, as from this hour. Twenty percent. I slash my salary. This damned country! The salaries
are too high! Too high for Tanzania!

"My salary! Do you know what my salary is? Five
thousand damned shillings a month! Five thousand damned
shillings in a poor country! The poor man who gets two
hundred shillings a month—do you know how long it's
going to take him to earn my damned salary? Twenty-five
years! It's going to take the poor man in this country, who
earns two hundred shillings a month, twenty-five years to
earn what I earn in a year.

"The damned salaries! These are the salaries which
build this kind of attitude in the educated people, all of
them! All of them! Me and you! We belong to a class of

exploiters! I belong to your class! Where I think three hundred and eighty pounds a year is a prison camp! Is forced labor! We belong to this damned exploiting class on top. Is this what the country fought for? Is this what we worked for? In order to maintain a class of exploiters on top?

"I agree with you! We are paying too much! Everybody in this damned country is paid too much—except the poor peasant. I'll slash the salaries! I agree with you! I'm glad you're so concerned about this country! Forced labor? Where do we get this language? The day I can give every worker in Tanzania three hundred and eighty pounds, we will have worked a revolution that has not been worked anywhere in Africa. The day that I succeed in giving everybody in this damned country three hundred pounds, we shall have worked a terrific revolution; we could stand, all of us, on top of Kilimanjaro and proclaim the Tanzanian revolution!

"Forced labor! Go, go in the classroom, go and don't teach. This we shall count as National Service for three hundred and eighty pounds a year. You are right, salaries are too high. Everybody in this country is demanding a pound of flesh. Everybody except the poor peasant. How can he demand it? He doesn't know the language. Even in his own language he can't speak of forced labor. *What kind of country are we building?*" He fairly screeched the words.

"I have accepted what you said. And I am going to revise salaries permanently. And as for you, I am asking you to go home. I'm asking all of you to go home. Rashid! You are responsible to see that they go home."

There was mild applause, presumably from those students who didn't realize what had happened. He expelled

31

them, three hundred and ninety-three in all, and sent them home.

SIR RICHARD TURNBULL, the last governor of Tanganyika: "He has rather a Gandhian streak, you know. He doesn't lack courage, but he will never grasp the nettle. He was very slow to realize that, when you rule, you hurt people's feelings; every act will benefit some and bring disadvantage to others. He has a tremendous adherence to principle. As Shaw said in his *Prefaces*, the man who would 'sell all and follow me' would create absolute chaos. Well, Julius would sell all and give it to the poor and rather enjoy the ensuing chaos. There's a shadow of a death wish in him. He likes to follow a principle to its logical end rather than its realistic end. But he's a bigger man than that suggests. He once told me how he would go to endless lengths to avoid quarrels. Only once or twice, he said, had he let it happen; he feared the humiliation of shouting and getting red in the face, and how ashamed he felt afterwards. The great thing about Julius was: he didn't want the spoils of leadership; he just didn't care about possessions. At one time, as I recall, he was smoking one hundred cigarettes a day; and when he found it was affecting his work, he cut it, just like that."

One of his staff assistants: "The staggering thing is how little he has changed. At Mwanza, there is a Nyerere Street. He says, 'It's named for my father.' The Dar City Council thought of taking down the Askari Monument and putting up a statue of the President. He said no. He doesn't like the personality cult. He doesn't believe in one-man government, he believes in consensus government. His way is to try to bring people around, as in the TANU National Executive committee meetings. They argue and argue and argue. He usually gets his way—because he argues. They could have a dictator here as easily as anywhere else; democracy is stronger here because the President is preaching it."

One of his ministers: "He starts by trusting a person. Then he lets you prove it. Or prove otherwise. He starts by showing interest in a human being. He absolutely believes the human being to start with. Then maybe he will discover you are a fool or a rascal; or maybe he will discover you're somebody he could get on with. Some people say, 'He likes to give you a long rope.' "

His friend Father Richard Walsh: "The last thing Julius Nyerere believes in is mandarins. He has a tremendous confidence in the innate goodness of people. I used to tell him, 'There's only one Nyerere in Africa,' and he didn't always believe it."

Colin Legum, the British journalist: "He was never afraid of losing his leadership in a cause he knew was right. He was prepared to stake his leadership on causes that were important. On questions of race and dignity, his immediate reaction, always, is emotional—sharp, stinging. And this creates problems for the diplomats who have to deal with him immediately afterward, because he is already deeply committed to the emotional position. And then always there is the second phase; the rational man takes over. And essentially he is a rational man."

His former colleague Oscar Kambona (a few months before he broke with Nyerere and went into exile in 1967): "He had two qualities, and he has them still, and I believe, if he keeps them, he will become a very great leader of Africa. One is his simplicity, his understanding of the other man's point of view. The other is his not caring about

33

wealth. He has no idea of wealth. The first time he went to the United Nations, he had old rotten suitcases. Clothes he doesn't worry about."

Oscar Kambona (a few months after he fled from Tanzania): "I can accuse the President and substantiate that he is hiding behind the façade of democracy, while quietly building himself into a dictator. This is the mind of a man enmeshed in a web of wickedness."

A Western diplomat (formerly assigned to an embassy in Kenya): "He should be in a university. He has to keep proving he's nonaligned, having so long been the darling of the British and the Americans. With Jomo Kenyatta, if you accuse him of being pro-British, he can say, 'After nine years of imprisonment by the British, I can judge that for myself.' But with Julius it's more difficult."

A Western diplomat (formerly assigned to an embassy in Tanzania): "There are many bridge players in this world who can take a good hand and get good results. There are few hands as poor as his."

Julius Nyerere (soon after he had broken diplomatic relations with the British government over Britain's Rhodesian policy, in 1965): "I have not changed. I was considered a moderate in the past because I stuck stubbornly to certain principles—two in particular. One was our method of winning independence. It was very clear in my mind that, because of the nature of the Trust Territory under the British, it was possible to win independence without violence. I stuck to it. I'm not non-violent in the sense of Mohandas Gandhi. But I feel violence is an evil with which one cannot become associated unless it is absolutely necessary. And so, in Western circles, they said, 'Julius is very good.' I don't think the Communists thought I was so good.

They accused me of being a stooge of the British, I think.
Secondly, I said racialism [racism] must never be a part of
our campaign for independence. I put my foot down.
Some of my colleagues were not happy about this 'purity.'
But I stuck to it, and the West said, 'Julius is very good.'
So I earned a good reputation—fine until independence.
But the same principle applies to Rhodesia. I wanted six
words out of Harold Wilson: independence 'on the basis of
majority rule.' And I suddenly became an extremist for
sticking to my nonracialism. Now I am an embarrassment to
Britain on Rhodesia, and I'm a bad fellow. My reputation
in the West is very bad just now. But sticking to principles
is not a mistake. Do they want me to say now, 'Racialism is
all right; let my people oppose the Indians who live here'?
No!"

IN HIS SPARE TIME Nyerere has translated two Shake-
spearean plays, *Julius Caesar* and *The Merchant of Venice*,
into Swahili. He received so many suggestions and correc-
tions from friends and Swahili scholars after publishing the
Caesar translation that he later revised it. Occasionally he
has exchanged poems, in the Swahili manner, with local
writers. Most of these poems are said to have patriotic
themes, but Nyerere has rarely discussed them; he once
said, "after some careful thought," that he did not think it
useful to make them public.

Most of his writing has dealt specifically with Tanzanian affairs, and has ranged from the 1967 Arusha
Declaration to a privately circulated memorandum to Tanzanian foreign service officers entitled "Argue, Don't
Shout," a gentle effort to soften the tone of diplomatic oratory. Two volumes of his speeches and papers have been

published. While assembling the material for the second volume, *Freedom and Socialism*, he decided to omit any passages from the extemporaneous speech to the complaining students in 1966. "I was too angry," he said.

In April 1967, he asked the parents of the expelled students to write letters to their regional commissioners stating that they were satisfied that "the student will be of benefit to the nation if he resumes his studies." Nyerere pardoned the majority of the students, saying he felt they had come to believe that Tanzania could only be built "through the religion of socialism and self-reliance."

"When the Christian missionaries tried to convert my father, he would listen to them and, after they had finished, he would preach to them, and then they would go away for good. When they said to the old man, 'Love your brother,' he would say, 'I agree with you.' The only thing the British had against him was his twenty-two wives."

"WE ZANAKI have two reputations among our neighbors," Nyerere has said of his tribesmen. "One, of being cunning, and the other, which follows the first, of being untrustworthy. People will say, 'A Zanaki friend will kill you'—which is not true. I don't know how we got that reputation. But certainly we are very independent-minded. As in such small communities, the people are very conscious of themselves, very proud of themselves."

The Zanaki are one of the smallest of Tanzania's one hundred and twenty-six tribes, numbering no more than thirty-five or forty thousand out of the country's thirteen million. Their homeland lies in hill country to the southeast of Lake Victoria and to the west of the Serengeti Plain, a starkly beautiful landscape of granite outcroppings, brooding skies and the magnificent colors of tropical Africa. The Zanaki raise cassavas, millet, corn, cotton, chickens, and, here and there, a few cattle. The soil is poor and the rains irregular, but, as Nyerere says, "The Zanaki know no famine."

"They are much more aggressive than most tribes, and noted for making mischief," says the Reverend Arthur Wille, an American Maryknoll father who founded the Roman Catholic mission at Butiama, the President's birthplace, in the early nineteen-fifties. "They love court cases. There are more killings out there in Zanaki"—or Zanakiland, the tribal area—"than elsewhere. The police in Musoma," the regional capital, "used to have a map with pins showing murders, thefts and other serious crimes. Zanaki was always a cluster of murder pins." The Zanaki have demonstrated their stubbornness to the Catholic fathers by their resistance to Christian teachings; after more than fifteen years of missionary activity, only three or four hundred Zanaki have been converted to Christianity. To the British colonial administrators, the Zanaki proved their truculence by their frequent quarrels with neighbors, and, specifically, by a riot they staged in 1952 in support of Ihunyo, their chief and rainmaker, whom the British were seeking to depose. "I don't think many other tribes would have dared," Father Wille has said, "or even thought of such a thing, at that time."

Unlike most African tribes, the Zanaki never had a chief until the Germans came in the late nineteenth century. Instead they had a *mwami*, or "rich one," whose function was to make rain. It was this rainmaking tradition, in part, that has led tribal historians to trace Zanaki origins to Buhaya, west of the Lake, where the rainmaker played an important role in tribal life. Indeed, there is a legend in Buhaya of a rainmaker who long ago was driven away for failing to make rain; and a similar story in Zanaki lore of a rainmaker who came from the west. Or it may simply be that the Zanaki migrated to the eastward a thousand years or so ago in search of food. The name Bazanaki—with the tribal prefix added—means, "Those who came with what?" The story is told of a stranger who drifted long ago into the village of Majita. The local chieftain asked, "*Baza na ki?*" ("What does he bring with him?") When told that the stranger had come with nothing, the chief hustled him on his way, to settle in what was to become Zanaki.

Some authorities believe that, in addition to his rain-making powers, the *mwami* of the Zanaki possessed certain secular functions; in case of war, he would order the warriors to the defense, and in victory he would collect a share of the spoils. By tradition, anyone who had killed and fled to the rainmaker's village was safe, pending justice. But the *mwami*'s executive powers were not extensive. "There was no chief," Father Wille has said. "The government was in the hands of the warrior class, the *erikura*. This group ran the tribe. Within it were the speakers, the *abagambi*—literally, 'those who speak.' When an important decision was to be taken, there would be a meeting of the *erikura*. Various speakers would present their opinions. These speakers were unusual people, but they had no power other than the ability to convince. After his advocacy, a speaker would revert to being an ordinary member of the *erikura*."

All this changed when the Germans arrived. They wanted chiefs to run the tribe and control its members, and instead of appointing one chief over all the Zanaki, they named eight headmen to run the various Zanaki communities. "The natural candidate," said Father Wille, "was the *omugambi*,"* the local speaker. In the village of Butiama,

* The singular form of *abagambi*.

39

the Germans picked Buhoro, but he was quickly succeeded by his cousin, Nyerere Burito. The name Nyerere, which means "caterpillar" in Ki-Zanaki, commemorates the fact that a plague of caterpillars attacked the Zanaki countryside in 1860, the year Julius Nyerere's father was born. The name is pronounced Nyuh-*reh-reh* by the Zanaki and most other Tanzanians, and Nyuh-*reh*-ree by most foreigners in Tanzania today.

The subtleties of Zanaki traditional government were utterly lost on the Germans. When they first reached Zanaki country, the *mwami*, a rainmaker named Monge, sent a messenger to greet them. The messenger was a wily fellow named Fundi Kenyeka, and he was the *omugambi* of Busegwe village. Eventually Kenyeka managed to convince the Germans that his son Kitara was chief of all the Zanaki. So Kitara became the chief, even though he was regarded as a pretender by the Zanaki, and he retained the post until after the Germans were driven out of Tanganyika during World War I. A paper in the Butiama mission library—unsigned, undated, but apparently written years later by an educated young Zanaki—describes the tribe's plight at the time of the British arrival. "All this happened while Monge was still alive, for he died in 1918. My elders explained that they themselves remembered these happenings, but no one dared at the time to complain, even Monge himself, because no one knew the new masters, and everyone was afraid."

The intrigues continued. Kitara's brother Isomba became chief, and Monge's son Ihunyo became *mwami*, and the two clashed. For six years, Ihunyo lived in exile on Kurukuba Island in Lake Victoria, having been convicted of trying to make rain by obtaining a human sacrifice. In

1926 he was allowed to return to Busegwe and two years later, following Isomba's overthrow, Ihunyo became the chief. In 1930 the post was abolished, and Ihunyo reverted to being merely the *omugambi* of Busegwe. His political status was no different from that of Nyerere Burito of Butiama village and the other *abagambi* of Zanaki. But Ihunyo alone remained the rainmaker.

Throughout the period of British colonial rule, the most numerous and complicated cases of inheritance to reach the courts in Musoma were the ones from Zanaki. This excerpt from the same unsigned paper gives an indication of what the British district commissioners at Musoma were occasionally faced with.

"The age of the (deceased) person was important. If the deceased had not passed through the first stage of *nyangi*, which made him an elder entitled to carry the *kiraburu*, the black oxtail, his heir would have been his father. There was an exception, not uncommon in Zanaki: if the father had disowned his son, perhaps because the son had turned cattle thief and the father had had to pay for his delinquencies, and the son turned to his *wajomba* (his maternal uncles) and they assisted him—especially if they bought him a wife—then they became his potential heirs. But once the man had passed *nyangi*, his senior heir, in the majority of cases, became his maternal uncle and the second heir his brother by the same mother, the latter becoming the senior heir if by chance he was older in years than the maternal uncle . . ."

In today's market, the price of a Zanaki bride averages about twenty cows, although it varies by location and circumstances. "In some places it's as high as thirty-five or forty cows," Father Wille has said. "And if you're talking

41

about an old man who already has a lot of wives, then you're going to be up in the high forties." It is not uncommon for a man to pay a dowry for a five- or six-year-old girl, perhaps making a deposit of five cows at that time. When she is nine or ten, the child may move to her husband's village, and at fifteen or sixteen will be formally married. "Polygamy," a long-time Musoma resident has said, "is the ideal of the Zanaki man. He looks forward to it, whether he can afford it or not." Julius Nyerere's half-brother Edward Wanzagi has eleven wives. "Julius used to kid him about his wives," a friend has recalled. "Edward would say, 'But I need them for work.' Julius would say, 'Buy a tractor.' But Edward treats them with a great deal of affection. To one he granted a divorce."

"Once," said Father Wille, "one of the television companies was up here, and they were in front of Edward's cluster of houses, where each wife has her own hut. A reporter asked Julius if he would explain why there were so many houses. Julius said, 'Well, they are for my brother's wives. He has eleven, I think.' They asked him what he thought of polygamy, and he said something like this: 'Ah, well, it is a popular custom in Zanaki. But it will pass, for economic reasons."

In Butiama, Chief Nyerere Burito died in 1942, at the age of eighty-two, and was succeeded by Edward Wanzagi, his eldest son. "If my father had followed tradition," Julius Nyerere has said, "a nephew would have succeeded him. It would have been my uncle or a nephew—a sister's son, although he didn't have one. But a nephew—sons of his maternal cousins, these we call nephews—and these might have succeeded him. And they would have taken my father's property when he died. But he decided not to be traditional in this matter of succession. He was practically retired before his death, and he appointed my brother Edward to represent him everywhere. He also tried to leave some of his property to his sons, but the tribe rejected this."

In the late nineteen forties, the British decided to reunite the Zanaki chiefdoms. "For years," Nyerere has said, "a number of educated people in the tribe had advocated amalgamation of the Zanaki, for we still had eight so-called chiefs, or headmen. Ridiculous! Even now, there are not more than forty thousand Zanaki, so there were probably fewer then. If we had one chief, I argued, it would be better for the tribe. Later I led the campaign, and actually succeeded in convincing them. But the problem was the person. The obvious choice was my brother Edward —but they didn't like him. Well, I couldn't press my brother. They asked me, 'Why don't you do it yourself?' I said, 'No, no, I can't be chief.'

"But while I was away in Scotland, they held a tribal convention, and the amalgamation took place. And I think they did the right thing. They picked an innocuous chief— Ihunyo, who was believed to be the rainmaker. This was his one qualification, but it was accepted by all the Zanaki. So, good. And they named two others as his assistants: my brother was to be his administrative assistant, and another young man his judicial assistant.

"Well, the work was being done by my brother. My brother is no nationalist, but he was pushing progress. The chief was useless. I mean—a rainmaker!" Ihunyo, moreover, was suspected of taking bribes; in 1932 he had also been involved in an arson case; and so, in 1952, the local British authorities decided to get rid of him and make Edward Wanzagi the chief.

43

The British district commissioner and his assistant called a meeting in a field near Busegwe, Ihunyo's village. "They were warned that there might be trouble," Father Wille has recalled, "and so they took a few police with them. And sure enough, a crowd of Ihunyo supporters had gathered, and most of them were carrying walking sticks. There was also a smaller group from Butiama and Buhemba, and they were supporting Edward Wanzagi. The D.C. could see it was a hostile group—people were waving their sticks—and he told Ihunyo to say, 'I won't start the meeting until you all put your sticks in front of the table.' Instead, Ihunyo said, in Ki-Zanaki, which the D.C. couldn't understand, 'Let's go!' and they attacked.

"The police shot over their heads, but it didn't stop them. The D.C. and his party managed to get to their cars. Edward Wanzagi was badly beaten. From Musoma, the D.C. wired the police mobile unit at Mwanza, and the assistant D.C. and Edward spent the night with the police rounding up the Busegwe leaders. About a hundred were later convicted, and Ihunyo himself died in jail. It's amazing how many chiefs died in jail. They just couldn't stand the confinement."

The incident occurred two days before Julius Nyerere returned to Zanaki after spending three years at Edinburgh, the first Tanganyikan to receive a graduate degree overseas. On his return he had lingered a few days at Dar es Salaam, then taken the thirty-six-hour train ride to Mwanza. The riot took place while he was waiting at Mwanza to catch the lake steamer to Musoma. "It was a completely tribal incident," Nyerere has recalled. "It happened on a Friday, and I arrived on a Sunday. They were all bandaged when they came to meet me at the boat. And so the chief was deposed. Before this, I had said we must have an elected chief; we couldn't have this rainmaker rubbish. It was my first election campaign, and we got our first elected chief, our first and last." Was Ihunyo deposed for corruption? "For uselessness," Nyerere snapped, betraying a touch of the young Zanaki reformer's zeal. "He was useless and corrupt."

Edward Wanzagi thus became the chief of the Zanaki in 1952. He held the post until a few months after Tanganyikan independence, when the chiefs were relieved of their political powers. They were allowed to retain their titles, however, and some were given local jobs. Chief Edward became the divisional executive officer, and continues to perform many of the same chores: collecting taxes, carrying out development projects and pressing the stubborn Zanaki to work for progress.

For generations the Zanaki hunted and waged war with bow and arrow, the arrow points needle-sharp and dipped in a black syrupy poison made from bark. Nowadays the larger plains animals that the Zanaki traditionally hunted for food, the impala, the zebra, the wildebeeste, are disappearing from the region. Chief Edward urges and cajoles his tribesmen, who have always raised cassavas, millet and corn for their own use, to grow cash crops, such as cotton, sisal and peanuts, as well. A few years ago he took part in the building of a self-help dam on a government-sponsored resettlement scheme nearby. A curiosity of contemporary Tanzanian life is that Chief Edward, who had never previously been outside East Africa, was taken on a two-week trip to China a few years ago to observe agricultural methods there. "Edward is a driver for work," a friend has observed. "He will say, 'Everyone is eating, but

45

no one is working, so eventually we will all starve.' Sometimes he despairs and says, 'I can't do anything.' He may schedule a meeting at nine, and nobody will show up, but he'll be there.'' No matter how hard he has worked in Zanaki, however, Edward Wanzagi has made little progress in winning over the people of Busegwe village, the home of Marwa the rainmaker, the son of Ihunyo. There the villagers still say, "Wanzagi is not our chief. Marwa is."

BECAUSE IT WAS RAINING so hard on the day of his birth, in March 1922, Julius Nyerere was named Kambarage, after an ancestral spirit who lived in the rain. The name Julius he took much later when, at the age of twenty, he was baptized a Catholic. When he was already sixty-one years old, Julius' father had taken a fifth wife, Mugaya, who was fifteen. Julius was the second of the four sons and four daughters she bore him, of whom six survived. By the time of his death, Chief Nyerere had taken twenty-two wives, most of them toward the end of his life, and left twenty-six sons and daughters. "There were many more," Nyerere's younger brother Joseph has remarked, "but many died." It is often said that Nyerere's character is similar to that of his eldest half-brother, Edward Wanzagi. But, according to Joseph, "there was only one of our brothers who was like Julius, and that was Burito. He was a little older than Julius, and they were great friends." Burito was a private in the British army in World War II. His family is not certain where he was killed. Joseph thinks Burito died in Burma, and Julius has the impression it was somewhere in Africa.

The cluster of hillside huts where Julius Nyerere spent his childhood lies in ruins today, returned to nature. A cement marker, surrounded by tall grass, bears the words in Ki-Zanaki: "Deceased Chief Nyerere Burito, ruled 1912, died 1942, aged eighty-two." The old chief was, in the absolute judgment of his sons and their friends, the most important influence in the making of Julius Nyerere. "His father was very slow, very careful, before acting," Julius' childhood friend Oswald Marwa* once said. "We thought this was the foundation of Nyerere." "He always insisted on giving people their rights," Chief Edward Wanzagi has said. The eight Zanaki chiefs would take turns presiding over the tribal court. "But people would not go to court if they knew another chief was presiding. If they knew he was presiding, there would be a long queue because they knew that from him they would get justice."

Julius Nyerere is especially fond of recalling the occasional confrontations between his father and the Christian missionaries. "To the extent that I have some humanity, I took it from my father. He would talk to the missionaries about never making revenge. He was a chief under the Germans, and when the British soldiers came down to Musoma from Kenya, his enemies tried to overthrow him. One man brought the soldiers to my father's house, and they beat him almost to death. Years later, somebody slipped into my father's tent late at night for asylum, and it was this man, his enemy. He had committed a crime, and the British were after *him* now. And the district commissioner was only a few yards away! But the old man fed him and hid him and next morning took him out several miles from the camp and said *kwaheri*, goodbye.

"To the extent that a man can be an upright human

* No relation to the rainmaker.

being, he was one. And"—jubilantly—"he couldn't see why having so many wives and children was sin."

It is sometimes said that Julius' mother, Mugaya, was his father's favorite. "No," Nyerere has said carefully. "She was not far from that. But no, it is not true. She was *one* of the more liked ones. Another, who died recently, was clearly the favorite, and perhaps my mother came next.

"The women all knew this, and accepted it. The position of the eldest is accepted, the position of the favored one is accepted. Oh, there are frictions, of course. He is a patriarch. It is difficult to explain to someone from a monogamous society; they think of women's jealousy as a natural thing. But in a tribal society, the women accept their position. In my own tribe, jealousy is something to be ashamed of. It's one of the biggest insults to say a wife is jealous, that she doesn't want her husband to have a big family and many children. It's like saying she dominates him. It's a terrible thing."

In certain tribes, it is customary for each wife to come forward with food, taste it and retire. "In our tribe, the wives bring food, and he will accept it and pick, pick, pick. Sometimes he will eat with the children and one of the younger women, and the other women will eat together. They would know he prefers a certain woman's food because she cooks very well. What they do not accept is the rejection of food. That is a terrible thing."

Despite the fact that Julius' father was a chief or headman, his pay was only 60 shillings a month. One of Julius Nyerere's sharpest memories is of the mud hut whose leaking roof his mother tried endlessly to repair on rainy nights. In later years, the cry for good houses with good roofs became one of his political refrains. "At least," he has often said, "we always had milk."

His childhood was thoroughly tribal. His teeth were filed in the Zanaki manner. Until he was twelve, he rarely saw a "European" or an "Asian," the East African terms for whites and Indians. Occasionally the Zanaki still fought with their neighbors, notably the dreaded Masai. The Zanaki, who defended themselves with their bows and arrows, were hardly a match for the spear-carrying Masai, but at long last they hit on a plan for avenging themselves. "When they first attack, we'll shoot in the air," a tribesman suggested. "The Masai will raise their shields to protect their heads. The second time we'll fire at the lower part of their bodies." The strategy proved to be devastatingly effective.

"Julius always tells of the time," Father Wille has said, "when the Zanaki were attacked by the Nguruimi, who had disguised themselves as Masai by painting their bodies red with ochre and by carrying spears. The Zanaki were terrified and fled. But later the Nguruimi made the mistake of boasting too much, and the Zanaki said in disgust, 'Ah, it's only the Nguruimi,' and beat them up."

"Under the British, hunting was regarded as poaching," Nyerere has said. "Well, we didn't like this, of course, so we hunted anyway. Once I went out with the elders to part of what is now the Serengeti. A boy of my own age and I, and one or two others, were left in the camp to look after the meat. And one afternoon I saw a car coming toward us. I thought, 'It must be the game warden! We are finished!' And we rushed out of camp. But it was only a gold miner who was poaching too.

"And I remember another time, when I must have been about eleven. As I told you, a tribal boy of eleven is much more grown-up than an urban boy of the same age. But still he is only eleven. Well, another boy and I had run away into the bush alone. And then we started back toward camp. Tribal youths are very good about directions—much better than Boy Scouts. Then suddenly we heard a voice calling my name, 'Kambarage, Kambarage.' I remember it vividly! As I opened my mouth, this boy put his hand over it and said, 'Don't answer. Your father is a chief. You don't know if this man is calling you to kill you. Let's go quietly until we find out if he is a friend or enemy.' " So they crept along until they recognized a friend of Julius' father's. "Imagine," Nyerere said, "a boy of eleven."

AT TWELVE, Julius was sent to school in Musoma, twenty-six miles away. "It was really my brother Edward who was responsible," Nyerere has said. "Ihunyo himself said I should go. There is a Bantu game, *bao*. It's a clever game, the best tribal game, I think. Well, Ihunyo was very clever at it. My father wasn't good enough for Ihunyo. One reason my father and mother got on so well was that she was the only one of the wives who played *bao*. And I was very good too. Well, one time when Ihunyo visited our house, I played him. I don't think I defeated him, but it was clear to him that I had some brains, and he told my father, 'This boy is very clever. He should be sent to school.' But my father had sent his first two sons already, and as for the others, he didn't see much point. The problem was, Which should he pick and which should he leave out?

"Well, Edward had married the daughter of a neighboring chief, and this girl got to know me very well. I was small, and was liked by my sister-in-law. So when Edward came home from Ikoma, where he was working for another chief, he also knew me well—better than he knew the other younger brothers. Eventually he adopted his wife's sister's son, Wambura Wanzagi, who was my own age. This boy had already learned to read and write, and he tried to teach me, but it was no good. He spoke Swahili, and I was completely tribal. One day the district commissioner came and met the boy. The boy was very clever, and was not afraid of Europeans. So the D.C. ordered my brother to send the boy to school. And my brother went to my father and said, 'I suggest you send Kambarage too.' So I was really chosen to accompany this boy. I was delighted. And right away, the next day, I left." What happened to Wambura Wanzagi? "He has disappeared, abandoned his wife and children. I don't know where he is."

NOT LONG AFTER JULIUS went away to school, his old father bought him a bride. This insured that, in case of the chief's death, Julius would still have been able to marry. Under the Zanaki system, he could have been left with no cows or other wealth; but no one else could inherit his bride. "Of my father's four bigger sons, two were already married, the third could have married at any time, and I was the fourth. So I was the only one who wasn't provided for. And my father was worried about his health. Besides this, my mother had had three daughters, and I was my mother's eldest son, and there is a tribal obligation to allocate the bride-price of a mother's daughters to her sons." Otherwise this money, like the rest of the chief's estate, would have gone to a brother or nephew. "I'd have been inherited by a nephew or an uncle," Nyerere has said, "and it takes a very long time before an inherited son is able to get married. He will be bypassed. The stepfather gives brides to his own sons first." As it turned out, Nyerere never married the girl his father bought for him. He sold his equity in his child bride when, years later, he became engaged to Maria Gabriel.

The year Nyerere returned from Edinburgh, he and Father Wille were driving to Chief Edward's *shamba* one day, when Nyerere yelled at a woman on the road. Then he explained to Father Wille, laughing, "She's my wife. My father paid cows for her."

"THERE WASN'T ENOUGH TO LEARN," Nyerere said years
later, recalling his first days at the Mwisenge School in
Musoma. He began to study Swahili at twelve and English
at fifteen; he scored first in the territorial examination of
1936 and advanced to the Tabora Government School.
"The British were trying to build a public school, which
of course is anything but public," Nyerere once explained.
"Originally Tabora was built for the sons of chiefs; it was
as close to Eton as it could have been in Africa—fagging,
sportsmanship, fair play, all that. If you went through it
for six years, and succeeded, that was really something.
When I took the examination at Musoma—it was a Standard Four exam, to get into Standard Five—there were only
two Standard Five's in what was then the Lake Province.
One was at Mwanza, but it was a blind alley. If you went
there, you were stuck. The other Standard Five was at
Tabora, and this led to Standard Ten. It was not a blind
alley."

Nyerere's training as a Catholic began at Musoma and
continued at Tabora. "It was an accident," Nyerere has
said, "in human terms, at least. I was a completely tribal
boy. But at Musoma, on Tuesdays and Thursdays, religious
instruction was given to those boys who wanted it. It was a
good practice; we still have it. Well, I was the friend of a
neighboring chief's son, who said, 'Why don't you come
with me to my class?' So I went. But I used to protest to

53

him about this peculiar teaching. I told him I couldn't believe in this bearded man, and I felt we should worship the gods we knew.

"But I wasn't baptized until several years later. The church thought I might succeed my father as chief—which was most unlikely." The assumption, apparently, was that a man could not be both a chief—at least not a polygamous chief—and a Christian. So the baptism did not take place until after Nyerere's father died in 1942. It was then that he took the name Julius. "It's silly that you have to take a name other than a tribal name when you are baptized. Later I investigated and found that the name didn't stand for a very good saint. Well, I mean, all saints are good, of course, but it didn't stand for a particularly well-known saint."

Nyerere's schoolmates at Tabora remember him as an ambitious, competitive boy, thin and wiry and small for his age. "If he didn't finish first, he could be very unhappy," a classmate has said. Nyerere thinks of himself as having been a rebel during his six years at Tabora; certainly he was a reformer. He was deeply offended by the special privileges accorded the prefects. "One of my biggest humiliations was trying to defend one of the boys in my house, Tembo. A prefect, I felt, had mistreated the boy by tying his hands. I took exception to this, I went to the headmaster, I said this was not justified. So the headmaster asked me to call them in. The prefect explained, the boy explained, and the headmaster took the side of the prefect—the side of the system. A prefect could do no wrong. The boy got four strokes with the cane, and I was to do it. I did cane him, but I wasn't too enthusiastic.

"I had already been in trouble with the prefects. They had decided the only way to save me was to make me a prefect too. But I never became head prefect. The teachers recommended me, but the headmaster vetoed it. He felt I was too kind for the job."

"We used to talk a lot about our homes," a classmate, Emanuel Kibira, has recalled. "Once, I remember, those of us who were from Bukoba told him we had eight chiefdoms in Bukoba. He said, 'You're lucky. Bukoba is very big. Eight is all right. But in our small tribe, which is the size of one chiefdom, we have eight chiefs. That's too many. Something must be done!' " Once the debating club, which Nyerere had founded, held a debate on the question of bride-price. "He didn't approve of it," Kibira has said, "but he was very interested in it because he had a wife already; his father had *paid*."

After completing his Standard 10 studies at Tabora, Nyerere entered Makerere College in Uganda. Since most students entered Makerere after completing Standard 12, the Tabora graduates had a difficult time at first. "Tabora was very good in biology," Nyerere has said, "and at Makerere we could compete with any boy in biology. I was very keen on it. And English I was all right in. But my real interest was—not politics exactly, but philosophical subjects—ideas, thought. John Stuart Mill's essays on representative government and on the subjection of women —these had a terrific influence on me. Twice I entered the East African literary competition and won first prize, and the second time I wrote on the subjection of women and applied Mill's ideas to tribal society." With friends he organized a campus chapter of the Tanganyika African Association, an organization that had been established in Dar es Salaam in 1929 as a social group for African civil servants; but Nyerere, already conscious of the special privileges enjoyed by Europeans in East Africa, used the campus branch as a club for studying political issues. He was graduated from Makerere in the class of 1945, and spent that summer building a house for his mother, who had been staying with an uncle since her husband, Chief Nyerere, had died three years earlier.

Nyerere received two teaching offers that year, one from the Tabora Government School, the other from the new Catholic secondary school, St. Mary's College, which was also located in Tabora. The Reverend Richard Walsh, who was the first director of St. Mary's, has recalled that the headmaster of the Government School told him, "You won't get Nyerere. He's coming straight to Tabora." "So," said Father Walsh years later, "we bet five bob." Nyerere accepted Father Walsh's offer at the urging of his friend Andrew Tibandebage, who was already teaching at St. Mary's. The government, as Father Walsh remembers it, then advised Nyerere by letter that "at a mission school, you won't get the same salary or pension, and if later you should transfer to a government school, you won't be able to count the years in the mission school toward your pension rights." Nyerere was furious and replied, "If ever I hesitated, your letter has settled the matter. The mission teachers are doing as much for Tanganyika as the government teachers are."

He taught biology and history at St. Mary's, and his salary was £6 5s. a month. In his spare time, he helped organize a cooperative store, an effort aimed at breaking the monopoly of the Indian merchants in Tabora, but the store was badly run and closed down a few years later in a minor scandal. In the evenings he taught English to the townspeople. He shared a house with Tibandebage and at night, with a group of friends that included Chief Harun Lugusha, talked endlessly about Tanganyikan affairs. Joseph Nyerere, who was twelve when his brother brought him to Tabora to begin his schooling, has recalled, "I used to listen to them talking politics. They talked for hours and hours—till four in the morning, sometimes."

As secretary of the local Tanganyika African Association branch, Nyerere was asked by the government to serve as a price inspector. "It was after the war, and goods were in short supply. The government wanted prices to be regularized, and so there was a price-control department. I used to go around the shops inspecting—not so much for overcharging, because it was very difficult to catch them on this, but to see that their price labels were displayed properly. My job was to report them. But the shopkeepers would say to me, 'You can do what you like, but you'll get nowhere.' And in fact, when I reported a violation, nothing happened. So I lost interest." His friend Oswald Marwa, who was visiting him at the time, has added, "He caught one merchant, but the case was dropped by the government. He was so angry he sent back his uniform: 'I'm not going to do it if justice is not done.' "

Through the African Association, Nyerere was beginning to take an interest in territorial politics. In April 1946 he went to Dar es Salaam for the first time to attend a general conference of the association; the meeting had been called to oppose a British Colonial Office proposal for the creation of a Central Assembly for East Africa. The Africans of Tanganyika feared that such a step would lead to an East African federation dominated by the white settlers of Kenya.

Rashidi Kawawa, who years later was to become

Nyerere's deputy in power, entered the Tabora Government School in 1948, and soon afterward saw Nyerere for the first time. "He came to our school to participate in a debate," Kawawa has said. "It was a competition between secondary schools, Tabora and St. Mary's, and he was so convincing that he converted us all—we all voted for his side. The subject was 'Wealth Is Better Than Education,' and he was against that, of course. He said, 'I chose the teaching profession in order to make people *understand*; and once you understand, then you are a happy man. Not because you are wealthy ; you can be a wealthy man but not a happy man . . .' But I didn't meet him that day. I was only eighteen."

NYERERE HAD LONG WANTED to continue his studies abroad, but had been reluctant to leave Tanganyika because his mother and younger brothers needed to be cared for. He had also been the victim of some subtle political pressure ; a local British official, according to Oswald Marwa, had written the Governor advising him that Nyerere should not be allowed to study overseas because he was politically minded and might be dangerous when he returned. Finally Nyerere's friend Father Walsh helped to arrange a government scholarship as well as a grant from St. Mary's for the support of Nyerere's family and his fiancée. A few months earlier, Nyerere had become formally engaged to Maria Gabriel, whom he had met in Musoma.

He reached London in April 1949. "The idea was that I should take a degree in biology," he once recalled. "I liked biology, and my boys at St. Mary's were doing well in it. It was my strongest exam subject, but not my strongest interest. So I had a debate with the Colonial Office, and they were kind enough to let me do as I wanted. At Edinburgh, my degree was in history and economics; my strongest subject was philosophy. I read a great deal. I had plenty of time to think. My ideas of politics were formed completely. It was my own evolution, but it was complete."

In an essay entitled "The Race Problem in East Africa,"* Nyerere wrote at the time: "There is too much hypocrisy in East Africa today. The European official and the European settler rule and maintain their prestige mainly by hypocrisy; their inner motives would hardly stand examination; the Indian trader makes his living by downright dishonesty or at best by sheer cunning, which is hypocrisy; the African clerk or laborer often disregards fulfilling his part of a contract and even a very educated African will pretend to love the Europeans where his heart is nearly bursting with envy and hatred." Recalling an incident in which a British minister had walked out of a meeting after an East African settler had said he would sooner dine with swine than with an African, Nyerere continued: "The statement by the settler was regarded by the white community in Tanganyika and Kenya as unfortunate, but everywhere the Minister was blamed for doing what he thought was the only thing he could do under such circumstances.

"The expression of hatred is not on one side; an African friend of mine once referred to the Europeans in East Africa as *mbwa hawa*—'these dogs.' Personally I welcome these outbursts; they show us the seriousness of the disease, they are like bubbles that fly off a boiling pot . . .

"The African's capacity for bearing insult is not really limitless . . . [Africans] cannot bear insult forever, and it

* Published years later in his book *Freedom and Unity.*

is well to remember that a day may come when someone may
want to incite them. How easy it is to inflame an insulted
people! I really shudder when I think of the terrible possibility—but it will not be a mere possibility if our white
neighbors insist on this vulgar doctrine of the Divine Right
of Europeans . . . A day comes when the people will prefer
death to insult . . . I hope and pray that such a day will
never come. But the European holds the answer. He has
only to will that such a day shall never come, and it will
never come . . . Africa is for the Africans, and the other
races cannot be more than respected minorities . . . Should
it come to a bitter choice between being perpetually dominated by a white or an Indian minority and between driving
that minority out of East Africa, no thinking African
would hesitate to make the latter choice."

Apparently Nyerere rarely discussed politics with his
friends at Edinburgh. He obviously liked the British, and
often remarked at how hard they worked, as compared with
the British colonials of East Africa. He lived at the British
Council residence, and on evenings and weekends often
visited a friend, Walter Wilson, and Wilson's mother, a
widow whose husband had been a medical missionary in the
Belgian Congo and Angola. Mrs. Wilson has recalled that
Nyerere delighted in the crossword puzzles in *The Scotsman*
and loved to play canasta and Lexicon. "English was only
his third language," she has said, "but he always seemed to
win." Nine years later, he invited her to Tanganyika's
independence celebration.

"I HAD HAD THREE YEARS in which to think," Nyerere has
said. "I had given up the politics of complaint, and was
ready to tackle the roots of the problem of colonialism."

Exactly when he fixed on the idea of working for independence he does not know. "No. There was no moment when it all clicked into place. It wasn't a sudden inspiration, I didn't suddenly see the light. It was not like the call of the Christians, 'I've been called!' At Edinburgh, I was certain I was coming back to get myself involved full-time in politics. I had made up my mind that my life would be political. I had been away three years; now I would give myself three years to look at the country before taking up politics fully. And I nearly did my three years. By 1953 it was quite clear to me: it must be the politics of independence.

"In 1953, Colin Legum and I went to a hotel in Dar es Salaam—I won't mention its name—and he asked me what I would have and I said beer. As I was about to drink it, the manager came running over. 'This is terrible,' he said, 'Africans are not supposed to drink here.' I was very angry! But it was very clear to me: it was absurd to talk about wanting to be able to enter hotels. This was not the point at all. This was a result of colonialism. I was refused a beer. So what? Not many Africans in this country cared about being served in hotels. It was just the problem of a minority that wanted to be accepted by the colonial club. Absurd! We had to distinguish between the issue of colonialism and the desires of Africans of my type to be accepted by their colonial masters. Should we have fought about being given a license to drink European beer? Should this have been the peak of our achievement? This approach was ridiculous."

NYERERE FLEW HOME to Tanganyika in October 1952. He landed at Dar es Salaam and had a reunion with his fiancée, Maria, and then proceeded by train to Mwanza and lake steamer to Musoma. There he was met by his family, including his bandaged brother Edward, and together they went on to Zanaki. "We started to build the house where the wedding was to take place," Nyerere's friend Oswald Marwa has recalled. "And when he began to make mud bricks, they all started to laugh. 'Why is he doing such work?' He said, 'I went for an education, everybody who has an education must work.' And then we put on the thatched roof."

During Nyerere's years at Edinburgh, Maria had taken a domestic-science course in Uganda and later taught at a Lutheran school in Moshi; then, at the urging of Father Walsh, who felt she should receive more schooling in order to be a suitable wife for Nyerere, she studied English at St. Joseph's Convent in Dar es Salaam. Friends recall that Maria refused to meet Nyerere at the Dar es Salaam airport on his return from Britain because, she said, "It is not a woman's place to run after a man." She also insisted that the wedding should not take place immediately. "We wait," she is said to have told him. "I want to know you better. I knew you before you went away, but I want to see if you have changed." "And so," Nyerere has told his friends, "I had to build our house first. I had to take off my Edinburgh suit and my shoes and with my bare feet mix the sand and cement, and not until I had built the house did I earn her respect." They were married at the Musoma mission on January 24, 1953, and soon after returned to Dar es Salaam.

Nyerere had been hired to teach history at St. Francis' College in Pugu, twelve miles from Dar es Salaam. At first he was paid £300 a year. "But after a little noise," he has said, "they raised it to four hundred and fifty pounds. I knew this was only three-fifths of what I would receive if

I were an expatriate. But I also knew it was more than I would have been paid for the same kind of work in England. It was more than Tanganyika could afford. And a thirty percent 'cost of living' allowance besides! Salaries were too high. It was one of the crimes of the colonial administration."

Within three months, Nyerere was elected president of the Tanganyika African Association. "It had been dormant," he has said, "and I felt it was my job to try to revive it." Most observers of the new Africa formerly believed that political consciousness came late to Tanganyika—later than to Ghana or Nigeria or even Kenya, where the Mau Mau rebellion broke out in the early nineteen-fifties. But the speed with which the independence movement developed following the founding of the Tanganyika African National Union in 1954 suggests otherwise. The clue to TANU's rapid growth lies partly in the homogeneity and stability of Tanganyikan society. The slave trade had caused a considerable uprooting of the population and re-settlement along the main trade route from Bagamoyo to Lake Victoria and Lake Tanganyika. Swahili, originally a language of the East African coastal peoples, was carried inland along the trade routes. In the days of German East Africa, the colonial government maintained a well-trained African civil service and transferred its employees throughout the territory. As a result of its history, both ancient and recent, Tanganyika as a candidate for nationhood had three distinct advantages over many of its neighbors. It had a large number of tribes, one hundred and twenty-six in all, of which none was dominant. Since it was neglected by the British in favor of Kenya, a Crown colony, the Trusteeship Territory of Tanganyika had only a small colony of

63

white settlers who tried to resist the rise of African nationalism. And it had Swahili, a genuine lingua franca. Only twice during the seven years he stumped the country working for independence, Nyerere has often recalled, was he unable to speak directly to the people.

In 1929 Sir Donald Cameron, a highly respected British governor, had established the Tanganyika African Association as a social organization for African civil servants. By the nineteen-forties, several of the TAA's stronger branches, including the one at Makerere College that Nyerere helped to organize, were delving into political issues, or at least were dealing with grievances connected with government service. In 1945 the TAA's leaders considered moving the organization's headquarters from Dar es Salaam to Dodoma, in the interior, because so many of their members were being transferred out of the capital. "If you had a big mouth, and talked too much," Chief Patrick Kunambi once explained, "the British moved you to a smaller place, and at that time quite a few of the members were concentrated at Dodoma." Rarely if ever did its members talk of independence in the early days. "Not of independence," one has said. "Of equality." By the time Nyerere reached Dar es Salaam in 1953, the TAA was little more than a social group once more. "Nyerere couldn't see much point to an organization that merely gave tea parties for every European officer who went home on leave," Chief David Makwaia has said. "This didn't appeal to him. He thought, 'Why have it?'"

Somehow Nyerere, a newcomer to Dar es Salaam, and a member of a small upcountry tribe at that, quickly assumed the leadership of the TAA. "He was one of the first university graduates in the Territory," Abbas Sykes has said. "And he came at the right time. Usually, if a man went away to university, when he came back he would not be one of us, he would be very sophisticated. But here was a man who had the same kind of education—higher, in fact, because he had an M.A. instead of just a B.A.—who was willing to be with his people. This humility—'I'm willing to serve you'—made everyone forget that he was from upcountry and that he wasn't a Moslem." There are almost as many Christians as Moslems in Tanganyika as a whole, but the coastal region is heavily Moslem.

The favorite African politician of the Governor, Sir Edward Twining, was Chief David Makwaia; and in Twining's eyes Nyerere soon became, as Colin Legum has put it, "the bad black because he wouldn't join the Twining club." Makwaia—whom Nyerere was later to call "our Hamlet" because, in Nyerere's view, Makwaia could never make up his mind whether or not to join the nationalists—had clashed with Nyerere and the other young TAA intellectuals as early as 1947. "He had it all," Abbas Sykes has said, "a black man with a white man's education. But he was so conceited. He would arrive by train from upcountry, go straight to the Legislative Council, and when the session was over, would go straight back to his chiefdom at Shinyanga. We would go to see him and he would brush us aside; 'I have to go to the chief justice's party now,' he would say, trying to escape from us. Once, in a discussion, he said, 'Look, boys, if you want to have *your* voice,' as if he were not part of Africa's voice, 'you fellows have to organize yourselves.'

"But *now*, we thought, we have got a fellow of the same

65

kind of education who is entirely different, who puts himself *below*, who discusses ordinary things with people." Later, when Nyerere was forced to resign his teaching job because of his political activities, his friends were even more impressed. "He showed he was prepared to sacrifice," Sykes said. "We said, 'Here's the man who has come to save us.' " In addition Nyerere, as a mission school teacher, was relatively free of government control, whereas most of the other TAA leaders were civil servants. And he was easily the best orator in the Territory.

"The fact that he came from an insignificant tribe," the former chief of a large tribe has said, "made him less identifiable to the big tribes, so there were no big blocs automatically set against him. It was also an advantage to have at the top a man who has the human touch, a man who can easily sell himself and his ideas." His leadership wasn't based on what he promised, as Chief Patrick Kunambi has said, "because Julius practically never promises anything." But he quickly transformed the organization. "The colonialists believed all we wanted was a square deal," Abbas Sykes's late brother Abdul once said. "Nyerere made us start to think: all we wanted was independence." With this goal in mind, Nyerere and his colleagues reorganized the TAA as a political party, TANU, on July 7, 1954—a day that has been celebrated ever since as *Saba Saba*, the seventh day of the seventh month. Nyerere, at thirty-two, was unanimously elected its president.

Among his earliest colleagues were the three sons of Kleist Sykes, who had been a corporal in the German signal corps during World War I, and had learned typing, shorthand and accounting; later he became a co-founder of the TAA and, in the words of his son Abbas, "one of the two or

three most highly paid Africans here." Other early TANU
members were Dossa Aziz and John Rupia, eighteen years
older than Nyerere, who was one of the territory's first African entrepreneurs. *Mzee* John had worked as a government
clerk and tax collector; then he bought a truck and became
a transporter of building materials. By the time TANU
was founded, he was the most prosperous African in Tanganyika, and he talked as eloquently of the virtues of hard
work as any Western capitalist: "What I want is that they
all work hard. Time is money! We can do big things in the
world if people work hard." He was the first treasurer of
TANU but, as he has said, "There was no money. The
treasury was our pocket." In the beginning, in fact, the
treasury was *Mzee* John himself. When Nyerere and his
TANU organizers would start out in the morning, Rupia
would ask them, "Do you have any power?" Then he would
dig into his pockets for money.

THE SAME YEAR, Sir Edward Twining decided to appoint
Nyerere to a temporary vacancy in the Legislative Council. The regular Legco member, David Makwaia, had been
sent to London to serve on a royal commission. "Julius was
very serious about it," his brother Joseph, who was living
with Julius and Maria at Pugu, has recalled. "He was
teaching full time and working in politics full time, sometimes walking twelve miles into Dar es Salaam to attend
meetings in the evening." His first Legco speech dealt with
the need for more schools: "By 1956, we shall still have
sixty-four percent of our children of primary age outside
schools . . . I do not think, Sir, this gives us any cause for
complacency." It was the period of the Mau Mau Emergency in Kenya, and Nyerere assured the council: "I am

67

certain that every African wants to see this country peaceful, because it is only through peace that he can get the
things he wants, and that is development." It would be a
mistake, however, to assume that Nyerere disapproved of
the Mau Mau in principle. He once said to Father Walsh,
"How do you explain it? The Christian faith put fire in the
bellies of the Africans in the eighteen-eighties. Now you're
reduced to pulling them into church. You don't spark the
dynamism. You're like the government: you thought we
were people without ideals, and lived only for our bellies.
But look at the Mau Mau up there: they're dying for their
ideals. The British thought they would win us over by building roads and schools. But those things alone will not satisfy us." A few months later, Nyerere let it be known that
he planned to oppose a government recommendation that
civil service salaries be increased. But before the debate
had begun, Makwaia was whisked back from London and
Nyerere was automatically unseated.

In August 1954, a U.N. mission visited Tanganyika
and subsequently published a report recommending that
the Territory be given a timetable for independence within
twenty or twenty-five years. The local authorities were infuriated by the mission and particularly by the pro-Afri-
can views of its American member, Mason Sears. A few
months later, TANU voted to send Nyerere to New York
to address the U.N. Trusteeship Council on the subject of
independence. Twining responded by sending a three-man
delegation to support the government's position. He also
urged Father Walsh (who by then had moved to Dar es
Salaam) to refuse to allow Nyerere to be absent from his
classes, implying that Nyerere's political activities verged

on sedition. Walsh refused. "If it's sedition," he demanded, "why isn't Nyerere in jail?"

As a result of the Governor's warnings, however, the U.S. government restricted Nyerere to an eight-block radius of the U.N. headquarters and limited his stay to within twenty-four hours of his appearance before the Trusteeship Council. Such gestures must have seemed foolish in the light of his reasoned appeal to the council on March 7, 1955. In behalf of his party, Nyerere said, he wanted to refute "the outrageous assertion . . . that the vast majority of the Territory's inhabitants were against the major political recommendations of that report"—that Tanganyika should be granted independence within twenty or twenty-five years. "What will satisfy my people is a categorical statement, both by this council and by the Administering Authority, that although Tanganyika is multiracial in population, its future government shall be primarily African. Once we get that assurance, everything else becomes a detail."

Nyerere had had trouble raising the money for the trip. "I almost didn't go at all," he has said. But *Mzee* John contributed 5,000 shillings, and a little more was collected from other friends. Rupia has recalled that, on the night before his departure, Nyerere stayed at Rupia's house in Dar es Salaam. The next morning they were all so nervous that they couldn't remember where Julius had left his suitcase. Finally, after turning the house upside down, they found the suitcase in the car trunk, where Nyerere had put it the night before. They dashed to the airport, and Julius barely caught his plane.

Father Walsh, who had cleared the way for Nyerere's trip, told him before his departure, "I think we're coming to the end of the road; one day you'll have to give up your teaching job." The headmaster of St. Francis' College, who was considerably less sympathetic than Father Walsh, told Maria during Julius' absence, "Your husband is causing our school to be threatened by the government. He had better decide whether he wants to be a teacher or a politician." A year earlier, the government had ruled that civil servants could not participate in TANU. By the time of Nyerere's trip to New York in 1955, the Governor had made it clear to the Catholic fathers that he felt no teacher in their employ should be permitted to engage in political agitation. As Twining explained it years later, a few months before his death, "Nyerere was in receipt of a salary paid by government. I said, 'We wouldn't allow civil servants to do this. Nyerere must choose between being a political leader and being a teacher paid by government. I can't have a man who is in receipt of a government salary, even if indirectly, being a political leader.' "

Nyerere resigned as soon as he returned, partly because he didn't want to get the missionaries in trouble. "But by then," he has said, "I was sure it would be absurd to go on teaching anyway. I really came back from the U.N. to say to the headmaster that in June I would go to Makerere to find a trained Tanganyikan teacher to take my place. But before that, he gave me a choice."

In April 1955, Nyerere took his family back to his Zanaki homeland to the house he had built for Maria three years earlier. He had received job offers from the government and from an oil company, but had turned them down. "I must be a free man," he said. In Musoma, he accepted a job as translator and tutor, at 700 shillings a month, from the Maryknoll Fathers, who were preparing to establish a mission in Zanaki. "I asked him if he would help me with the tribal language, Ki-Zanaki," Father Wille, who was to direct the new mission, has said, "and so he moved into Musoma; he stayed with Oswald Marwa, and he taught me every day. He translated some catechisms and a teachers' manual for the catechism. He offered to try to do a translation of the New Testament into Ki-Zanaki. No, there still isn't one. What he did translate was a reading from the Gospels for every Sunday in the year. And he taught me—oh, from nine until twelve-thirty, and from one to five. He used to exhaust me, he has tremendous intellectual energy. We were using *Teach Yourself Swahili* as the basis for the Zanaki grammar. I think there are seven classes of verbs in Swahili, and he would say, 'My language has twelve classes —this class in Swahili is similar to this one in Zanaki,' and so on. I used to be amazed he could remember it so well, because he had left tribal life when he was twelve and had never really gone back to it. He might say, 'I'll have to ask my mother,' or Oswald.

"Then we would have tea and talk about what he was going to do. He would say, 'There's no problem getting independence. The problem is preparing for it.' His greatest worry was what would happen afterwards. He once said, 'Those Baganda' "—the members of the largest tribal kingdom in neighboring Uganda—" 'I'm sure Britain would give them independence tomorrow if Uganda were united. *I'd* get them united, and then I'd put on the brakes.' I'm sure if someone else had appeared, Julius would gladly have gone back to his books. He was a scholar at heart. He would say to his friends, 'Why don't you go and read something?' Sometimes he would talk about the Masai. He had no sympathy for the way the British had romanticized the

71

Masai, he said the Masai would have to develop like every-body else. 'They're going to have to fall in line.' He would say, 'My people—it's a vicious circle: not enough food to do a day's hard work, and not enough money to buy good food.' He said he knew they would have to build a strong Presidency into their constitution, and yet somehow pro-tect the individual, a big problem."

In February a new Legislative Council had gone into session, this one based on Twining's multiracial "parity" policy under which "Europeans," "Asians" and "Africans" had roughly equal representation among the unofficial members of the council. Despite the fact that the Tangan-yikan population was more than 98 percent black African, Nyerere recognized the new formula as a modest advance. But he was infuriated a few months later when he learned that the Twining government proposed to divide certain funds gained from the confiscation of German properties during World War I in the same way—£711,000 for Euro-pean education, and equal amounts for Asian and African schooling. Nyerere fired off a letter charging that such a method of distribution was "inexplicable" in view of the Territory's racial make-up: 22,000 Europeans, 80,000 Asians and 8,000,000 Africans. "The advocates of parity have a duty," he wrote, "to see to it that its application does not make it look absurd and unjust." It would be far better, he said, to use the full amount to expand higher education without regard to race.

Occasionally, wearing a white shirt, khaki pants and carrying a walking stick, he held TANU meetings. "He had a big meeting at Butiama," Father Wille has recalled, "and he brought up the point: 'If anybody tells you we will throw out the Europeans and the Asians after *Uhuru*—that

72

is wrong. We all know Mr. Patel, over there. And we all know Father Wille and the Mennonites. We respect them, we need them.' " The government, however, had been keeping a close eye on him. Oswald Marwa, who was an assistant district officer, had been asked to tell Nyerere to report to him regularly—an easy matter, since the Nyereres were staying with Marwa. Once the provincial commissioner, the senior official in Musoma, asked Marwa, who was acting as TANU's local treasurer, to bring him the TANU books; but after inspecting them, he merely suggested a few bookkeeping techniques. Occasionally the police asked Nyerere's old friend Emanuel Kibira, who by then was headmaster of the Musoma School, how much money Nyerere had.

"During those months at Musoma," Father Wille has said, "Julius was kind of lost, I think. This was a time to rethink his life. He was a great admirer of Gandhi; he wanted *no bloodshed*. He fully expected to go to jail sooner or later. The house he had built Maria near Chief Edward's village had only a thatched roof, so I loaned him the money —a thousand shillings, I think—for a corrugated-iron roof. He was concerned that, if he should be imprisoned, Maria might have difficulties; a grass roof requires repairs. He got Oswald, who was doing all kinds of construction work, to put it on for him. Well, I never pressed him for the money. But on his third trip to the U.S., a couple years later, he appeared on TV, and when he got home he gave me a check and apologized for taking so long to repay, but said, 'Really, Father, I haven't had any money, and I got this for my appearance on television.' "

He also tried to fight the corruption in the Musoma hospital. "He knew the African drug dispensers were forcing people to pay for the government medicine they were giving out—a widespread form of petty graft, even today. So he sent in a child with a marked twenty-shilling note, and arranged for a police officer to check the dispenser immediately afterward. But the fellow was clever—he insisted the child change the bill and bring coins, so they didn't catch him."

When reminded of the incident many years later, Nyerere exclaimed, "Yes, I failed. The fellow escaped." Then, in an aside to his secretary, he murmured, "It's not easy catching corrupt people."

In August 1955, Nyerere was visited by Oscar Kambona, a young colleague from TANU headquarters in Dar es Salaam. Kambona has recalled, "Julius had left us in April, and until August we never had a word from him. Not a word! So in August, the TANU Central Committee asked me to find out how he was, and to take him three hundred shillings. So when I got to Musoma, I found him sitting on the floor reading a book about Gandhi. I told him of our troubles and gave him the three hundred shillings and, to my astonishment, he gave it to his brother Joseph to buy a cow—to give to *me* for a feast! This made a tremendous impression on me. We began to talk, and we decided to hold a public meeting and try out the non-violent technique. The district commissioner refused us permission to hold the meeting, but we said we would hold it anyway, and two hours before the scheduled time they said it was all right."

During the visit, the two men talked about TANU's rapid growth in the preceding six months, and Nyerere told Kambona that he would return to Dar es Salaam in September or October. After leaving Musoma, Kambona took the lake steamer to Bukoba and then to Mwanza, where

Paul Bomani, another close colleague, told him Nyerere wanted him to return to Musoma. But Kambona also received a telegram from Dar es Salaam advising him that the entire TANU Central Committee had threatened to resign. So he took the train to Dar es Salaam. As Kambona told the story years later, John Rupia, who was serving as committee chairman in the absence of Nyerere, had made the members angry. "John was very outspoken always, he would say, 'This is rubbish!' So I went to all the members and told them, 'Look, you can all write down your versions of the fight, and we'll settle it after independence.' Then I told them I had brought *money* from Bukoba—ten thousand shillings!—and that Julius would be coming back soon, and so they forgot about the fight."

THE SHY, BROODING, EMOTIONAL KAMBONA was born in 1928 in a corner of southern Tanganyika somewhere near the Mozambican border. His tribesmen, the Nyanja, were cousins of the Zulus of South Africa; they had wandered northward until their migration was checked by the Hehe of central Tanganyika. Unlike most of his contemporaries, Oscar was the son of educated parents. "My grandfather was a chief," Kambona has said, "and when the missionaries asked him for a boy to teach, my grandfather sent only a slave. Later, when he saw how the boy was benefiting, he sent his own son, my father. And my father became an Anglican priest. My mother, who also had been sent to school, was always arguing with my father's father. He wanted his grandchildren to look after the cattle, and he complained that school was making us tame. But my mother insisted. She read us stories about Booker T. Washington. She told us about all the big American Negroes.

75

"Our paramount chief had been given his chieftainship by the Germans. He ruled us for forty years against the intrigues of all the factions, including my grandfather's. He balanced the factions against each other, and the man he feared most was my grandfather. Late in his life, my grandfather became an Anglican priest too, and I always felt the chief encouraged him in this out of fear rather than love. He got the missionaries to move my grandfather out of the area.

"My grandmother was an exceptional woman. She almost came to rule. When my father would be ready to be transferred to another post, his mother would go first to the new post to see the chiefs and make arrangements for her son's arrival. Sometimes she would sit in the courts, and sometimes she would veto the court proceedings. She was very powerful. She had enemies. And she was poisoned and died. Yes! When I was twelve or thirteen. A sub-chief did it. The tribe wanted to bury him alive, according to the custom of the time. But my father urged them not to do this." And so the man was simply deposed.

Kambona's pursuit of schooling, as he tells the story, was a seemingly endless series of rebuffs and misunderstandings. At the mission school, where classes were taught in the tribal language, he was punished for using English words, he has claimed. "Even in Standards Seven and Eight, we had only two periods of English a week. I wanted to go to an English school, but I was rejected because I was already in a vernacular 'stream.' The bishop wanted me to become an Anglican priest, but my father refused because I was the first son, and so I was to become a grade-two teacher, a vernacular teacher."

7 6

The story of Kambona's eventual transfer to an English-language school, as he describes it, reveals both the extent of his hunger for education and his youthful cunning. "I was determined to go to secondary school, but I was rejected by them all. A new one was being built at Dodoma, with Australian and New Zealand missionaries, and they agreed to take me. But the fees were very high: I was to pay three hundred shillings a year, and my father was earning thirty-five shillings a month, with a family of six. So I went to the bishop. I said, 'Look, Bishop, I know you've tried. If a school admitted me, would you help me to go?' He said of course he would, but he thought no school would do it. Then I gave him the letter I had received from Alliance School! Well, he was very cross, he prayed for me. But then he said that, since he had promised, he would help. He gave me the three hundred shillings."

After two years at Dodoma, Oscar moved on to Tabora, where he spent the most difficult and apparently the most painful years of his schooling. "Twice I was almost expelled. The first day I was at Tabora, the headmaster, Mr. Blumer, said, 'Well, who is Oscar?' He saw me and said, 'I want you to cut off your hair by tomorrow morning, and cut it every two weeks thereafter.' He was one of the most *dictator* headmasters I ever met. At first he disliked me, but then we became friends. At Tabora I didn't do very well. I thought my English schoolmistress was against me. She didn't realize that my English was weak. At Dodoma, three of my teachers had been ill, and we didn't have the attention we needed. She said awful things to me. I began to take a keen interest in reading magazines, and she thought I spent too much time on them."

77

When he had finished at Tabora, Kambona became a teacher at the Dodoma school, transferred for a while to a nearby teacher training college but resigned because he decided the college authorities were not trying to help him get a scholarship to Britain or the United States.

Back at the Dodoma school, Kambona met Kanyama Chiume, a fellow teacher who was later to become a member of the government in neighboring Malawi before fleeing into exile in Tanzania. Kambona has given this account of how the two young men became interested in politics: "Every Saturday we went up the hill to a cave, the two of us. Chiume would stand up and address the audience, and the audience was me. Then we would break for tea. And then I would address the crowd, and my audience was Chiume. We would discuss how to organize a youth league, how to draft a constitution.

"Well, this was during Mau Mau in Kenya. One Saturday the Bishop"—the one who had sent him to school years before—"and the district commissioner and the headmaster came to the cave. Unfortunately it was I who was speaking. And Chiume said, 'Go on, go on,' and I went on, 'The British government must leave this country,' and so on, and Chiume was clapping. The bishop said, 'Let us pray'—for us to renounce hate. We joined in the prayer—for them to see our cause. They were angry, yes; they banned us from further preaching; all the teachers had taken turns preaching. But the bishop had great understanding." As he told the story twelve years later, Kambona added, "Just yesterday, someone told me his grave is in Dar es Salaam, and it needs attention."

Then, leaving his teaching career behind, Kambona moved to Dar es Salaam. He arrived soon after the founding of TANU and became a full-time party organizer. "I used many tricks," he has recalled with great enthusiasm. "I'd ride the buses, and talk to people at the stops, and then jump back in. I'd get a leader of a tribal group or a social group to buy memberships for all his members or friends." And by August 1955, he concluded, leaving the impression that the extraordinary rise of TANU had been largely a one-man feat, "we had one hundred thousand members!"

"We've never accepted the arguments of 'readiness for independence'—that people were not ready to govern themselves. That is like saying to an individual, 'You are not ready to live.' How do you say to a nation, to a people, 'You're not ready to be human'? It's part of humanness that people should govern themselves. It is incompatible with our being human beings that we be governed against our will."

"I THINK I REMAINED much more philosophical than political," Nyerere has said. "I wouldn't tackle things like discrimination. I just said, 'It is wrong for one people to govern another,' and everything else fell into place. So they called me a moderate. I believe I was a big extremist—that we must jolly well be independent! But probably this philosophical way removed the bitterness from the campaigns. I was not saying, 'Today a man was refused beer,' but just, 'We must govern ourselves.' Well, politically, this is the wrong way. In the Lake Region, the colonial government was saying, 'There are too many cattle.' I said, 'We can't campaign against cattle destocking because we may have to destock when *we* come to power.' There was one TANU man in Iringa who campaigned against cattle dipping.* He

* Immersing them in a trough filled with a parasite-killing solution.

made dipping *extremely* unpopular. I was very angry with him! But politically, of course, you exploit every grievance."

Nyerere returned to Dar es Salaam from Musoma in October 1955. During the next six years, until independence in December 1961, he toured upcountry Tanganyika almost continuously. TANU's Land-Rover, with license plates DSK 750, became a familiar sight throughout the Territory. "When he came to Bukoba," Miss Barbro Johansson, a Swedish missionary who campaigned with TANU, has said, "he and I would ride in the TANU Land-Rover, and the police would be in another. We had an understanding. If we had a puncture, they would stop to help; if they did, we would."

On his first trip to Mbeya, Nyerere found the police primed as if for a riot. "What are they expecting?" Nyerere asked in astonishment. He went to the police station himself, and was given permission to hold a meeting for TANU members only. Then the TANU party went to a local mission to borrow a loudspeaker, but the missionary couldn't decide whether it would be politic to lend them one. "It's up to you," the district commissioner told him. "So to play it safe," recalled Joan Wicken, who was visiting Tanganyika on a research fellowship, "the missionary said no. Eventually the police lent the TANU chaps their own loud hailers. And then, to my surprise, the police, including the inspector, saluted him. In his speech, he said, 'We are fighting against colonialism, not against the whites.'"

On a tour of the Usambara mountains, Nyerere drove eighteen miles in a rainstorm to speak to the people of Kimweri village, only to discover that the local chief had sabotaged his visit. "We were not welcome," Bibi Titi Mohamed, the early leader of the national women's organization, has said. "The chief was a stooge of the British. He had made them all drunk with *pombe*. So we drove back to Korogwe for the night." The women of Kimweri were furious with the chief for wrecking the meeting and particularly for getting their men drunk, and they refused to cook the evening meal. "We are on strike," they said. "Why don't you go and eat at the chief's house?" So the villagers sent a delegation to Korogwe and, over Mrs. Mohamed's objections, Nyerere agreed to return. "Listen, we must be patient," he told her, "we can't mind too much if we are chased away." So they drove back to Kimweri and, said Bibi Titi, "this time the *Mtemi* did nothing."

In Bukoba, Nyerere first met Miss Johansson when his throng of followers accidentally trampled the hedges and flowerbeds of her school. In the beginning, she has recalled, Nyerere complained of his sudden notoriety: " 'We must stop this, this singing of Nyerere songs.' " She told him, "You have to take this as a sacrifice for the sake of your work." The following year, there were great banners on the road to greet him. "I said to him, 'What do you think when you see your name in letters as big as a man?' He said, 'I beg your pardon?' I repeated my question and he said, 'Oh, I don't even see it.' "

Often, in the years after 1958, Nyerere rested at the Iringa home of Marion the Lady Chesham, the American-born widow of a British farmer. "There was no red-carpet stuff, no nonsense," Lady Chesham has said. "Such an easy visitor. I'd just tell the servants, '*Baba* Julius is coming.' He read the U.S. Constitution in my home. He said, 'Ha! They were the same average age as we—and people say we are too young!' " In that period, Lady Chesham performed an invaluable service for Nyerere and his colleagues; she served as their liaison with the Governor, Sir Edward Twining. "He *had* to see me," Lady Chesham has said, "because I was the widow of a peer of the realm."

TANU continued to grow at a remarkable rate: from one hundred thousand members in 1955 to half a million by 1957. "In a sense," Nyerere has said, "we had won the battle by 1957." Although he opposed TANU, the Governor was painstakingly even-handed in the way he treated it; he occasionally punished individual TANU branches for breaking the territorial laws, but at no time did he ban the entire movement. So Nyerere was always free to speak in one region if not another; at one point he was banned for several months from addressing public gatherings, but TANU meetings were not affected.

"When he first spoke in Iringa, there were fifty people," Lady Chesham has said. "By 1958 there were six thousand." A British friend who, a few years earlier, had taken Nyerere to Labor party meetings in London at which forty party members might dutifully show up, was embarrassed to discover that Nyerere's own meetings in Dar es Salaam were drawing as many as thirty thousand by 1957. Miss Mary Hancock, a peppery little Englishwoman who had come to Tanganyika in 1940 "to help the black people, as we called them then," has recalled, "Oh, that man, how he thinks! The civil servants in Musoma couldn't see why I remained his friend after he declared for *Uhuru*. We civil servants had to be careful, you know—we couldn't attend political meetings. I would say, 'He's my friend. If you can't differentiate, I *can*.' Well! You should have seen the civil servants change when it became clear that he was winning. They would ask me to invite them for tea with him, when he was visiting Musoma, and I'd say, 'Why should I? You wouldn't even talk to him before.' "

Yet TANU's transformation to a national movement came none too soon, for the politics of Africa were changing more rapidly than anyone then realized. In 1955, the U.N. Visiting Commission had urged the British government to promise independence to Tanganyika within twenty or twenty-five years. At the United Nations two years later, Nyerere himself asked for independence within twelve years; and in 1959 he reduced it to five years. But *Uhuru* came in December 1961. In 1958 the Governor of Tanganyika paid a visit to the Belgian Congo. He later recalled, "The Governor [of the Belgian Congo], a pocket Napoleon, told me, 'We admire what you British are doing in Tanganyika, of course. But aren't you going about it too quickly?' Well! Eighteen months later . . ." Eighteen months later, the Belgians recklessly settled their accounts in Central Africa by granting the Congo an independence for which it was tragically unprepared.

SIR EDWARD TWINING, a blustery idealist, was governor of Tanganyika for twelve years. He ruled from Government House with a strong will—"like Robert Morley playing the sultan," a Tanganyikan once said. In his early years as governor, he had deeply pleased the Hehe tribe of central Tanganyika by arranging, through a German museum, the return of the skull of a famous Hehe warrior, Chief Mkwawa, whom the Germans had slain in battle forty years before. It was a shrewd and magnanimous gesture, but Twining apparently had some private doubts as to whether the museum had sent him the right skull. When the Hehe asked him, "How can we be sure this is our chief's skull?"

85

Twining assured them, "Well, won't you recognize him?" An old man said, "*I* will. He had a great bump on the right side of his forehead." Twining told friends later, "My heart sank." The old man studied the skull for at least two minutes, turning it around and around in his hands for what seemed to Twining an eternity. At last he said, beaming, "*This* is our Mkwawa."

Twining never got on well with Nyerere, whom he dismissed as a racialist. "I've seen Twining so mad about Julius, he forgot he had gout," Father Walsh, who was a close friend of both men, has recalled. "In December 1954, I was with Twining at his lodge at Lushoto, his leg wrapped up in his chair. Oh, he was angry, he just wouldn't listen to me. He said, 'Nyerere is not intelligent, he's just an emotionalist.' I said, 'All revolutions in the world have been inspired by men of emotion.' Twining was the last of the Kipling era, one of the greatest men I've met. But he was from the world of Kipling. They sang a Kipling hymn at his funeral, "Lest We Forget, Lest we Forget." He was the last of the empire builders, and Julius was the first of the radicals, and so they clashed. Both were honest, both were idealists. Twining said, 'He's trying to pull the chair out from underneath the British Empire!' He said, 'I'll destroy that man'—but of course he had gout, remember."

Another man who was close to both Twining and Nyerere was the polished David Makwaia. "It was difficult for me," Makwaia has since recalled. "One tended to be regarded as a stooge of the colonialists. But Twining once said to me, 'I've been trying to meet Julius Nyerere socially. He has kept promising he would turn up, and he never turns up.' Julius said, 'He is quite right. If you are going up there, I'll go,' and I took him to Government House that day at six P.M. Only one servant was present, and he quickly disappeared. Lady Twining was not there. I recall that both of them were reluctant to start the discussion. Then Twining, having poured himself a gin, said, 'Look, Julius, what do you want to drink? I'm having a gin, what about you?' Julius said, 'What about you, Chief?' I said, 'I suppose I can break the law in Government House and get away with it.' Julius said, 'Well, I'll have a small beer.'

"I said, 'Now, you wanted to talk. Why do you seem so shy?' Twining said, 'I feel the president of TANU and the Governor should discuss matters of state, because whatever I do will have some bearing on what Julius Nyerere wants to do.'" They began by discussing the terms "multiracialism" and "nonracialism." "Then," Makwaia continued, "I said, 'You have said you are preparing Tanganyika for self-government or independence, and Nyerere is demanding there be a timetable. What is your objection to that?' Julius said, 'David is quite right. We would be very happy if the colonial government could state the number of years until independence.' Twining said, 'I'll tell you in confidence. I'd say fifteen or sixteen years from now, this country should attain independence. But you cannot expect me to say that in public.' Julius said, 'Why not? That is exactly what we want; and we would then work for it.'"

Many years later, Lord Twining reflected on Tanganyikan politics from his apartment in Ashley Gardens in London. "The mandate was the foundation of our policy," he said. "It stated that we should bring Tanganyika to self-government and independence, but it set no time limit. We refused to have a timetable. The last visiting commis-

87

sion, in 1955, said it should be within twenty-five years. In 1958, I said I thought it would be within twelve or fourteen years. My policy was based on the accepted policy of the British government: nonracialism, with a gradual program of turnover to African control; a plan of carefully graded objectives. Now Nyerere's was a rabid African nationalism. Nothing in it about nonracialism: he wanted one-man–one-vote immediately! I told Nyerere, as long as they didn't break the law they could do as they wanted. But it got out of control; some TANU branches set up their own courts! Well, I thought Nyerere was a nice chap. Mild, moderate, intelligent. He would agree with me, and go off next day and address thirty thousand people and say the opposite. He is a very shrewd politician, an emotionalist, and that was the sort of stuff they wanted. But he is not greedy, not corrupt; I think he is a good man."

Long after the independence fight was won, Nyerere made this assessment of Twining: "He was one of the greater governors—to the extent that I can appreciate colonial governors. If one were to write a history of the colonial period, I would give an important place to Twining, and to Sir Donald Cameron; they were the most prominent.

"Twining came at the wrong time, and he stayed too long. But you must give him credit: he had ideas. But he had a fault. Who is the Turk referred to by the English poet Pope, 'Like the Turk he likes to rule alone, and does not like another near the throne'? Well, *he* was governor, and he didn't like anyone to tell *him*. He did good things. The British did little to develop this country, but to the extent that development took place, it was pushed by Cameron and Twining. The deep-water berths in the port are from Twining's time; the new Dar es Salaam airport is Twining; the tarmac road to Morogoro, the big school at Iringa, all Twining.

"Politically, he didn't like anyone near the throne. He saw some European settlers thinking of establishing here the kind of empire they had in Kenya, and he put a stop to that. There would be one voice, and it would be that of Government House! One voice and none other! I respect him. But we clashed as early as 1954. In his vague mind, I stood for racial dominance, and his party was 'multiracial.' By 1955 he realized he couldn't fight us alone, and he tried to revive the European voice—but it was too late."

TANU's TABORA CONFERENCE in January 1958 was one of the pivotal events of the pre-independence period. In December 1955, Twining had sponsored the formation of the "multiracial" United Tanganyika Party as an opposition to TANU. Two years later he announced that the first elections in Tanganyika would take place in 1958; in each of the ten constituencies there would be three members of the Legislative Council—one African, one Asian and one European, and each voter would vote for a candidate of each race. Most of the TANU leadership thought the party should boycott the elections; Nyerere argued at the Tabora conference that it should participate.

Nyerere's brother Joseph has recalled that, at the beginning, Nyerere was supported by only one member, the delegate from Tanga. "All the other delegates, more than two hundred, said no, we should boycott the elections. The debate had gone on for two days, and the last day I wasn't at the meeting. That day there were only two speakers— Bhoke Munanka and Julius. Well, I had the impression

89

that the whole country was against our contesting the election. So when I came back and was told that we were going to participate, I said, 'But how can we, when there were only two who wanted it? How could they decide like that against the wishes of the people?' And I went to his place in the evening, and I said, 'You dictator!'

"Julius said, 'OK, I know you are fired up, now sit down and I'll tell you. If we don't participate this year, the UTP is going to win. All members will be returned unopposed. And TANU will be fighting from the outside. The only thing we could do is send a petition to the Colonial Office explaining our position; the Colonial Office would send a commission of inquiry; and the next election would be three or four years later; and by that time the UTP would be firmly established. We might get our independence by 1970 or 1975.

" 'But suppose we do contest it. Everybody says that TANU will elect only ten members, but that's not true. We also have Europeans and Asians who are friends of ours and will support us. We'll have thirty TANU-supported members. Then we'll fight from the inside *and* the outside. We'll demand a new constitution. In a few months we'll have self-government, and we'll be independent by 1961.' "

Joseph reflected on his brother's powers of persuasion. "Julius is not hurried in reaching a decision. We'll discuss it. Then he will say, 'OK, now let's go out for a beer, or take tea.' Then we'll come back and he will say, 'OK, tomorrow,' and you go on like that until he has convinced you."

ON MAY 27, 1958, the TANU newssheet *Sauti ya Tanu* published an editorial by Nyerere cautioning party members to refrain from violence. "The reason why lunatics have been trying to provoke the people into violence," it said, "is the fact that they know we are virtually invincible if we remain a law-abiding organization . . . Fellow Africans, be on your guard. The enemy is losing the cold war because he has no argument against our case. Don't give him that chance. Don't be provoked into violence. Be as calm and good-humored as you have always been." The editorial then singled out two district commissioners for criticism; it charged that one D.C. had put a chief on trial for "cooked-up reasons," and accused another of trying to undermine TANU. However mild such comment may seem to have been, the colonial government saw fit to file three counts of criminal libel against Nyerere on the basis of the editorial. The case dragged on for almost three months. In the end, Nyerere was found guilty, and was given a choice of paying a fine of £150 or serving six months in prison.

Many observers felt the authorities had behaved unwisely in pressing the case. Even Twining, in later years, blamed the incident on "an obstinate Irish attorney general" and added, "Under the British system, a governor can't interfere, any more than he can interfere with the chief justice." Whatever the truth of this statement, it was generally assumed in Tanganyika that Nyerere would seize the opportunity to become a "prison graduate" like most other African nationalist leaders. Indeed, Nyerere's friends recall how he wrestled with the decision. Resting at Lady Chesham's farm, he would say lightly, almost jokingly, "Shall I go to jail? Every other Prime Minister has gone to jail. But I *can't* go to jail—it's an election year."

The trial coincided with another important event, the

retirement of Twining and the arrival of a new governor, Sir Richard Turnbull. A tall, thin, erudite man, Turnbull had served as chief secretary in the Kenya government during the height of the Mau Mau Emergency. He took the oath of office on July 15, a week after Nyerere's libel trial had begun. To the surprise of virtually everyone in Tanganyika, Turnbull invited Nyerere to Government House for a talk on July 24, more than two weeks before the trial ended. "The British made a mess of the trial," Turnbull has said. "Tremendous feeling had been aroused. I had been through four years of the Emergency in Kenya, and I didn't want to go through that again. I couldn't wait for the judgment. I sent for him."

A friend recalls that Nyerere said at the time, "When I went to see Turnbull, I thought I should say something polite, so I said, 'I thank you for what you intend to do for Tanganyika.' But Turnbull put it aside. I took a deep breath and thought, 'Thank God, this man is shy. With him I can probably work.' "

Nyerere said in later years, "Turnbull could have fallen into Twining's footsteps and gotten into real trouble, because the political movement was now very militant. I was determined to go to jail. The showdown had come, and we were in the mood to fight. I expected that he would invite me to talk with him, but I thought he would wait until the trial was over. But he didn't wait. Well, I respect people even if they represent systems I am fighting. And also, we realized he had inherited difficulties not of his own making. I felt after our first discussion that it was absurd to precipitate crisis for the sake of crisis." He chose to pay the fine. As Turnbull has put it, "He did a very generous thing: he gave up the martyr's crown."

92

* * *

IN THE CAMPAIGN THAT YEAR, Nyerere ran for a seat in the Eastern Province against Chief Patrick Kunambi, who had fallen out with the TANU National Executive committee and decided to run as an independent. In one incident, TANU supporters broke up a meeting of Kunambi's by throwing rocks. "I know Julius was very upset about this," Kunambi has said. "No, he didn't speak to me about it. He finds it difficult to talk about such things. He understood, I understood, that's all." In Dar es Salaam, Nyerere campaigned for the TANU candidate against a European named Tyrell, whose campaign slogan was: "You all know Tyrell." "We all know Tyrell," Nyerere said in his speeches, mimicking and animating the line until his audiences shook with laughter. "Who doesn't know Tyrell? Oh, we know Tyrell, all right." As Nyerere had predicted, TANU and TANU-sponsored candidates won all the seats they contested; Nyerere himself received 2,600 votes, as compared with 800 for Kunambi. The following March the Governor increased TANU's role in the government significantly by giving it five of the twelve ministerial posts. It was on that day that Nyerere, with victory so clearly in sight, celebrated with his colleagues Amir Jamal, an Indian, and Derek Bryceson, an Englishman, by "jumping around the room, first on one foot and then the other," as Bryceson once described it, in a burst of joy.

Pounding away at his main theme, *uhuru na kazi*, freedom and work, Nyerere cried, "We cannot go around the world begging for money. We must work for the things we want. This is God's ordinance—not Nyerere's." Condemning the traditional practice of giving petty bribes to chiefs and elders, he declared, "The people can no longer

93

afford to see justice purchased with gifts of goats and chickens."

When he attended a conference of independent African states at Addis Ababa in 1960, Nyerere delivered a study paper in which he said that the creation of an East African federation was so important that, if necessary, Tanganyika would be willing to have its independence delayed so that it could become independent with Kenya and Uganda simultaneously, and could federate with them immediately. An aide released the paper to the press by accident, and it quickly became apparent that Nyerere had not cleared the statement with his party leadership. "Every major TANU official in Dar called us to say that Nyerere couldn't have said such a thing," a former editor of the Tanganyika *Standard* has said. But Nyerere took responsibility for the idea, and later explained, "I felt we should become one country. The question was how? When? I argued that the best time to achieve federation would be at the time of independence—we could combine the freedom movement with the unity movement. Freedom was popular; unity could be popularized. You would be asking the states to achieve something, whereas after independence you would be asking them to surrender their sovereignty, and that's not easy. My point was: Don't wait until the day the flag goes up. So I said, 'We in Tanganyika will delay our independence until Kenya and Uganda get popularly elected governments.' But my friends [the British] didn't see it that way."

In the elections of August 1960, TANU candidates won seventy of the seventy-one seats in the new House, and Nyerere was called to form a government. "But success must not go to our heads," he told his followers. "We must not become big-headed with ideas as big as Kilimanjaro, forgetting the past and future." In March 1961, a constitutional conference was held in Dar es Salaam; in May, Tanganyika achieved full self-government and Nyerere became prime minister. As a concession to the Colonial Secretary, Iain Macleod, Nyerere agreed that Tanganyika should first become a monarchy, with a governor-general representing the Queen; only later did many of his colleagues realize that they would wait a full year before Tanganyika would become a republic within the Commonwealth.

A British journalist, John Collier, has recalled dropping by for a beer one day at Nyerere's six-room government bungalow in Dar es Salaam's Seaview district. "Yes, it's a beautiful view," Nyerere reflected, "but that car is in the way. Will you move it, John?" No, he had never learned to drive, Nyerere said wryly; why should he bother, when there were always so many people around who wanted to drive for him?

By this time, Nyerere's views on African affairs were being solicited regularly by the British and American press. For years afterward, journalists in East Africa fondly retold a possibly apocryphal story about the time a British reporter pleaded with Nyerere to rephrase a point he was making in more colorfully African language. "Oh, I don't know," Nyerere is supposed to have said. "You do it, you're good at that sort of thing." The reporter quoted Nyerere as saying that unless African leaders could find ways of meeting the aspirations of their people, "we shall fall, as surely as the tickbird follows the rhino," a line widely quoted thereafter. "Not bad," Nyerere said.

One of Nyerere's first acts as prime minister was to

suspend the practice of supplying Tanganyikan laborers to South Africa's gold mines. The new policy cost Tanganyika £500,000 a year, but Nyerere regarded it as morally unavoidable. A few months earlier he had written: "In South Africa, the white man behaves like a man at a sleeping giant's throat. He dare not relent his grip for fear of the consequences. This fear drives him to suicidal madness and he tightens his grip until the giant wakes up feeling the pain." He was also beginning to speak of the nonalignment that would become a cornerstone of his foreign policy: "We shall not allow our friends to decide who our enemies shall be."

"Julius and TANU were very inexperienced in those days," Sir Richard Turnbull has said. "In Ruanda-Urundi, they supported the wrong people, the Watutsi, who had the quarrel with the Belgians, on the principle that the enemy of my enemy is my friend. In point of fact, the Watutsi were the immigrant aristocrats, the Hamitic overlords, the fifteen percent in Rwanda, while the Bantu peasantry were the other eighty-five percent.

"Two things I used to reflect on: One tends to underestimate the terrible poverty of Africa. One may say, 'Why don't the young men of Africa go back to the villages?' But how can they, when they don't have even two hundred pounds to buy fertilizer and essentials? The terrible drain of poverty.

"And secondly, the nature of the African family. There are no old-age benefits; the old and ailing have to be looked after. So when one acquires wealth, everybody shares it. As chief minister, Nyerere sometimes had as many as forty people staying there. Oscar Kambona once

96

complained to me that his relatives took his clothes; he had gotten a new suit, and his father had taken it. Well, Julius found this terribly demanding, all these people wanting jobs, and Maria with forty people. All we could do to help was to paint his house frequently, and that meant pushing them all out. Of course this happens everywhere in Africa; corruption is sometimes explained in these terms, the hordes of hangers-on who have to be taken care of. Julius never complained, but I know it was a burden to him."

The wives of the diplomats and civil servants gave "knife and fork" parties for the African wives so "they wouldn't be embarrassed using them," as a Briton later explained it. But the practice ceased abruptly after Rashidi Kawawa condemned it as "a blow to African customs." Turnbull has recalled that he used to teach Nyerere informally, sometimes using Herbert Morrison's *Essence of Parliament*. "When dealing with an African," Turnbull has said, "it's always better to quote a Labor man."

"We the people of Tanganyika," Nyerere had said in a Legco speech two years earlier, "would like to light a candle and put it on top of Mount Kilimanjaro, which would shine beyond our borders giving hope where there was despair, love where there was hate, and dignity where there was only humiliation." On the night of December 9, 1961, climbers planted such a torch on the summit of Africa's highest peak, while in Dar es Salaam, five hundred miles away, seventy-five thousand Tanganyikans and their guests, including the Duke of Edinburgh, participated in the ritual of independence. At exactly midnight the stadium lights darkened as the British flag was lowered and the green, black and gold colors of Tanganyika were raised.

And then, as Nyerere had long warned, the real problems began. Toward the end of Tanganyika's first turbulent year of independence, Nyerere was asked what he felt was the most significant thing his country had accomplished. "We have learned this hard fact of life," he said, "that there are no shortcuts to our aspirations."

THE TWELVE MONTHS that began on December 9, 1961, when Tanganyika became independent, and ended on December 9, 1962, when it became a republic, have been characterized by Sir Richard Turnbull, who stayed on as governor-general, as "the year in the wilderness." It began with an unexpected series of deportations. The British manager of the Palm Beach Hotel in Dar es Salaam asked four Africans—one of whom, he later learned, was the mayor of Dar es Salaam—to leave the hotel bar. He was immediately served with a deportation order. At an inn in Korogwe, three Britons got into an argument with a young African who turned out to be a parliamentary secretary. All three were deported. At Lindi, a Swiss citizen who had lived in Tanganyika for nine years was similarly expelled. According to the government, he had pinned an *Uhuru* badge to his dog's collar and "paraded the animal in front of the people . . . He was heard to say that his dog was just as good as the people who were celebrating independence." What alarmed the British press was not the fact that the Tanganyikan government had reacted angrily to racial incidents, but that it had expelled the individuals, usually on twenty-four hours' notice, without giving them a chance to answer the charges. "For once," said *The Economist,* Nyerere "showed an inept touch and did not ensure that justice was to be done." "It may be," said the *Guardian,* "that an African leader has to behave as a racist occasionally even

though he is not one, and to talk like a politician even
though he is a statesman. It may be that racism, like small-
pox, is best prevented by vaccination." Even in Tanganyika, many observers seemed to believe Nyerere was simply
allowing the party a bit of self-indulgence. "One principle
outweighed all the rest: to avoid a quarrel with the party,"
Turnbull has said. "The law provided that [the deportees]
had some recourse to the courts. This wasn't allowed
them." But, he added, "there were the rich Indian merchants in their Mercedeses, and there were the privileged
Europeans, and the Africans were still in the same position,
with nothing changed. What had they but national pride?
The rash of deportations was very offensive to the national
spirit, but it let off some steam."

Unhappily, the twenty-four-hour deportation became,
in Tanganyika as elsewhere, a symbol not only of the African's rise to power but of the arrogant and even whimsical
use of that power. (In Kenya a few years later, the government obliged one of its Cabinet ministers by expelling his
American-born wife on a few hours' notice; the charge
against her was "disaffection toward the Kenya nation.")
But it was a practice for which Nyerere never apologized.
"For many years we Africans have suffered humiliations
in our own country," he said at the time. "We are not going
to suffer them now." A few years later he added, "I think
we were definitely right. You go through two stages in these
colonial countries. One is when midnight comes; the clock
strikes, and you are independent. Fine. But then begins a
whole process of changing conditions and changing people.
I had been talking to the people, telling them that the second
process would not be easy. I'd been saying over and over,
'*Uhuru na kazi*,' work, work, work, long before independ-

ence. Getting the people ready for the next stage: 'Don't expect miracles, don't expect a better house after midnight.'

"But," he continued, chopping his words in anger, "one thing *must change* after midnight: the attitudes of the colonial people, their way of treating the Africans as *nothing*. This must change after midnight. The colonized are now the rulers, and this man in the street must *see* this! If they have been spitting in his face, now it must stop! After midnight! This cannot take twenty years! We had to drive this lesson home."

Such incidents continued as evidence of the abrasive tension that remained. The following year, the Safari Hotel at Arusha was ordered closed without warning; its twenty-eight guests, mostly whites, were given an hour's notice to find other lodgings. The government's complaint, it turned out, was that the hotel had insulted Guinea's President Sékou Touré, who was in Tanganyika on a state visit. On the previous day, when Touré's party, led by Oscar Kambona, arrived at the hotel for lunch, nobody stood up as the distinguished visitor passed through the lounge; guests said they had had no idea whom the party consisted of. Peter Walwa, the regional commissioner, complained that the hotel had neglected to display national flags or other decorations, and in addition had served "a poor meal." "When we came into the hotel, an attitude of mind showed up," said Oscar Kambona, "and we thought it was time we showed an example. One thing an African will never stand for is this lack of dignity accorded him as a human being. We are very sensitive to no appreciation of our dignity." Inevitably, the foreign press criticized the Tanganyikans for their hypersensitivity and arrogance; the local white community tended to blame Kambona and Walwa and to take refuge in the thought that Nyerere, had he been present, would have smoothed things over. The Safari Hotel was allowed to reopen a few months later.

In a somewhat similar incident, sixty-nine members of the government and party applied for membership in the Dar es Salaam Club, a squat old relic of colonialism. The club refused to take them, but implied that the applicants might be accepted later if they were properly proposed and seconded. Of the club's nine hundred and eighty members at the time, only nine were Africans. By late 1963, the club had become the subject of angry parliamentary debate. "Here is a club which even President Nyerere cannot enter," shouted one M.P. "We don't know what's going on in this club, either. For the sake of our security, it's time the club was closed down." But Job Lusinde, the Home Affairs Minister, assured him that the government was watching the club's every movement: "Our security is such that even if a group of people meet in a hidden place for subversive activity, they will be found out. We wait until the iron is hot, and then we strike." Eventually the government decided to dissolve the club and take over its assets. Since the club had been started by Germans before World War I, explained Lusinde, it was former enemy property and should have been confiscated long before. "This," declared a jubilant M.P., "is real African socialism." The club's veranda thereafter became a favorite meeting place of Tanganyikan politicians. As in the Safari Hotel case, Nyerere remained aloof from the controversy; a few years later, when the reorganized club fell into bankruptcy, he promised personally to see that its bills were paid.

*   *   *

ONLY SIX WEEKS after Tanganyikan independence, the London *Sunday Telegraph* carried a report that Julius Nyerere had resigned as prime minister. When shown a copy of the paper, according to the Tanganyika *Standard*, Nyerere "read the first few words, laughed loudly and said, 'Oh, boy.' " He laughed again after reading a reference to Oscar Kambona as "one of Nyerere's strongest opponents" and told the *Standard* reporter, "You can say I read it and laughed."

The next day, however, he announced that the report was true. "Today I relinquished my position as prime minister," he said. "Before doing this, I myself selected a new team of ministers, with Mr. Rashidi Kawawa at its head." He had decided to devote himself to the rebuilding of the party, he explained, because he believed this was the best way to achieve "our new objective—the creation of a country in which the people take a full and active part in the fight against poverty, ignorance and disease." In addition to an able government, he said, the country needed a "strong political organization, active in every village, which acts like a two-way all-weather road along which the purposes, plans and problems of the government can travel to the people, at the same time as the ideas, desires and misunderstandings of the people can travel direct to the government. This is the job of the new TANU." He knew such a step was unusual, he said, but added, "We do not believe it is necessary for us to copy the institutions of other countries. We do believe we must work out our own pattern of democracy." He asked Tanganyika's friends abroad to "understand these changes and not to try and read into them a different significance than they have."

His request notwithstanding, Nyerere's resignation

was widely interpreted as a strategic retreat. "It looks as if Mr. Nyerere has met a too-common fate among African moderates," said the *New York Times*. "The swiftness with which pressures from more radical and nationalistic elements rose against him and drove him out of office is disquieting." A better-informed judgment was offered by *The Economist*: "If anyone had been asked to prescribe a nightmare formula that would do the most harm to the reputation of Tanganyika throughout the world, he could hardly have improved on the concoction brewed in Dar es Salaam this week." Even Jomo Kenyatta, in nearby Kenya, said he had heard "with great sorrow" of the resignation of his "dear friend." In Dar es Salaam, journalists interpreted the series of deportations as evidence of discontent within the party; they also noted the recent inclination of *Uhuru*, the party's Swahili-language weekly, to adopt a strident, racial tone; it had referred to the country's Indians as "snakes" and to the remaining British officials as "the prophets of colonialism." Indeed, the resignation became the first in a series of not-quite-explained incidents that were to become an odd hallmark of Tanganyikan politics.

If Nyerere had in fact had a serious quarrel with some members of the National Executive committee in the weeks following independence, he has never admitted it publicly. "I had known a month earlier that he might do it," Turnbull has recalled, "but I hoped that he was being unnecessarily pessimistic." There is no doubt, however, that Nyerere regarded the rebuilding of the party as the most urgent task facing the country; and that, when he told the National Executive committee of his plan, it took him some three days to win their consent. "We had deliberately tried to discuss nothing but *Uhuru,*" he has said. "But then the nation was asking, 'What next?' I couldn't sit here. I had to answer the vital questions."

The following morning he called in Rashidi Kawawa, who was a Minister Without Portfolio at the time. "And," Kawawa has recalled, "he said, 'Look, Rashidi, you are the Prime Minister from right now. Take the chair.' I got the shock of my life! Yes, we had given him the green light [to resign] the previous evening. He argued with us for four hours that night; but he didn't tell us when he wanted to do it. This shocked everybody. He is always dramatic, you know."

"He was very agitated," Amir Jamal has said. "He had already gone through the agony of the decision. He said, 'I'm asking Rashidi to become Prime Minister, and all you fellows are going to stay on.' "

When Nyerere told the Governor-General that he had finally decided to resign and that Kawawa would succeed him, Turnbull pointed out that Kawawa was scheduled to leave on a trip to Nigeria that very evening. "I said they'd better not let him get off. They hadn't thought of this." Turnbull was also disturbed about the effect the announcement would have overseas. "Julius was awfully bad at handling his public relations. I told him, 'Look, this will have to be very carefully explained to the world—in the towns here, in Britain, in the U.N., and in other African countries; you must tell each of them, and in a slightly different way. You must get your public relations chaps to work on it.' And I told him to tell the overseas staff by cable. But they didn't do any of this. The Tanganyikan High Commission in London didn't know for a week. They didn't know if Julius was ill, or what."

105

Despite the lingering confusion, Nyerere never regretted his action. Several years later, long after he had returned to office as President of the Republic, he was asked if he thought he had been right to resign so suddenly after independence. "No question about it," he said. "If I made any mistake, it was that I came back." His listeners laughed, but he was deadly serious. "I was convinced my function was to lead the masses. If I regret anything, it is that it would be difficult now to go back to the masses. It changed the tone of the country. I will not say we are therefore different from other East African countries, but I think we are different from what we might otherwise have become. If this country has anything, it has a sense of purpose. I think my actions in 1962 helped give it that sense of purpose. I think it's the best thing I've done for this country."

Nor have his friends ever doubted that he made the right decision. "As a result of that resignation," Amir Jamal once said, "nobody will ever accuse him of hanging on to power for the sake of power. They know they're dealing with a very serious man."

RASHIDI KAWAWA was born in 1929 to a family of elephant hunters. "My father inherited this profession from his father, and he from his father," Kawawa has said, "and I learned it from my father." He belonged to the Ngoni tribe of Songea district, but grew up in several places in Tanganyika, including Kilwa and Nachingwea, because his father, a government game scout, was frequently transferred.

After his graduation from the Tabora School, where he heard Nyerere debate the merits of education over wealth, Kawawa became a clerk in the social welfare depart-

ment in Dar es Salaam and, by accident, a film actor. The
department had imported a film-producing unit from South
Africa and had begun to make films of its own. "Well, I
was a young man, you know, it was very exciting, so I
decided to play a part in a film. I was given the leading role
in a picture called *Bitter Cassava*. It was a story of a country boy who was attracted by town life and misled by it,
and who decided to go back to his village. Another film was
called *The Ship Is Sailing*. It was about a village girl who
was misled by a town boy. She went to Mombasa and was
abandoned by the boy. She decided to go back home and
found that her fiancé had married somebody else. So she
bewitched her old fiancé's wife, you see, and she was found
out and taken to jail. That was her fate."

Later Kawawa worked in a camp where some of
Kenya's Kikuyu tribesmen were being detained during the
Mau Mau Emergency in Kenya. "At first the Kikuyu were
very suspicious, they thought I was a spy. But then they
discovered I could be very helpful. I organized them into
committees, and took their complaints to the camp commander."

During his travels throughout the Territory, Kawawa
helped to organize meetings of the Tanganyika African
Government Service Association (TAGSA), in which his
father had been active. As TAGSA's president, Kawawa
helped raise money to send Nyerere to the U.N. in 1955.
"But please," Kawawa cautioned Oscar Kambona, "when
you receive the money, just give me a receipt, don't write
'Given to TANU,' or I'll be in trouble." In October 1955 he
became general secretary of the Tanganyika Federation
of Labor, and the following year he resigned his civil service
job and joined TANU. From then until independence,

TANU and the TFL worked closely together. The brewery strike of 1958 was led by Nyerere himself. "If you drink beer, you drink the blood of your own people," Nyerere told his TANU audiences. "And it worked," Kawawa has said. "We paralyzed the beer bars everywhere, and within a month they had to give in to our wage demands."

From the day he took office as prime minister, Kawawa insisted that he was merely sitting in for Nyerere. "He is the Father of the Nation," said Kawawa, "and as president of TANU he is the most powerful and important man in Tanganyika. I am a member of the party, and I am always guided by it." After his election as President, Nyerere named Kawawa Vice-President, and Kawawa has since remained his closest political ally.

JULIUS IS BACK WITH THE PEOPLE, reported a headline in the *Standard* soon after he resigned as prime minister. In the Lake Region, he complained that too much money was being buried in the ground, and told of a man at Shinyanga who had shown him £500 in ant-eaten notes. "We shall have a bank here," Nyerere declared. Still arguing for East African federation, he shouted, "If we want more places where we can have prime ministers, let us Balkanize Africa even more. Let every tribe go to the United Nations. You have no idea how many votes we would have from Tanganyika if that happened." In words strikingly like those of his Arusha Declaration five years later, he said, "Our emphasis must be on what we ourselves can do. We must produce more cotton, more coffee, more tobacco, and if, without too much government assistance, people can build a dam or a school or a road, they must do it. This is what we can rely on—not outside assistance."

Under the self-help program, villagers all over the country donated a day's work a week to a community project—a new road, a well, a school or clinic. According to one government announcement, the population built $2,500,000 worth of projects during the first half of 1963, for which the government donated $200,000 in materials. To understand the enthusiasm of many villages, a visitor had only to spend a day that year at a place such as Kibamba, fifteen miles west of Dar es Salaam, where two hundred villagers hoed and hacked at a new roadway to the rhythm of drums and castanets. One man, seemingly berserk with exuberance, raced back and forth through the crowd waving his pickax like a bayonet. There were, miraculously, no casualties. Prime Minister Kawawa, who had arrived to hoist a few ceremonial shovelsful of earth himself, seemed slightly put off by the pandemonium. "I think I have made you too joyful," he said. "We are all sweating," boasted the local TANU official, "from the Prime Minister down." Much of the early excitement faded when villagers waited in vain for the government to send a roof for a new community center, or a teacher for a new school. If he could repeat the experience of the early months of independence, Nyerere said later, "I'd try to make better use of the people's enthusiasm—try to give more guidance about where a road should go, or whether a school should be built."

SIX MONTHS AFTER INDEPENDENCE, the government abolished the powers and salaries of the hereditary chiefs. "The reason the chiefs were not absorbed into the nationalist movement," a former chief has said, "was primarily due to their own short-sightedness. Most of them were too closely

109

identified with the British authorities; and there were growing tensions between the old chiefs and the younger, educated ones. 'They are ambitious,' the old men would say,
when the young ones favored change. The colonial administrations found the chiefs useful in trying to carry out
policy, and also as scapegoats if things went badly." For
example, he recalled, the chiefs in Sukumaland—the region
of Tanzania's largest tribe, the Sukuma—were pressured
into supporting a plan for cattle destocking. "To the
peasant, his cattle were his wealth. He couldn't care less
if they were only skin and bone. Any effort to reduce his
cattle simply meant the government was trying to make
him poorer. Well, the old chiefs started accusing the
younger chiefs. 'They want you to get poorer,' the old
chiefs would tell their people. It was Machiavellian—a case
of hunting with the hounds and running with the hares.
Many of the younger chiefs decided to wait and see, and
they got caught in the process. The nationalist movement
was able to label them anti-people. As long as the chiefs
had any power, they could be a headache to TANU. So it
was expedient for the TANU government to get rid of
them."

Another former chief has said, "There was feuding
in Nigeria and Ghana between the chiefs and the demo-
cratically elected governments, and problems of double
loyalties. To avoid these problems, TANU decided to abol-
ish them altogether. TANU's aim was to streamline the
government from the top down to the village level, and re-
taining the chiefs would have made a break in the direct
line."

The only chief who survived as a powerful political
figure was Abdullah Fundikira. A conservative and a tradi-

tionalist—who, in fact, had once said of himself, "I am tradition"—Fundikira became minister of justice and later was the first chairman of the Tanganyika Development Corporation. He was resented by many of the TANU leaders, including Kambona. At Cabinet meetings, Sir Richard Turnbull has recalled, "I used to sit and watch Kambona hating Fundikira." He continued, "Fundikira was the doyen of the chiefs' corps; he was reserved and dignified, with a suggestion of the divine right of kings about him. I think he was contemptuous of some of the younger politicians, who were noisy and undignified. When an African is embarrassed, he often takes refuge in the guffaw. At Cabinet meetings, I would see them laughing their heads off at some insoluble economic problem, and would turn to see Fundikira looking at them."

Eighteen months after independence, Fundikira was arrested on charges of corruption; he was accused, as chairman of the National Agricultural Products Board, of having accepted £2,500 "to incite him to do something in relation to granting an agency for purchase of produce to certain merchants." Fundikira denied the charge, and was acquitted. In December 1963 he resigned from TANU, saying he disagreed with some of its basic policies. Later he rejoined the party and subsequently became chairman of the East African Airways Corporation.

WHEN PARLIAMENT reconvened in mid-February 1962, with Nyerere seated among the backbenchers, the government offered legislation to convert the system of land ownership from freehold to leasehold. In a paper entitled "Ujamaa," in which many of his ideas about African socialism were explained, Nyerere wrote: "To us in Africa,

111

land was always recognized as belonging to the community." Man's right to the land "was the right to use it; he had no other right to it, nor did it occur to him to try and claim one . . . The foreigner introduced a completely different concept, the concept of land as a marketable commodity. According to this system, a person could claim a piece of land as his own private property whether he intended to use it or not. I could take a few square miles of land, call them 'mine,' and then go off to the moon . . . Such a system is not only foreign to us, it is completely wrong . . . Unconditional or 'freehold' ownership of land which leads to speculation and parasitism must be abolished."

Shortly thereafter, the government announced the details of the new republican constitution that would go into effect on the first anniversary of independence. Under the new constitution, a President was to be elected by universal suffrage; the President would then appoint a Vice-President who in turn would preside over the National Assembly, or Parliament. Having an elected President, rather than a governor-general representing the Queen, said Kawawa, would "provide a new focus for loyalty" and would be "more capable of inspiring a sense of loyalty in the people." "The pattern of dictatorship emerges in Tanganyika," cried the London *Daily Express,* and there was widespread criticism that the strong powers handed to the Presidency could lead to authoritarianism. Reflecting his British tutelage, Nyerere told Parliament that "the ultimate safeguard of the people's freedom is the ethic of the nation." What was needed, he said, was a national ethic that enabled the government to say, "We cannot do this, this is un-Tanganyikan," and the people to say, "That we

cannot tolerate, that is un-Tanganyikan." Without such
an ethic, said Nyerere, "no constitution, however framed,
could insure that the people would not become victims
of tyranny." As for political campaigning, he told the Assembly, "it is not a traditional African practice. It smacks
of pride, vanity and sometimes stubbornness. A man standing before the public outlining his good qualities—this is
a shameful thing."

IT WAS A FOREGONE CONCLUSION that Nyerere would become TANU's candidate for President. He combined elec-
tioneering with his TANU duties, stopping only at those
villages that had undertaken self-help projects. In the
November election he polled 98-1/10 percent of the vote.
Not long after that, a visitor asked him if he had been
surprised to receive so high a percentage of the vote.
"Why?" he replied sharply. "I would not have been surprised to have received ninety-nine and nine-tenths percent.
We are a united people. I would not have been surprised
for America to have had only one party in the beginning.
You would have said, 'We've got to win the war and get
this stupid King George out! The most important thing is
unity! The issue is, should we be led by a monarch three
thousand miles away?' We Tanganyikans want to govern
ourselves. This is no issue. We laugh at the happenings
in Kenya"—where, a year before independence, the two
major parties were in conflict. "We say to the Kenyans,
'You have no sense of priorities—one hundred percent
unity is the answer.' My ideas of democracy are Western.
I never questioned the two-party system until I was confronted with the problem in Tanganyika. Is it necessary
for a democracy to have a two-party system? I said no.

It's no good standing on Mount Kilimanjaro and shouting our disagreement."

For much of the preceding year, Nyerere had been pondering the meaning of a one-party system in a democracy. "What nonsense it is to have elections on this basis," he would tell his colleagues, "because people do not in fact have any choice. It's not democratic. So what do we do?" A friend has recalled, "He would scribble a draft, and play around with it, and this went on for several months."

Following the November 1962 elections, Nyerere announced that the National Executive committee had voted to ask the party's national conference to open party membership to non-Africans, and to grant "complete political amnesty" to all persons who had been expelled from TANU since 1954. "We were not racialist then, but we were realistic," he said. "We were the Africans of Tanganyika fighting for our rights. Our aim was to be racial in composition and nonracial in policy." But as early as 1955, he said, the policy had become an embarrassment; that year the party had voted to accept any Tanganyikan who was half-African. In early 1963 Amir Jamal became TANU's first non-black member, and Derek Bryceson became its second.

As for the other change, Nyerere explained, many members had been expelled in the past for failing to support TANU candidates, but the party realized that under a one-party system such practices made no sense. "We realize you can't have an election in Tanganyika between TANU and another organization, so it will have to be between members of TANU."

It was not until after the 1965 general elections, however, that Western criticism of Tanganyika's one-party system began to subside. Sir Richard Turnbull has said, "None of us realized at the time that the one-party state is the natural and proper way of governing a country like Tanganyika. How can there be two parties? Maybe in ten years, if they develop differing economic programs. But the dominant thing is national pride and feeling, and raising the level of the people." The key point, as Nyerere wrote in a pamphlet called "Democracy and the Party System," was that parties such as TANU "were not formed to challenge any ruling group of our own people; they were formed to challenge the foreigners who ruled us. They were not, therefore, political parties, i.e., factions, but nationalist movements."

Would the country develop a two-party system at some later stage? "It does not necessarily follow," Nyerere said in 1964. "It could become a multi-party country, but I see no necessity for that. We are rejecting the idea that only a two-party system can be a democracy. The philosophical concept of freedom is not a matter of mechanics." He was also rejecting the notion of his Western friends who were "making allowances for us to go through an undemocratic period in the beginning." He added, "But look, brother, this is not right. We must not be undemocratic even in the beginning."

"I MUST CONFESS," said a British resident of Dar es Salaam in late 1962, "I don't quite understand this security mania." "The ferocious desire for total unity," wrote the correspondent of the *Times* of London, "has led the government to introduce precautionary legislation out of all proportion to the mouse that squeaks defiance." And so it seemed. The opposition to TANU, insofar as it existed at all, consisted of a few dissident trade union officials and one or two tiny political parties. Nonetheless, the government in 1962 pushed through Parliament a labor law virtually banning strikes, and, under a certificate of urgency, a preventive detention law enabling the government to imprison without trial any person it deemed dangerous to the national security. "We feel that while this country is peaceful," Nyerere said, "its roots are not really all that deep." A few months later he explained further: "We know this law could be a convenient tool in the hands of an unscrupulous government. The point is, preventive powers are assumed by democratic governments at times they consider such powers necessary. Britain had such a regulation in wartime, India has one which she recently used. We hope we misjudged the danger. We don't want to use this drastic law. This is a huge country, with five hundred miles of coastline and borders with seven nations. And we have *eleven hundred men* in our army. Eleven hundred men! Our security is in the hands of the Almighty! I have no money for a large army or a large police force. But I can put this law on the statute books. It's a safeguard. And I think it has done some good."

The "Africanization" of the civil service was already under way. Several hundred Britons had left Tanganyika with their "golden handshakes" or "lumpers"—severance pay amounting to as much as $28,000 a man. By the end of 1963, roughly half the senior- and middle-grade posts were held by Africans, but there were many vacancies. Many of the Africans were insufficiently trained; many of the Europeans were newcomers on short-term contracts.

Since independence, the trade union leaders had

pressed for accelerated Africanization. The head of the railway workers union, Christopher S. K. Tumbo, had threatened a strike; in Parliament he had called the white civil
servants "mercenaries." In April 1962, presumably to
get rid of him, the government sent him to London as
Tanganyika's new high commissioner. In August he resigned, however, dropping hints that he didn't really have
to work for a living. In September, when the detention bill
was passed, Nyerere spoke with uncharacteristic vehe-
mence: "What is to be done to traitors? A man from Tanganyika, a poor country, to have money sufficient to keep
him going without employment for the rest of his life?
Where did he get the money? What do we do with such a
person?" By that time Tumbo had started his own political
group, the People's Democratic party, but in late November he slipped across the border to Mombasa, Kenya, where
he became a press agent for a cement factory.

The other opposition party was the African National
Congress, whose leader, Zuberi Mtemvu, accused Nyerere of
plotting to "introduce neocolonialism" into newly independent African states. In May 1962 he announced a three-stage
plan—"cool, warm and very hot"—to obtain a "purely
African government" in Tanganyika within twelve months.
For several months the government prevented the ANC
from holding meetings, but lifted the ban in time for the
November elections, in which Mtemvu was Nyerere's chief
opponent. Mtemvu drew 21,276 votes to Nyerere's 1,127,-
978. A few days later Mtemvu asked to rejoin TANU.
"The most significant result of the election," said a TANU
statement, "is the refusal of our people to have anything
to do with racialism."

* * *

THE CELEBRATION of *Jamhuri* (Republic) in December 1962 was much like the ritual of independence a year earlier. At the National Assembly, an African sergeant-at-arms bellowed "Mistah Speakah!," and carrying the mace, entered the chamber. He was followed by the be-wigged Speaker, the chief justice and, finally, to the roll of a nineteen-gun salute, the Governor-General, who delivered his farewell address and prorogued Parliament. At a midnight ceremony another tattoo was played, fireworks were set off, and schoolchildren marched forward to slay the papier-mâché dragons of poverty, ignorance and disease. Nyerere, now President, moved into State House.

Most of the first year had been devoted to domestic problems; the emphasis of the second—in addition to a series of official visits to West Germany, the U.S., Canada, Algeria, Scandinavia, Guinea and Nigeria—was on African affairs. Nyerere ridiculed existing African boundaries as "ethnological and geographical nonsense": "It is impossible to draw a line anywhere on the map of Africa which does not violate the history or future needs of the people." At the Afro-Asian Solidarity Conference, held in Moshi in February 1963, he said, "As we emerge successfully from the first 'scramble for Africa,' so we are entering a new phase—the phase of the 'second scramble' . . . The events in the Congo have demonstrated that it is possible for a colonial power to leave by the front door, and the same or different external forces to come in by the back . . ." At the founding session of the Organization for African Unity at Addis Ababa in May, he told the delegates, "The real, humiliating truth is that Africa is not free; and

118

therefore it is Africa which should take the necessary collective measures to free Africa."

In June, Nyerere met in Nairobi with Jomo Kenyatta of Kenya and Milton Obote of Uganda, and the three announced that they had agreed to inaugurate an East African federation before the end of the year. "We cannot create a continental government overnight, but we can start in East Africa," Nyerere said. But the talks broke down at the ministerial level, and by the end of 1963 Nyerere was calling the failure to achieve federation the major disappointment of the year.

Some observers speculated that the June 1963 announcement of federation had been a cynical attempt to induce the British government to advance the date of Kenya's independence; Kenyatta, in fact, once implied as much. "If it was a pressure technique, it was quite unnecessary," a former British diplomat has said. "Britain was as anxious for Kenya's independence as the East Africans were." The Tanganyikans have insisted, however, that this was not the purpose of the negotiations, and that at least several of the Kenya delegates—notably the late Tom Mboya— were as determined to achieve federation as the Tanganyikans were.

Both Kenya and Zanzibar became independent in December 1963.

"IF YOU DON'T BELIEVE in human equality, quit the party," Nyerere had said the previous July. "Those who do not believe in the principle of human brotherhood had better burn their membership cards." Africanization was a kind of discrimination, he said, but was "justifiable" to redress

119

past inequities. But on January 8, 1964, in a critically important move, Nyerere announced that the government's two-year-old policy of Africanization was being ended. Thereafter, he said, Tanganyikan citizens of all races would be equally eligible for government jobs. "It would be wrong for us to continue to distinguish between Tanganyikan citizens on any grounds other than those of character and ability to do specific tasks. We cannot allow the growth of first- and second-class citizenship. This action is not taken for the sake of people with brown or white skins, but for Tanganyika."

The announcement was harshly denounced by trade union leaders in Tanganyika, and was tragically misunderstood by the men of the Tanganyika Rifles. It was a prelude to the most serious crisis of Nyerere's life.

In the meantime, four days later, revolution broke out on Zanzibar, twenty-four miles away.

JULIUS NYERERE'S FRIENDS recall that he had long worried about the closeness of Zanzibar to the Tanganyikan mainland. "If I could tow that island out into the middle of the Indian Ocean," he had said a few years earlier, "I'd do it." At a dinner party in Dar es Salaam a year or two before independence, he had remarked that he thought one of Tanganyika's biggest problems in later years would be Zanzibar. "No, I'm not joking," he said at the time. "An alien monarchy, with the sons dabbling in politics. It's very vulnerable to outside influences. I fear it will be a big headache for us."

If Nyerere's friends were skeptical of this prediction, it was partly because Zanzibar Town in those years seemed like nothing so much as a magnificent old theater set, a relic whose grand but evil history had passed it by. It was also a tiny place, compared to the territories of the East African mainland, consisting of two principal islands, Zanzibar and Pemba, with a total population of 319,000 and an area of only 1,020 square miles. Zanzibar Island, which lies twenty-four miles off the Tanganyikan coast, is fifty-three miles long and twenty-four miles wide at its broadest point.

But Zanzibar had always seemed more menacing to the mainlanders than its dimensions warranted. In an earlier time, the island's Arabs used to say, "When the pipes are played on Zanzibar, all Africa east of the Lakes must dance." It was a proud boast and an accurate one, for Zanzibar was the base from which the Arab slavers and traders set off by dhow for Bagamoyo on the mainland coast, and on by caravan toward the Great Lakes of Central Africa. Zanzibar was the center and the symbol of the Arab tyranny in East Africa, the marketplace and shipping point for the mainland's exports—its rhino horns, ivory and human beings. It was also the point from which the great explorers, Burton, Speke, Livingstone, Stanley, set off on their expeditions to the interior.

The Arabs and Persians visited it from ancient times, the Portuguese took it in 1503, and the Arabs of Oman seized it in the seventeenth century. In 1832 the ruler of Oman, Seyyid Said bin Sultan, moved his capital to Zanzibar, bringing with him the cloves that were to become the island's major export crop. He also brought the sultanate's red flag that survived as the flag of Zanzibar until January 12, 1964. Toward the end of the nineteenth century the Germans explored and annexed some sixty thousand miles of what had been regarded as the sultan's mainland territories. Faced with the prospect of having an aggressive European power as a neighbor across the channel, the Sultan of Zanzibar willingly submitted to the protection of the British Crown in 1890.

During the seventy-three years that Zanzibar remained a British protectorate, its territories included a ten-mile-wide strip of land that ran for fifty-two miles along the Kenya coast and included the port of Mombasa. This land was administered by Kenya but remained a part of the sultan's dominions, and the Zanzibar government received £11,000 a year in rent for it.

Zanzibar's decline coincided with the gradual abolition of slavery. In 1872 the slave trade was banned within the sultan's dominions, but the island remained dependent on slave labor to work the Arab-owned clove plantations. In 1897 all slaves who "cared to apply" were freed. By 1963, the year of independence, there were few visible traces of the heritage of slavery except for the Anglican cathedral that stands as a memorial on the site of the slave market. Zanzibar had become a tranquil but marvelously vivid place, pungent with the aroma of cloves and other spices, a land of coral beaches and iridescent palms and the decaying remnants of lost rulers. Old Arab guides took visitors to see the Beit-El-Ajaib, the "House of Wonders"; to the residence where David Livingstone spent several weeks preparing for his last expedition; to the Jubilee Gardens beside the ocean wall. A world asleep, or so it seemed; a place where British civil servants, in tropical shorts, worked until midday and spent the long afternoons at sailing and other sports, and evenings at the English Club. But even then there were a few forebodings. There had been, for example, the riots at the time of the 1961 elections in which seventy persons were killed. Of these, sixty-nine were Arabs.

For a visitor, it was no easy task to distinguish between the Arabs and the Africans on Zanzibar. Of the island's population of 319,000, 650 were "Europeans"— mostly British, with an occasional German, Italian or Greek; 20,000 were "Asians"—Indians, Pakistanis and Goans; 50,000 were classified as Arabs; and the rest as black Africans. Some called themselves Shirazis, claiming to be descended from Persians who visited the region in ancient times. Of the Arabs, a few were pure-blooded and looked, in fact, like creatures out of *The Arabian Nights*.

123

Most, however, were as black as the Africans. As a British resident explained at the time, "The way the local people sort it out, those who belong to the Arab Association, or *used* to, are classified as Arabs."

There were three political parties in Zanzibar. The oldest was the Zanzibar Nationalist party (ZNP), which had been founded in 1956 from the ranks of the Arab Association. Much of its membership was African but its leadership was purely Arab, and practically every Arab in the island belonged to it. The party was loyal to the Sultan and flew his red flag as its own. The party's leader, Ali Muhsin, was a former civil servant and an educated man. He was also something of an Arab sentimentalist, and was rumored to advocate the establishment of a loose Moslem union with Somalia, Sudan and Egypt. He rejected any notion of association with East Africa, and his declaration that "Zanzibar shall not become a district of Tanganyika" had a strong appeal to many Zanzibaris, particularly the Arabs. The ZNP's hierarchy contained most of the educated men of Zanzibar; primarily for this reason, the British clearly favored the party over its rivals.

Also within the ZNP was a brilliant young leftist named Abdulrahman Mohamed Babu, who returned to Zanzibar in 1957 after spending five years in London. He became the general secretary of the party and the organizer of its youth wing. Partly because he had visited China and the Soviet Union and partly because he edited a small newspaper, *Zanews*, that was sponsored by the New China News Agency, Babu was long regarded as one of East Africa's few certifiable Communists. The 1961 rioting frightened the ZNP's leaders, and caused them to send several groups of Babu's youth wing members to Cuba for military training so that, in the event of further trouble, they would be able to defend themselves.

In 1962 Babu was jailed for fifteen months on a criminal-libel charge. Shortly after his release the following year, he had a quarrel with Ali Muhsin over how many parliamentary seats the ZNP would allot to Babu's youth wing leadership in the elections that year. Accordingly Babu resigned, taking his youth wing with him, and established the *Umma* ("Masses") party. By this time a number of Babu's followers had returned from Cuba, and signs reading ZANZIBAR SÍ, YANQUI NO were beginning to appear in such places as the American consulate. The improbable blend of Communist political agitation with the traditional soporific spell of Zanzibar led one Western diplomat to observe, "It's as if part of Fantasyland had slipped its moorings. The leftist front here amounts to about forty people."

The British authorities, who regarded Babu as a firebrand and a rogue, sought in 1963 to curtail his political activities overseas by withdrawing his passport. But the resourceful Babu paddled to the mainland by canoe, talked the Tanganyikans into giving him an emergency passport, and showed up in London to attend the Lancaster House conference at which the Zanzibari constitutional details were settled. Then he paid a visit to Peking and arrived home shortly after independence.

The second major political organization in Zanzibar was the Afro-Shirazi party (ASP), which was founded in 1957. It was the island's black African nationalist party, and it had links with mainland parties such as TANU. Its president was Abeid Karume, a big, burly, uneducated former dock worker and boatmen's union official whose forebears had come from Nyasaland. Another leader, and an enemy of Karume's, was Othman Shariff, a Makerere College graduate and a veterinarian. A third was Kassim Hanga, who had shared a London flat with Oscar Kambona for a while in 1958, and later studied in Moscow. He returned to Zanzibar in 1961 and became the party's deputy secretary. The party suffered grievously from a lack of educated leadership. One British Labor party member, after meeting the hulking, unprepossessing Hanga in 1958, concluded, "If this is a leader of the ASP, the ASP is not the party we should support."

Yet it was clearly the most popular party in Zanzibar. In the June 1961 elections, the ASP received 49-9/10 percent of the vote, the ZNP 35 percent. But each won ten seats in the Legislative Council. The remaining three seats were taken by the Zanzibar and Pemba People's party, which received 13-7/10 percent of the vote. The ZPPP had broken away from the ASP four years earlier after a personality clash between Karume and the head of the ZPPP, Mohamed Shamte. It was Shamte himself who broke the tie in 1961. The wily old Shamte cast his vote in Legco for the ZNP, thereby permitting the party to form a government. Shamte demanded and received a handsome reward for his cooperation: he became chief minister.

The Afro-Shirazis were angry at the election outcome; they felt victory had been snatched from them by the Arabs and their Sultan with the connivance of the British. As a constitutional monarch, the Sultan was supposed to be above politics; but his young son Jamshid, who was best known for his love of sports cars and speedboat racing, had openly favored the ZNP. "At the moment," a British dip-

126

lomat commented, "the Sultan is not serving a very useful purpose, and if he were, he might not remain."

The Sultan, Seyyid Sir Abdulla bin Khalifa, died suddenly in July 1963, and his son Jamshid succeeded him. The soft-spoken Jamshid lasted barely six months.

The Afro-Shirazis, as well as their allies in the mainland governments, urged the British authorities to reshape the constituencies to ensure that the party with the largest popular vote would lead Zanzibar to independence. The constituencies were in fact redrawn, and the Afro-Shirazis assumed that they would be the beneficiaries. "I'm certain," said Othman Shariff, "that we can get seventeen seats." But the July 1963 elections, held under the watchful eyes of several hundred British marines, produced a repetition of the 1961 stalemate. The Afro-Shirazis polled 54 percent of the popular vote but took only thirteen seats. Together the ZNP and the ZPPP won eighteen seats, and Mohamed Shamte became prime minister. At the independence conference in September, the British tried to persuade Shamte to form a national government of all three parties; but Shamte refused.

The independence celebration on the night of December 9, 1963, was attended by visitors from seventy countries, including the Duke of Edinburgh and the Aga Khan, but none of the East African heads of state chose to attend. "We appreciate that *Uhuru* does not mean distribution of loot," said Shamte. "There is no loot to distribute." To many Africans in Zanzibar the occasion was called *Uhuru wa Waarabu*—Arab independence day.

THE GOVERNMENT of Prime Minister Shamte was jittery from the beginning. It seized the passports of several opposition leaders, and is said to have handed out weapons to many Manga Arabs, who were fiercely loyal to the Sultan. It also speeded up the process of "Zanzibarization" of the police force, whose ranks had previously been filled largely with mainland Africans, including a number of Makonde tribesmen from southern Tanganyika and northern Mozambique. These discharged policemen remained on the island, unemployed and embittered.

Then, in early January, the government banned the Umma party and appeared to be on the verge of arresting Babu, but Babu escaped to Dar es Salaam. "I had been charged that week with possession of a weapon," he explained later. "It was a very old gun that my child had found in a garden. I had made a speech two weeks before, and they said I had attacked the Throne [of the Sultan]. I heard they intended to put the two matters together and make a charge of treason. They intended to arrest me on Thursday at four in the morning. But a policeman I knew tipped me off, so I went to Dar es Salaam to get a lawyer. I didn't want to be arrested over there and not have a lawyer to fight it." Babu's three-year-old daughter had been killed by an automobile a few days earlier; there were rumors that the police had hoped to arrest Babu after the child's funeral, but he failed to appear.

The Afro-Shirazi leaders, who had worked closely with Babu since his resignation from the Nationalist party the previous July, were convinced that the government would arrest them as soon as it was finished with the Umma leadership. An ugly fight had broken out within the Afro-Shirazi leadership, meanwhile, between Othman Shariff and Abeid Karume. Shariff attacked Karume as "an utter fail-

128

ure" and demanded that he resign as party leader. There were also rumors that Shariff was negotiating with Prime Minister Shamte, who happened to be his brother-in-law, and might try to form a new coalition party.

"We had all speculated about how long it would take for trouble to arise," a former British civil servant on Zanzibar has said. "I guessed it would come in the second quarter of 1964. The ministers had decided they would not recognize Umma, and the A.S.P. youth element had said, 'Right, we're next for the block.'

"Immediately before this, the ministers had been very touchy. Some thought the Makonde tribesmen, with their bows and arrows, were plotting. It scared the daylights out of the locals. Then the ministers thought bombs were being landed to the north. I thought we were chasing wildcat rumors. Or it could have been a smoke screen—to get part of the force out of town. We had long pressed the ministers to make an agreement with the British for defense. In event of trouble, the East African mainland countries would obviously have been the best source of help; but the Zanzibar government couldn't get that support. We told them, 'You must mend your fences.' "

Sultan Jamshid said, much later, "On Saturday [January 11] a friend told me, 'There will be trouble tonight or tomorrow.' I had planned to go hunting for wild pig. I called a minister and told him. You know, people in the outlying districts were the ones who had been in danger in June 1961, when seventy people were killed. He assured me everything was all right."

Babu, who by that time was in Dar es Salaam, has said, "On Friday I heard over here in Dar es Salaam from some-

129

one—a member of the Afro-Shirazis—that something would happen very soon. Well, you know, you always heard those stories. But I thought this might be true."

"This was the whole point," Julius Nyerere remarked later. "The ASP was a popular movement. [In earlier years] I kept telling the British to do what I was convinced they would do in Kenya and Tanganyika." It was clear, he said, that they would yield to African majority rule on the mainland. "But I kept saying I was afraid about Zanzibar. That in their *very British way*, they would feel they were fulfilling their function if they handed Zanzibar over to the Sultan. I said, 'Yes, of course we are prepared to deal with a ZNP government—but the Zanzibar people will not accept it.'

"I did say to the Americans, 'Look, you tell the British: they must do in Zanzibar what I know they will do in the rest of East Africa. They must not cook up things in Zanzibar!' [Iain] Macleod was the one British leader who understood what I was talking about. I thought, good. In no time, he was out as colonial secretary, and we went back to [Duncan] Sandys.

"In May 1963, Sandys was right here in this office. I said, 'Of *course* we'll cooperate with whatever government they have, but we don't believe the Nationalists can be elected if you don't cook things up.' He said"—mimicking Sandys' smooth, patronizing tone—" 'Mr. Nyerere, why don't you like the Sultan?' He said, 'Our lawyers have told us, we didn't have a sound legal claim on the coastal strip of Kenya. The Sultan was extremely decent with us. He asked only that the Kenya government look after his citizens there.' I said, 'Fine, Mr. Sandys. If you had no legitimate

right to stand on the Kenya coast, you have no legitimate
rights on Zanzibar either. Why don't you pension him?'
   "This was the eleventh hour!"

IT STARTED late Saturday night, January 11, 1964, on the
last weekend before the beginning of Ramadan. The narrow
streets were crowded with townspeople, and the Afro-
Shirazis were holding a dance at the Raha Leo community
center. Despite the festive air, many Zanzibaris were ap-
prehensive; one African was told by a friend, "Go home
early and sleep very soundly tonight." In late evening,
the field police on duty at the Mtoni mobile force armory
were ordered to town, four miles away, to stop some rioting.
The order could have been based on a genuine report, but it
was more likely a ruse to get the policemen out of camp.

   Sometime after midnight, bands of men attacked and
overwhelmed the guards at the Ziwani police armory, on
the outskirts of town, and then at the Mtoni camp, seizing
hundreds of machine guns and automatic rifles. Both Ziwani
and Mtoni had fallen by five o'clock. By six, the only real
resistance was coming from the Malindi police station near
the harbor in Zanzibar Town. "I didn't sleep that night,"
Sultan Jamshid said later. "At about one-thirty I heard
shots. Around nine they called me and said that all was lost,
and that I should go to the boat in ten minutes." Under the
protection of the Malindi station, Jamshid and his party
escaped on the steamer *Salana* and were later transferred
to the Sultan's yacht, the *Seyyid Khalifa*, in the Zanzibar
Channel.

   An hour or two earlier, Prime Minister Shamte had
asked the British High Commission to send troops to Zanzi-

bar. It was, as a British diplomat later described it, "a rather hysterical request." He added, "Of course, there was no defense agreement between Zanzibar and Britain. H.M.G. was under no obligation at all. No, Britain never had any intention of responding to the request of a government that no longer existed." Nor does there appear to have been any chance that Shamte could have gotten support from any East African country, since this would have involved the use of troops to put an Arab government back into power over an African state. Shamte also sent a small plane to Pemba Island to bring back weapons, but the road to the airport was blocked before the plane returned. At 2:10 on Sunday afternoon, radio operators along the East African coast heard the Zanzibar tower operator say, "This is getting serious. A truckload of thirty men has just driven up. An armed party is down below. I'm going down to meet them now." The Dar es Salaam operator replied, "Best of luck." The government of Zanzibar had fallen on the country's thirty-fourth day of independence.

NOBODY KNEW exactly who the rebels were. By Sunday afternoon one embassy in Zanzibar was calling it an Afro-Shirazi takeover; another reported that "the Afro-Shirazis are providing the bodies, and Umma the brainpower." On Sunday evening, a man who identified himself on Radio Zanzibar as "the field marshal" announced in Swahili that the Afro-Shirazi party and the three-month-old Umma party would form a new government. He said that Zanzibar had been declared a republic, and that the President would be Sheikh Abeid Karume, the Afro-Shirazi leader. Curiously enough, he also called on Karume to "come back and take your job."

The next day the field marshal introduced himself as John Okello, a name previously unknown in Zanzibari politics. He announced that the Sultan had been banished for life and that his palace and property had been confiscated. "His foot may never touch our soil again." Amid reports of widespread fighting in the *shambas*, the field marshal asked the Tanganyikan government to send a planeload of medical supplies, and called for nurses to return to their hospitals.

In Mombasa, Kenya, an American destroyer, the U.S.S. *Manley*, which was in East Africa on a good-will visit, was dispatched to Zanzibar to pick up the employees of a U.S. satellite tracking station, and on Tuesday morning the *Manley* reached Dar es Salaam with ninety-nine evacuees, including fifty-three Americans. Two Dutch students on the *Manley* said they were convinced that a rebel leader who wore a green cap and claimed to be a "Persian" was in fact Cuban. Some thought they heard him speaking Spanish. Throughout the week, a number of persons arrived in Tanganyika with similar reports, giving rise to the early headlines that Zanzibar had become, overnight, the "Cuba of East Africa." Even a visiting U.S. diplomat claimed to have talked to a "definite Spanish-speaking type." But who was in charge? Karume had been away from the island at least once since the shooting began; Babu had been in Dar es Salaam during the entire period; and nobody had ever heard of Okello.

Every night the field marshal ranted wildly over Radio Zanzibar. "I shall take severe measures," he declared. "Eighty-eight times more severe. There will be no divorce. Anyone who gets a divorce will be given sixty-five strokes. The Sultan was a devil. Imperialists and capitalists are

133

devils. Do you reject these devils?" Another night he shouted, "It is I, the field marshal, who speaks. You will see how we hang people and burn them like chickens. Others will be cut into pieces and spread on the streets. Others will be thrown into the sea, and others will be tied to trees and shot. Anyone who tries to be a hypocrite will be punished by fifty years. Anyone looting even a bar of soap will be liable to eight years. I can make one hundred grenades an hour." To an Arab named Harusi he vowed, "Kill yourself and your sons or we will do it for you."

On Monday, Karume had appealed for peace. On Tuesday, Okello said four former ministers would be hanged. On Wednesday, Karume contradicted him: there would be no hangings and no reprisals. On Thursday, Karume flew to Dar es Salaam with Babu and Hanga to urge Nyerere to recognize his regime and provide some mainland policemen to help restore order. Okello, apparently unaware of Karume's trip, said he had made Karume President and that Karume had played no part in the revolt. That night he declared himself President, with Karume as his deputy. Later he denied that he had made such a statement.

By this time, East Africa was full of contradictory rumors about John Okello. He was said to have received military training in Cuba; he was reputed to be a former Zanzibar policeman. Everyone agreed that he spoke Swahili with a mainland accent and that his apocalyptic words had the strange quality of an Old Testament prophet gone mad.

On Thursday afternoon, on the fifth day of the revolution, Okello arrived at his headquarters, the yellow-stucco Raha Leo, the radio station and community center where the Afro-Shirazis had held their dance on the previous

Saturday night. In front, hundreds of Africans milled around, scraps of yellow or green cloth pinned to their shoulders; many swung rifles carelessly. At the front door, two women waved guns and knives at visitors. Next door was a hastily improvised camp where scores of frightened pure-blood Arabs were being held. When the field marshal appeared in his black uniform, the crowd cheered, shook his hands and shouted, "*Jamhuri, Jamhuri!*"—Republic, Republic!

Upstairs, a few steps from the radio studio where he spoke several times a day, Okello welcomed his visitors and, with the help of a translator, spoke at some length about himself, seemingly with relish. Like his radio oratory, his words had a dreamlike quality; but unlike the broadcasts, they were simple and without rancor except when he spoke of the Arabs. He was twenty-seven, he said, a Lango tribesman from Uganda who had moved to Kenya and had served for three years in the Mau Mau, rising quickly to the rank of brigadier because "I had the power of interpreting dreams." He said he had moved from Kenya to Pemba Island five years earlier, had become a house painter and had taken an interest in Afro-Shirazi politics. He had planned the revolution by himself, he said, training small groups of people in rural areas by using pieces of wood as practice guns. "I started the revolution," he said, "because I heard that the Arabs were slaughtering the poor Africans." The first attack, he said, was made with pangas, knives, and bows and arrows. He had named the new cabinet on Sunday night without consulting Karume and Babu, he claimed, and he implied that he didn't care much for Babu. He hadn't even told Karume about the revolution beforehand, Okello said, lest Karume try to stop it.

135

He rambled on about other matters. His new government would be "entirely democratic and won't lean to any bloke." Or did he mean bloc? His visitors laughed, and he smiled shyly too. Whom did he most admire among living men? Churchill and Khrushchev. He had never visited Cuba or anywhere else overseas, he insisted: "I never had enough money to go to Nyasaland." It was a not unreasonable statement, since many Zanzibaris of African origin had come from Nyasaland (now Malawi).

It was a strange interview, but his visitors came away with two impressions. In the first place, Okello seemed clearly to have the support of the little army of unprofessionals who lingered around the Raha Leo. The trained and uniformed young men outside the Zanzibar Hotel, to whom Okello's name meant little or nothing, were a different breed; these were Babu's Umma members, with their beards, berets and occasional words of Spanish, who had joined the revolution sometime Sunday morning. Secondly, Okello seemed to believe what he was saying. The story about his participation in the Mau Mau was bizarre, especially for a Ugandan and a man who was a member of neither the Kikuyu nor a closely related tribe. But who could say? Could an interpreter of dreams have insinuated his way into the Mau Mau?

In the years since 1964, the new leaders of Zanzibar have gone to elaborate effort to deny that John Okello played any significant role in the revolution at all except for his radio broadcasts. On the first anniversary of the fighting, *The Nationalist*, the TANU-supported newspaper in Dar es Salaam, managed to publish the "first authoritative story" about the revolution without once mentioning Okello's name.

136

* * *

THE SITUATION ON THURSDAY had been somewhat complicated by the illegal arrival of seven Western newsmen—four Americans, two Britons and a Canadian—by dhow from Bagamoyo. It was also the day that Karume, Babu and Kassim Hanga had flown to Dar es Salaam to plead with Nyerere for recognition and to ask for his help. Evidently they succeeded, because the first of three hundred Tanganyikan field policemen began to arrive a day or two later. The young American chargé d'affaires, Frederick Picard, had spent much of the afternoon discussing the journalists' case with the amiable Othman Shariff, who had been appointed minister of education in the new government—to his great surprise, in view of his recent open fight with Karume over the Afro-Shirazi leadership. In the early evening, Picard, Shariff and several of the newsmen sat drinking beer in a corner of the Zanzibar Hotel lobby.

Suddenly the bulky Karume strode into the room, followed by half a dozen of his revolutionary colleagues. Standing over Picard, he bellowed in his broken English, "Why are you causing us trouble? Why are you interfering in our affairs? Why? Why? You Americans, why did you evacuate your people without telling us? Why do you not recognize us?" Picard protested gently that he had informed the Zanzibaris of the withdrawal of U.S. citizens, but Karume railed on. Abdul Aziz Twala, one of his younger aides, snapped, "We have wasted enough time. We do not need the Americans." Then Karume shouted at Picard, "You have called our ministers and interfered in our affairs. Get out of here in twenty-four hours—no, twelve hours." Picard, running after him, asked, "You mean you want me to take my staff and leave?" Karume replied, "Go

137

to your house and do not leave it." Karume stalked out, and Picard was led away by revolutionary soldiers.

The precise reason for Karume's anger at that moment was never explained. It was true that Picard had had close ties with the deposed government and was also friendly with Othman Shariff, Karume's enemy. It was also believed that, in the evacuation of the Americans earlier in the week, Picard—presumably for humanitarian reasons—had withdrawn one or two Zanzibaris who were friendly with the old regime and who had been employed by the American embassy. Karume was undoubtedly upset about Okello's latest broadcasts, and was presumably annoyed by the arrival of the seven Western journalists. As Babu later explained, with a hint of amusement, "The reporters coming by dhow without proper papers—how could they do that? Suppose we did that in America? Would they have tolerated our landing in America that way? And it could have been very dangerous. The Sultan was still in those waters, and we thought there was a danger that he might go to Pemba and set up a government there, and we were trying to push him out of those waters. So, to have a load of foreigners arrive suddenly by dhow, of course they were accused of being spies, of course it was dangerous."

The next day Picard was declared *persona non grata* in Zanzibar and was flown to Dar es Salaam. The journalists and a number of British residents were evacuated the same night to Mombasa, Kenya, on the British survey ship H.M.S. *Owen*. In Washington, five days after the revolution, a State Department spokesman concluded, "We just don't know what's going on. The situation is impossible to grasp." He was skeptical about reports of Cubans on the island, however, and noted that Hanga was supposed to be

Soviet-trained, Babu Chinese-trained and Okello a Cuban-trained freedom fighter. "If these reports are true," he said, "no wonder nothing from Zanzibar makes sense."

The revolution appears to have come without warning to the mainland governments. Nyerere had expected trouble in the future but apparently knew nothing of the conspiracy that succeeded. He told one visitor a day or two later that he had called in Babu on Sunday, the day of the coup, and Babu said he didn't know what was happening, either. Oscar Kambona said in later years, "The revolution itself was a complete surprise to us; I think also to most Zanzibaris."

Despite the confusion on Zanzibar, the Kenya government recognized the revolutionary regime on Monday afternoon, scarcely thirty-six hours after the fighting began. Kambona had flown to Nairobi and Kampala on Sunday; he telephoned Nyerere from Nairobi to advise him that Kenya and Uganda were granting recognition immediately, and urged Nyerere to do the same. Nyerere said no. He couldn't be sure that Abeid Karume and the Afro-Shirazis were in control, he said, and he didn't like the violence. Friends have said that Okello's radio broadcasts worried the Tanganyikans and further contributed to the delay. Kambona also told Nyerere that Kenya had decided to refuse permission for the Sultan to land his yacht at Mombasa; Kambona said he assumed Tanganyika would also deny him entry. Again Nyerere disagreed. As it turned out, he allowed Jamshid and his party to land in Dar es Salaam late in the week and to remain until preparations had been made for them to fly to London.

On his way back to Dar es Salaam early Sunday afternoon, Kambona is said to have called the Zanzibar airport

139

tower, which had not yet been taken by the revolutionaries. "You bastard," said the tower operator. "We asked you for help six hours ago. Where are your troops?"

RECONSTRUCTING THE EVENTS of the Zanzibar revolution with certainty is not yet possible because most of the principal characters still have important reasons for obscuring part of what happened. All the Afro-Shirazi leaders claim to have played a part in planning the revolution. The official Zanzibari version, in fact, is that the coup was a project of the Afro-Shirazi party under the guidance of Abeid Karume; this version takes little notice of Okello because his presence became an embarrassment and because he was not a member of the party leadership. John Okello's account, on the other hand, as narrated in the "autobiography" he published in Nairobi in 1967 with the assistance of the East African Publishing House, is that Okello conceived of the revolution on his own, trained a small army in secret, gained the support of some Afro-Shirazi youth league members in the final week of preparation, and led the attack himself.

The confusion is compounded by the fact that two or more coups may have been in the planning stage as of January 1964. Many observers in East Africa believe that the Afro-Shirazis, probably with the support of the Umma party and perhaps with unofficial Tanganyikan backing, were preparing to launch a coup a few weeks later.

The best judgment that can be made at present is that the revolution of January 12 was planned by a group of persons who called themselves the "Committee of Thirteen." The group, which was formed a few weeks before the revolution, included several members of the Afro-Shirazi youth

140

league; among them were Seif Bakari, the head of the youth league; Said Bavuwai and Said Washoto; all later became members of the Revolutionary Council. The committee probably also included Yusef Hemidi, who became the Zanzibar army commander soon after the revolution. It did not include Abeid Karume and probably did not include Kassim Hanga; in fact, it may not have included any of the members of the revolutionary cabinet that John Okello announced on the evening of January 12. Nor did it include Edington Kissasi, the senior African superintendent of police, whom the revolutionaries awakened on the night of the attack and promoted to police commissioner.

The committee assembled a band of several hundred fighting men, and trained them in small groups hidden in the bush and among the palms. They had no weapons except their pangas, sticks, and bows and arrows. In recruiting members, the leaders relied heavily on Africans of Kenyan and Tanganyikan origin, many of whom had been discharged from the police force by the Shamte government. Among the mainlanders was John Okello, a Ugandan who had lived on Pemba and had in fact served there as a local branch chairman of the Afro-Shirazi party. For at least four or five months, and probably longer, Okello had been living on Zanzibar Island, where he worked as a house painter and stonecutter. He also ran a small coral quarry on the east coast of the island. He was not well known.

There are at least three versions of how John Okello came to prominence in the revolution. The first is that a few days before the revolution, the leaders of the committee recruited Okello because they wanted somebody who could blow up the ammunition storage area at Mtoni in case the attack should fail; among his many past jobs, Okello was said to have worked with explosives in a Kenya mine. A few hours before the fighting began, somebody attempted to ease the tension among the group by asking, "What rank would you like after our victory?" Okello, taking the question in earnest, is supposed to have replied, "Field marshal," and everyone laughed. For a man who later claimed to have lived and fought with the Kenya Mau Mau, it was a logical enough answer, since the Mau Mau organization was full of forest fighters who called themselves field marshals.

The second version—Okello's own—is that he had been training a handful of freedom fighters ever since the previous July and that in September he got in touch with Seif Bakari, the head of the Afro-Shirazi youth league, and joined forces with him. On the night of the attack, Okello wrote, the men cut the barbed-wire fence and entered the Ziwani compound, and then all but thirty or forty fell back afraid. It was then that the fanatical Okello, believing himself called by God, rushed forward, seized the rifle of a sentry and killed him with its bayonet, thereby giving the rebels "the first modern weapon in our revolution."

The more or less official explanation is that Okello was picked by the coup leaders as a scarecrow; they hoped that his mainland accent, not to mention his terrifying rhetoric, would frighten the island's Arabs into surrendering because it would make them think that Kenya and Tanganyika were behind the revolution. One European who was in Zanzibar at the time has said, "They *did* make use of Okello to frighten Arabs, I think. The Arabs thought him a superhuman devil. They're superstitious people, and he scared them more than airplanes could have done. After twenty-four hours, I don't think they thought of resistance. But I'm skeptical; I can't imagine anybody in the Afro-Shirazi

142

leadership thinking up such a scheme. Babu could have, but he wasn't there." Babu, who never claimed to have been part of the coup at the beginning, has said, "Okello was taken in, a short time before the revolution, because of his accent. To enhance the prestige of the revolution. As soon as he got hold of the mike"—a sputter of laughter—"he couldn't leave it."

Karume himself, minimizing Okello's role, has said, "He was here for labor. Radio was free. Anyone going to radio to announce anything he wants. During revolution, we had no field marshal here." Then he turned to his Afro-Shirazi colleagues and roared with conspiratorial laughter.

It is impossible to prove or disprove Okello's record as a battlefield hero. But it is difficult to believe that Okello's position of power following the revolution was based solely on his radio performances. Sometime just before or after January 12, the Committee of Thirteen was enlarged to fourteen to include Okello. When the Zanzibar *Gazette* of January 25 published the names of the thirty members of the Revolutionary Council, it listed first the members of the government and then the members of the Committee of Fourteen, starting with Field Marshal John Okello.

There is ample evidence that the rebels were poorly trained and organized. After seizing the armories, they fell to looting. They allowed the Sultan to escape, failed to capture the airport until about twelve hours after the fighting started, and never bothered to take the Cable and Wireless office at all. They had no direct help from outsiders, either from the mainland or overseas; the "Cubans" were the young men of Babu's Umma party who joined the attack sometime Sunday morning. A Briton who observed some of the early fighting was convinced that the rebels

143

had no rifles or other modern weapons until they captured the police arsenals. "When we went into town two days later," he has said, "the only weapons I saw at roadblocks were the .303 rifles from the armories—bolt-action, ten rounds before reloading. Okello, I think, had a Sten gun, and had had pictures taken of himself with it. And there were a few automatic pistols. All these came from the arsenals. It was at least two weeks later before weapons of Communist origin began to appear."

For several days after the Sultan's escape, the revolutionaries feared that he would land at Pemba and try to organize a resistance, or at least tarry there while he attempted to get military support from Britain or the mainland. But Jamshid, a placid young man with seemingly little taste for leading armies, has said that such a plan was never considered: "We didn't know our friends in Pemba were in control."

Several of Abeid Karume's political enemies have claimed that the Afro-Shirazi leader was unaware of the coup beforehand and that he fled the island sometime Saturday night, either because he didn't know who was leading the rebels or because he didn't want to be on Zanzibar if the attempt failed. This, however, is not true. Two British residents—John Cameron, an architect, and his wife—started out early Sunday morning on a fishing trip, unaware of what had happened during the night. They were stopped by the rebels near the Mtoni armory, north of town, and were driven to the Raha Leo, which was already being used as the revolutionary headquarters. There they met Abeid Karume, who was wearing slacks and a sport shirt. He seemed surprised to see them. "I've given strict orders that no Europeans be arrested," he told them. "I'll arrange transport back to your house."

A few hours after this, Karume did in fact slip away to the mainland in a small boat. His reason for leaving at that point, when the fighting was almost over, is not at all clear. Could he have failed to realize that the revolution had already succeeded, or was he alarmed by Okello's sudden power? Karume himself has said, "I went to Tanganyika to explain to Julius Nyerere how the revolution took place." But could he not have telephoned? The phones were working that morning, as were the telegraph lines. Again he has explained, "Julius Nyerere delayed to recognize our government, and the Sultan was requesting Tanganyikan assistance." But the Tanganyikans had not yet had a chance even to discuss the recognition question. Instead Karume left in a boat—a dugout canoe, some say—and spent most of the day on a rough sea, reaching Dar es Salaam exhausted in the early evening.

Kassim Hanga, whose post in the new government was first announced as prime minister but was quickly changed to vice-president, insisted in later years that the Tanganyikans had known about the revolution beforehand. He himself had flown to Dar es Salaam a day or two earlier, he said, to forewarn his old friend Oscar Kambona. He also claimed that the revolution had almost taken place twice previously—in late December and on January 7—but that on neither occasion had the time been right. He further asserted that he and another Afro-Shirazi, Abdul Twala, had spent two months in Tanganyika in late 1963 being trained in the use of firearms by a Tanganyikan policeman. No other sources ever confirmed any of these details. If

145

they were valid at all, they might have referred to an Afro-Shirazi coup that was to have taken place sometime later in 1964.

In any case, Hanga left Zanzibar for the mainland on Sunday a few hours after Karume. He also traveled by small boat. His purpose, Hanga said later, was to get more rifles.

That night in Dar es Salaam, Karume met with Nyerere, who felt Karume's stabilizing influence was needed on the island and urged him to go home immediately. On Zanzibar, Okello meanwhile was announcing the names of the new cabinet, and was calling on Karume to return. Oddly enough, none of the Zanzibar officials in Dar es Salaam that evening could remember Okello's name. Okello referred to himself that night as "the field marshal" and "Field Marshal *Huyu*"—a Swahili word meaning "this man" or "X"—and didn't announce his real name until the following day.

Unable to fly back to Zanzibar because the airport was closed, Karume and Hanga enlisted the aid of a European named Misha Fainzilber, who was engaged in the fishing business and had been friendly with the Afro-Shirazis in Zanzibar in previous years. So at two o'clock on Monday morning, twenty-four hours after the revolution began, the group left from Silver Sands, a small resort north of Dar es Salaam, in Fainzilber's glass-bottom boat. The crossing took them six and a half hours because the engine broke down en route. When they finally arrived at Kizim-kazi on Zanzibar in the early morning, the whole village came down to the shore to welcome them. The new leaders of Zanzibar requisitioned the schoolteacher's car and drove straight to the Raha Leo, where they were greeted by Field

Marshal Okello and sat down with him to a big meal. Then Karume and his cabinet retired to another room.

Nobody will ever know how many Zanzibaris died during the week of the revolution and in the unsettled period that followed. "Okello said nine thousand, nine hundred and ninety-nine, didn't he?" asked a European who formerly lived on Zanzibar. "And Karume said about twelve hundred? My guess is somewhere in between. Maybe six thousand, mostly in the outlying districts."

In the public mind, the symbol of the bloodshed was John Okello. A week or two later, a Briton who had known Okello as a house painter on Zanzibar had a dream in which Okello was painting the Briton's new boat, not with a paint spray but with a machine gun.

TEN DAYS AFTER the revolution, the Anglican bishop of Zanzibar, the Right Reverend Niall Russell, was finally able to return to Zanzibar Island from Pemba, where he had been marooned by the fighting. On the boat with him was Field Marshal Okello, who had been making a triumphal visit to his former home. "He was very respectful," the bishop later recalled. "He asked me to read Matthew Twenty-three to him—about the scribes and the Pharisees. He said to me, 'I don't mean all those things about burning people in oil, you know.' I said I thought it was time to quiet things down, and he said, 'Nobody tells me these things.' I invited him to come to church, and he did come once; he sat very quietly. He was very convinced he had been sent by God."

JULIUS NYERERE'S ANNOUNCEMENT in early January 1964
that he was ending his government's two-year-old policy
of Africanization, and that citizens of all races would henceforth be equally eligible for government jobs, produced a
chorus of angry protests from trade union leaders. The railway union promised to resist the policy change "at all
costs," and the head of the local-government union accused
Nyerere of taking the country "back to the colonial days."
He added, "If Tanganyika is to gain respect outside by
neglecting its indigenous citizens, then we don't want that
kind of respect."

Nyerere was preoccupied with the Zanzibar revolution
during the week of January 12. On Sunday night he saw
Karume at State House and urged him to return home
immediately. On Tuesday he flew to Nairobi to see Prime
Minister Kenyatta. On Wednesday the Sultan of Zanzibar
landed in Dar es Salaam to await transport to London, and
left four days later. On Thursday Nyerere saw Karume in
Dar es Salaam for the second time that week. Apparently
he promised help to Karume in restoring order and bolster-
ing the new regime, because, by the following weekend, some
three hundred Tanganyikan field policemen were being
flown to Zanzibar for temporary duty. Although nobody
realized it at the time, their absence upset the existing power
balance between the army and field police in the Dar es
Salaam area.

The weekend of January 18–19 was calm enough for Nyerere to devote some time to ceremonial duties. He unveiled a plaque after officially opening a new swimming pool at the Missions to Seamen in Dar es Salaam, and he gave a check for £3,000 to the Algerian ambassador for the victims of recent Algerian floods. On Sunday night he had a chat with Field Marshal John Okello, who had come over to Dar es Salaam for a brief rest, and urged him to work in good faith with President Karume.

A few hours later, at 1:50 A.M. on Monday, January 20, the British commander of the Tanganyika Rifles, Brigadier Patrick Sholto Douglas, was awakened at his home near Colito Barracks, some ten miles north of Dar es Salaam, by the sound of bugles and sirens. Dashing into the street in his pajamas, he saw a dozen of his officers rushing down the hill to the camp. At the foot of the hill, he later learned, they were arrested by enlisted men armed with rifles and Sten guns, and were locked up in the guardroom. Half of his army—the eight-hundred-man First Battalion —had mutinied.

Collecting his wife and six-year-old daughter, Douglas ran out the back door of his house and through the brush for a mile and a half, borrowed a car from a friend and drove into Dar es Salaam. The city was quiet. Leaving his wife and daughter with the Australian high commissioner, Douglas drove on to the home of an army staff officer in the suburb of Oyster Bay, just north of the capital. There he tried desperately to reach Nyerere and Vice-President Kawawa by telephone, but couldn't get through. Then he called Oscar Kambona, the External Affairs and Defense Minister, and asked that three DC-3s be sent to Tabora, four hundred miles away, to bring back elements of the

Second Battalion, which, so far as he knew, was still loyal to the government. Kambona agreed. Moments later, Douglas learned that the mutineers had already blocked the road to the Dar es Salaam airport, thereby separating the pilots from the planes.

Fearing that the post office had also been seized and that the mutineers could trace his telephone calls, Douglas ran from house to house in Oyster Bay. As he dashed into one house, a group of soldiers roared past in a Land-Rover, shooting wildly at the front door. Douglas quickly exchanged his uniform for a checked shirt and khaki pants, ducked out the back door, jumped hedges and walls, ran straight through the house of the German ambassador, and finally reached the residence of the British high commissioner, where he remained in hiding for five days.

Nyerere narrowly escaped. Douglas had telephoned the police inspector general, who walked to Rashidi Kawawa's house on the State House grounds and awakened him, and the two ran on to State House together. "We had a lot of trouble persuading the President to leave," Kawawa has recalled. "He wanted to stay and argue with them. He wanted to ask them, 'What is the problem?'" (Nyerere's colleagues have pointed out that he once went straight into the middle of an Indian riot at Douali and talked the rioters into going home. His friends were appalled; one said to him later, "My God, Julius, if one stone had touched you, there wouldn't have been an Asian left alive the next day." "I know!" he said. "But I didn't think of it at the time.")

"The argument," another friend of Nyerere's has said, "was over preventing him from going out to talk to the mutineers. His wife was on her knees to him. His security men helped Bhoke Munanka get him into the basement, with Maria pleading. And one of his security men then walked slowly down the State House drive to stall the mutineers. 'It's not the President you want, it's your minister,' he told them. 'Why don't you go see Mr. Kambona?' " While this argument was taking place, Nyerere and his wife and Kawawa were leaving the State House grounds by another entrance.

The President's younger brother Joseph was awakened by a neighbor, who warned him, "Don't go to town. There has been an army revolt." Joseph drove to State House, where soldiers stopped him and said, "You can't go in there; State House has been taken over." Joseph told them, "OK, you can take over State House, but you can't take over my mother," and drove through the gate. Inside he found his mother unharmed. As he started to leave, one of the soldiers recognized him as the man who had recommended that soldiers should be asked to work in the fields. "That's the fellow," said one, "who says we should go to Kilombero"— the huge sugar estate. So they arrested him and took him to Colito Barracks.

For most of the next two days, Nyerere remained in hiding somewhere in Dar es Salaam. Where he stayed during that brief period has never been disclosed, and has remained one of the more tantalizing minor mysteries of the country's political history. There have been endless rumors: that he took refuge in a mission, a church or an embassy, in a hut on the beach or a ship in the harbor, or that he went as far as Arusha or even Nairobi. "No, it was not a ship," Rashidi Kawawa has said. "I don't think it is appropriate for me to tell you where; we went to a place where we felt safe and could get information from time to time. Then

later, when everything was all right, we came back."
Nyerere was criticized for failing to keep in closer touch
with his people, and he himself admitted later, "I think I
made a big mistake." If such an admission implies that he
would behave differently in the event of another mutiny
or coup, the lesson he learned was probably a fallacious
one; his quick disappearance that January morning may
have been responsible for the preservation of his government and perhaps even his life.

THE FIRST DAY. The mutiny was led by a small group of
soldiers, mostly noncommissioned officers, whose aim was to
get rid of the British officers. The Europeans didn't understand their grievances, they said; one soldier testified later
that he joined the group—which called itself the Army
Night Freedom Fighters—because an officer had recently
ordered the "slaughter" of some chickens the men were
keeping; the henhouse, he complained, wasn't clean enough.
The soldiers also demanded an increase in basic pay from
105 shillings a month to 260 shillings; even a houseboy
was paid 150, they said. At a meeting late Sunday night,
the conspirators decided to proceed with their plan immediately. "Today," said a soldier named Pius Francis, "we
shall give back Mr. Kambona's teachers."
   Having seized Colito Barracks, the mutineers broke
up into several groups and drove into Dar es Salaam. One
group, led by Sergeant Francis Hingo Ilogi, forced its way
past the guards at State House and tried to find the President. Failing in this effort, Hingo's men drove to Oscar
Kambona's house and brought him back to State House.
There, in the gatehouse, Hingo told Kambona, "We have
locked up our officers. We do not blame you ministers, be-

153

cause you are civilians. You do not know a soldier's difficulties. If you will come with us to hear the men's complaints, the officers will be released." Kambona agreed to go with them to Colito. As a precaution, however, he drove behind the army Land-Rover in the police commissioner's car.

At Colito, Hingo told Kambona the soldiers wanted the army Africanized immediately—and completely. Kambona replied that such a plan was already being considered, but that he had to settle certain problems in the Defense Ministry first. He asked them to choose some representatives to discuss the soldiers' grievances in Dar es Salaam. Several men shouted, "Shoot him!" and "Beat him up!" and Hingo insisted, "No. We want everything today."

Seeing that the mutineers were determined to remove the British officers immediately, Kambona asked them who they thought should be the new commander of the Tanganyika Rifles. "I remembered from the Congo," Kambona has said, "that the worst thing is to have an army without officers." Somebody shouted "Nyirenda"—Alex Nyirenda, the Sandhurst-trained and very polished young officer who had planted the *Uhuru* flag on the summit of Mount Kilimanjaro on December 9, 1961. The suggestion was quickly shouted down; "Nyirenda is a European," said one man. Then Second Lieutenant Elisha Kavana was nominated, and was accepted by all. "When they urged Kavana to take over," Kambona has said, "I told him he must do it. They forced Douglas' brigadier's cap onto Kavana's head. I was surprised at how bitter they were."

Kambona then refused to sign an agreement on the new appointments until he had had a chance to consult the President, so he and Hingo's group drove back to State

House for a second time. Soldiers lined the State House drive, but none had entered the building itself. Some wanted to go in with Kambona, but Hingo restrained them. Nyerere had left State House at least two hours earlier; but Kambona, after remaining inside for a few minutes talking with the President's aide-de-camp and also the President's mother, emerged to tell the mutineers that Nyerere had agreed to their demands. "Liar!" someone shouted. "The President is not inside." But the group seemed satisfied and returned once more to Colito Barracks, with Kambona again following in the police commissioner's car.

This time, following a meeting in the education center, Kambona agreed to the removal of the British officers and arranged for their immediate transport to Nairobi. At one point, some said later, he reassured the frightened British wives that their husbands were safe and that he personally would look out for them. Before noon Kambona succeeded in getting all or most of the mutineers back to their barracks. Later he called some of the soldiers back to Dar es Salaam to restore order after looting and rioting broke out. In Magomeni township, an Arab shot two soldiers and two African civilians, one of whom had been looting the Arab's shop. Angry soldiers fired mortars at the Arab's house, then killed him and his six-year-old daughter as they ran from the flames. Five other members of the family were burned to death inside. According to the official count, seventeen soldiers and civilians were killed in the rioting.

Earlier in the day, Kambona had asked the Kenya government for assistance in putting down the mutiny, but the request was soon withdrawn by Job Lusinde, the Home Affairs Minister. In a broadcast to the nation, Kambona announced, "This is your Minister of External Affairs and

155

Defense. The government is still there . . . There has been some misunderstanding between the Africans and the British officers in the Tanganyika Rifles. At my intervention, the soldiers have now returned to Colito Barracks." Curiously, he failed to mention Nyerere at all, perhaps because he simply didn't know where Nyerere had gone. The subsequent statement by George Rockey, Nyerere's British press secretary, that *"Mwalimu* is safe, well and in command," was thus not altogether reassuring. Throughout East Africa there were rumors that Kambona was in the process of seizing power; even later, some of Kambona's enemies asserted that he had been working with the mutineers but had become alarmed by the depth of their anger and by the fact that Nyerere had escaped, and had pulled back. The best argument against this thesis is that, if he had had the soldiers' support, there was very little to have prevented him from staging a coup that day if he had chosen to do so. Kambona interpreted such rumors as further evidence that he was disliked and misunderstood by many Europeans. "The British looked to Mr. Nyerere as the moderate leader," he has said. "They felt my image had been boosted by the events that day, and they were angry."

Kambona soon realized that the crisis was not yet over. "At first," he has recalled, "the soldiers seemed very happy that the British officers had been removed. They cheered me." At the funeral of the two soldiers who were killed by the Arab, however, Kambona noticed that Hingo Ilogi was acting strangely. "He wouldn't talk to me or even look me in the eye. I suspected further trouble, and put on security men to track him."

THE SECOND DAY. The government learned that the Second Battalion of the Tanganyika Rifles had mutinied at

Tabora shortly after receiving news of the mutiny of the First Battalion at Colito Barracks. In the midst of the Tabora rebellion, a cable arrived from Oscar Kambona announcing that he was naming a new battalion commander, Mirisho S. H. Sarakikya, a mountain climber and runner who, while attending Sandhurst, had set an academy record by running the mile in four minutes and eighteen seconds. Sarakikya, who was under arrest at that moment, asked the mutineers' permission to read the cable, and told them to read it aloud. Then he ordered them to stand at attention, unfix their bayonets and unload; and they obeyed him. That night he arranged for the evacuation of ten British officers and noncoms.

Sometime Tuesday morning, presumably at the place where he had gone into hiding, Nyerere tape-recorded a short speech that was broadcast in the evening. In three minutes of tense Swahili, Nyerere urged his countrymen to remain calm. "Yesterday was a most disgraceful day," he said. "Some people went around spreading rumors and claimed that I was no longer here, and that there was no government. Such rumors make a little trouble seem much bigger than it really is." Didactically he added that rumor-mongering was "a sign of not being grown-up, a grown man is calm," and closed with a bitter comment: "My hope is that we shall never see such a disgraceful day repeated in Tanganyika."

"But where *is* he?" many Tanganyikans asked after hearing Nyerere's terse message, and some wondered if he had been taken prisoner by unknown enemies. As a precautionary measure, the British government prepared to send two thousand additional troops to East Africa. The frigate *Rhyl* was already standing by off Dar es Salaam,

157

and the carrier *Centaur* sailed from Aden with six hundred marine commandos aboard. Almost unnoticed in the excitement, Sultan Jamshid of Zanzibar reached London by plane from Dar es Salaam.

THE THIRD DAY. Suddenly Nyerere reappeared Wednesday morning. Riding with his wife and Job Lusinde, he toured every section of Dar es Salaam from Magomeni, where some of the worst rioting had occurred, to Kiungani, where an Indian shopkeeper greeted him warmly : "*Karibu, Baba.*" At TANU headquarters a crowd sang the party song, "Tanu yajenga nchi." At every stop Nyerere said, "What happened is a disgrace, but it is over, and there's nothing to be afraid of." People peered uncertainly from their houses ; some waved timidly. Once, after six people scurried away at the first sight of his procession, Nyerere walked after them saying, "Why did you run away? There's no reason to be afraid."

THE FOURTH DAY. Nyerere held a press conference at which he spoke about the effects of the mutiny and took the blame for failing to keep the public better informed. "It would be foolish to pretend that these events are unimportant," he said, "or that they have not damaged Tanganyika's reputation overseas." In reply to questions, he said that the soldiers' demands for higher pay were being discussed, and that he did not expect to call in British troops : "We can handle our own situation." Then he was asked if he intended to punish any of the soldiers in the revolt. He smiled thinly, paused for a full five seconds, and replied, "Thank you very much, gentlemen," closing the conference. The awkward pause underscored the predicament he faced at that moment ; his government had accepted a lawless solution, had capitulated to the mutineers and had no way of punishing them. The soldiers had simply returned to their barracks. "There is nothing the government can do," a Western diplomat said that day, "to prevent them from seizing Dar es Salaam again tonight if they want to."

That evening at Karimjee Hall, Nyerere received a five-minute ovation before delivering a lecture sponsored by the Dag Hammarskjöld Memorial Foundation and entitled "The Courage of Reconciliation." "It dealt with law based on enforceable power," as one of his aides said later, "and it was given at a time when he had no enforceable powers himself."

During those days, one of his friends has said, Nyerere "was pretending that the problem would heal itself; he expected the soldiers to be as shocked by the seventeen deaths as he was." On Thursday he issued a directive to the men of the First Battalion to put on their dress uniforms. "I wanted to see if they would respond to an order," he said later. They refused.

THE FIFTH DAY. Negotiations between the government and the army were breaking down, and the soldiers were becoming rebellious again. On the previous Monday, the mutineers had lacked a political leader and even a political motive. Now there were reports that trade union leaders had been meeting with the soldiers at Colito Barracks, and that the unions were planning a general strike for the weekend. There were also rumors of a plot at Morogoro, headquarters of the plantation workers union. According to one story that circulated later in Dar es Salaam, a woman sitting in an outhouse in a Morogoro garden had heard two men conspiring against the government, and had called the police.

The Tanganyika army mutiny had sparked similar

159

but less serious rebellions in the armies of both Uganda and Kenya. At the first sign of trouble, Uganda's Prime Minister Obote and Kenya's Prime Minister Kenyatta requested British military assistance. Nyerere was extremely reluctant to take similar action. It has long been said that he was not convinced of the existence of a conspiracy against the government until someone showed him a list of the proposed Cabinet that the plotters had prepared; but Nyerere has specifically denied this. "The thing that finally convinced him," Kambona once said, "was that one of his friends was approached by the conspirators and asked to be the new Vice-President."

In any case, Nyerere called the acting British high commissioner to State House at 5:30 P.M. and requested military assistance. Kambona then went to the high commissioner's house, where Brigadier Sholto Douglas had been in hiding all week, and asked for his help. That night Douglas and another officer took a launch from an isolated beach to the *Centaur*, which had arrived from Aden and was lying offshore. By the time Douglas boarded the carrier at 2 A.M. on Saturday, he learned that the British government had approved the action.

THE SIXTH DAY. At 6:20 A.M., six helicopters lifted sixty British marine commandos from the *Centaur* to the playing field just south of Colito Barracks. At 6:30 the carrier and the destroyer *Cambrian* began firing attack airbursts to frighten the Tanganyikan soldiers. From a distance of fifty yards, Douglas told the soldiers over a loudspeaker that he had resumed command, and ordered them to come out of the barracks with their arms in the air and to sit down in the road. He was giving them ten minutes to reply, he said, and began a countdown in Swahili. Then the marines fired at the guardroom with a rocket launcher, tearing away part of the roof and breaking windows. Immediately the soldiers began to surrender; one hundred and fifty appeared within ten minutes, and another hundred and fifty in the next hour. "By seven-thirty it was all over," Douglas said later, "although we spent the morning rounding up stray men who had fled into the bush." Three Tanganyikan soldiers had been killed and five wounded; there were no British casualties. No incident has illustrated more dramatically the vulnerability of the young African states; the Tanganyikan mutiny had been started by no more than forty men and was put down by sixty British marines.

British troops in Uganda and Kenya had acted simultaneously that morning. In Uganda they drove before dawn from the Entebbe airport to Jinja Barracks, where they overpowered the guards and took the mutineers captive. At Lanet Camp in Kenya, where troops of the Eleventh Battalion of the Kenya Rifles had seized arms Friday night, the British Royal Horse Artillery arrived at dawn, captured the armory and disarmed the soldiers. As of Saturday morning, British troops were protecting three East African governments from their own armies.

Early that morning, a frightened Tanganyikan soldier had appeared at the Dar es Salaam office of the East African External Telecommunications Company. He wanted to send the following message, he said, to the Secretary General of the United Nations, U Thant: TANGANYIKA RIFLES CAPTURED BY UNKNOWN TROOPS HELP QUICKLY SEND U.N. TROOPS. The message was to be dispatched at the "priority" rate and was signed "Lieutenant Colonel Ilogi, Commanding Officer." Testifying at the trial of the mutineers four months later, Michael Wright of the cable company said the man had appeared "very distressed." Wright was unable to identify him positively as Sergeant Francis Hingo Ilogi.

MANY OBSERVERS OVERSEAS thought it curious that mutinies had broken out in three East African armies at almost the same time, and only a week after the revolution on Zanzibar; but no evidence of an inter-army conspiracy was ever found. All three armies had previously been components of the King's African Rifles, and their men had certain grievances in common. Tanganyikan officials tended to blame their British officers for having failed to keep the government better informed. "I think the mutiny could have been avoided," Rashidi Kawawa once said, "if only the army commander could have told us the truth, which he did not. There was no proper system for telling us the thinking of our own army." For their part, many of the British officers felt Kambona had mismanaged the army and failed to understand military discipline; on one occasion he had talked to the enlisted men, in the absence of their senior officers, and invited them to air their grievances. Most diplomats in Dar es Salaam believed Kambona had behaved well during the week of the mutiny, however, although the rumors about his deviousness continued; when one London newspaper referred to him as "Moscow's man in East Africa," Kambona sued for libel and won.

On Saturday afternoon Nyerere denounced the ringleaders who had tried to "intimidate our nation at the point of a gun," and explained to his people why he had had to call in the British to punish an army that had "tasted the poison of disloyalty and disobedience." A friend of Nyerere's, recalling how he had once remarked, "The British have been through the furnace, we have never been through it," asked him after the mutiny, "Is this the furnace?" "Yes," Nyerere said, "a little of it." He had always been fond of saying that, in the long struggle for independence, not a single life had been lost; in the week of the mutiny, at least seventeen were killed. "The whole week," said Nyerere, "has been one of most grievous shame for our nation. It will take months and even years to erase from the mind of the world what it has heard about these events this week."

In the days that followed, Nyerere disbanded the First Battalion and dismissed hundreds of soldiers from the Second. He also discharged about 10 percent of his five thousand policemen. He rounded up more than four hundred persons, mostly trade unionists, for questioning; by late February the government had arrested five hundred and fifty people under the preventive detention act, but the majority were quickly released. He disbanded the Tanganyika Federation of Labor and founded the National Union of Tanganyika Workers, with his Labor Minister as general secretary. He appointed a new army commander, Captain Mirisho Sarakikya, and promoted him to brigadier. He increased the soldiers' wages to almost exactly what the mutineers had asked: from about $15 to $34 a month. He sent a telegram of thanks to the British government, and then called an emergency meeting of African foreign and defense ministers to discuss "the grave danger to the whole continent" posed by army revolts. The meeting, in effect, absolved him of blame for calling in the British troops, and endorsed his plan for borrowing soldiers from other African states until his own new army had been trained. In early April the British troops were withdrawn, and were replaced by the Nigerian Third Battalion under Lieutenant Colonel James Pam, who was to die two years later in a coup in his own country. Sergeant Hingo Ilogi was sent to prison for fifteen years for his part in the army mutiny; thirteen other soldiers received five- and ten-year sentences.

ONE DAY IN FEBRUARY that year, Nyerere spoke about the damage caused by the mutiny. "This is a very proud country," he said. "Our country feels let down very much. It's a double shame—shame at being let down by our own men, and shame at having to call in the British. It's clear as anything to me—the British should be here as short a time as possible."

The mutiny had caused Nyerere to ponder what kind of army his country should have. "The King's African Rifles never taught the men to become soldiers of Kenya, Tanganyika and Uganda. They were just battalions with British officers. So what did we do when we took over? We changed the uniforms a bit, we commissioned a few Africans, but at the top they were still solidly British. There were no African field-grade officers. We had inherited an impossible situation. You could never consider it an army of the people. When I suggested, 'Here are these able-bodied men, why can't they help in building bridges?,' the officers answered"—he affected a clipped British accent— "'These are soldiers!' I said that in wartime, British soldiers built bridges. They replied, 'Wartime is different.'

"An army, I think, must accept the political ethic of a country. Our army didn't know what our political ethic was. The British allow political dissent within their army, but that's part of their ethic. I had some of the British officers to dinner here, and one of them talked politics to me. He said he was voting socialist against the Tories. Well, that's fine. But can you imagine a KADU colonel"—KADU being Kenya's opposition party at the time—"in the Kenya army? If we had an opposition here, the damned fellows would be overthrowing the government the next morning. Here the opposition would be subversive. *On that day* [during the week of the mutiny] *they were talking with the army.* Where is the future opposition leader I can call in, as Lord Home can talk to Wilson? Whom I can call in and say, 'Look, brother, here is the security situation as I know it'? There is no such thing here.

"*I* don't need to be convinced of the need for an opposition. The West should talk to the opposition, not to me. It should tell them, 'If you want to be the opposition, don't be subversive, don't be disloyal.'

"One of the soldiers said during the mutiny, 'How can we overthrow the damned government? It's too popular.' Can you imagine that?" He repeated the question, obviously pleased with it. "What we need is the kind of criticism that pushes a good government. I got a letter recently implying that I hadn't kept a promise I made in 1958. This is the kind of opposition you like."

His goal, he said, was "an army that understands the problem of building a nation, not an army isolated from the people." Some of his friends had protested that he should not build a political army, he said. "But to me a political army is simply one that accepts the political ethic of its country."

In retrospect, the mutiny seems to have marked the zenith of British-Tanganyikan relations in the post-colonial period. When asked why he believed the British rescue of the Tanganyikan government had failed to create better relations on a sustained basis, Sir Richard Turn-

165

bull replied, "No independent country likes to see its army put down by sixty young men. Of course we had the equipment. But it was a great humiliation for Julius and Tanganyika. Nobody likes having a good turn of that sort done to them. People don't like to be helped in that way."

Looking back on the mutiny four years later, Julius Nyerere said with growing confidence, "The recovery is complete—and early. The mutiny was a strike of the army people, and it went out of control. It shocked the country. But every cloud has a silver lining, as the British say. It enabled us to build an army almost from scratch. Many institutions we have inherited, but the army is something we built ourselves."

President Nyerere wishes it clarified that the word Tanzania should be pronounced Tan-za-ni-a, with the emphasis on the penultimate syllable, as is the practice with the Swahili language.
—State House announcement, *November 1964*

In the uneasy weeks following the Zanzibar revolution, the three hundred Tanganyikan field policemen remained on the island. Their stated purpose was to help the Zanzibaris restore order and guard against an Arab counter-coup, but the more important effect of their presence was to bolster the regime of Abeid Karume against other revolutionary elements. The new President announced a fortnight after the revolution that Zanzibar had become a one-party state; the one legal party was, of course, the Afro-Shirazi, so Abdulrahman Babu went on the air immediately to say that his Umma party was joining the ASP.

Almost from the beginning, the new government began the seizure and distribution of large quantities of Arab plantation holdings to African peasants. It also nationalized the island's "racial" clubs while Duncan Sandys, the British Commonwealth and Colonial Secretary, was having tea in one of them, the English Club. "No," he replied later, in response to a reporter's question, "nothing would surprise me on Zanzibar." In another symbolic and highly popular action at about the same time, Karume burned the island's few remaining rickshaws at a ceremonial bonfire, promising £100 in compensation to each rickshaw owner. He had long advocated an end to the degrading practice in which men worked as animals, he said, but the previous government had laughed at him.

During this unsettled period, while hundreds of revolutionaries carried weapons carelessly in the streets and killings continued intermittently in the remote districts, the British community of five hundred dwindled to less than fifty. At least seven hundred Arabs and five hundred Indians fled the island. Dhows that were authorized to carry thirty passengers were loaded with as many as one hundred and fifty. One such dhow went down off the coast of northern Kenya; only the captain survived.

On February 20, Field Marshal John Okello flew to Nairobi, where, at a press conference, he denounced foreign "devils" and said he was willing to start revolutions in southern Africa wherever the colonialists were still in power. Then he went off to Uganda to see his family. When he reappeared in Dar es Salaam a few days later, he denied that he was Field Marshal Okello; his name was Gideon Baker, he said. He was lingering in Dar es Salaam waiting for Abeid Karume, Okello later explained in his autobiography, but Karume failed to arrive. After four or five days Okello heard a rumor that he was unwelcome in Zanzibar, so he flew to the island to find out what was happening. At the Zanzibar airport he was greeted by Karume and the rest of the Revolutionary Council—armed, as usual. Karume bundled Okello into a Tanganyikan government plane, saying Nyerere had something to tell them, and the two flew back to Dar es Salaam. The following morning, when Okello was taken to State House, Nyerere said to him,

"There have been some misunderstandings. Does the government belong to you or Karume?" Okello answered with oracular ambiguity, and the next day Karume returned to Zanzibar alone. When he finally managed to see Nyerere a week later, Okello wrote, Nyerere told him that Karume wanted him "to go to my home in Uganda and rest for six months, after which time the question of my returning to Zanzibar would be reconsidered."

Okello complained that he had no money and had even left his suitcase at the Zanzibar airport the week before; and what about his three months' army pay? Oscar Kambona brought him the suitcase the next day, but nothing else. "The Sultan had been well received in Britain," Okello wrote sorrowfully, "and my own brothers had expelled me. I caused the Sultan to lose his regime, yet my fate was much worse than his."

Okello wrote how he then wandered, penniless, from Nairobi to Uganda. He failed to mention, however, how he happened to come into possession of a new Peugeot sedan, which he wrecked completely on March 14 while driving to Uganda. Some observers in East Africa have suggested that a former Kenya politician bought him the car; others have theorized that the suitcase from the Zanzibar airport contained his unofficial retirement pay. On April 7 Okello wrote a letter to Karume and received a cable from the principal immigration officer in reply: YOU ARE INFORMED THAT YOU ARE AN UNWANTED PERSON IN ZANZIBAR.

THE SPEED WITH WHICH the new Zanzibar government welcomed technicians and aid from China, East Germany and the Soviet Union dismayed many East Africans who had supported the overthrow of the Arab regime. Having rec-

169

ognized the Karume government as quickly as possible after the revolution, the Soviet Union sent a freighter loaded with trucks, mortars, antitank and antiaircraft guns as well as small arms. In late February, Babu announced that Zanzibar had accepted £185,000 in aid from China. "That's only the beginning," he said. Colonial names were replaced by Communist ones; within a few weeks a stadium had been renamed for Mao Tse-tung and a school for Fidel Castro, and Chinese doctors had begun to practice the art of acupuncture at the V. I. Lenin Hospital.

The Zanzibaris were doubly angry with the West. They resented the early press reports that Zanzibar had become the "Cuba of East Africa," and they were particularly annoyed that Britain, the U.S. and many other Western countries had withheld recognition. The West German government sent a Foreign Ministry official to Zanzibar in early February; he returned to Bonn convinced that the Zanzibaris had agreed to establish relations with West Germany and not East Germany. Shortly after that, however, the Zanzibaris admitted an East German chargé d'affaires to the island, and Hassan Moyo, Zanzibar's Acting External Affairs Minister, dismissed a West German protest as "presumptuous."

The sole remaining American diplomat on the island, Donald Petterson, drove around town with two Tanganyikan policemen as guards. His main chore was looking after the NASA tracking station, as well as the homes and property of the station's evacuated American employees. Every day at 9 A.M. and 3 P.M. he talked over an open telephone line with the U.S. embassy in Dar es Salaam.

On February 19, President Karume impatiently ordered the British high commissioner and the acting U.S.

170

chargé d'affaires to leave Zanzibar within twenty-four hours because their countries had not recognized his regime. Recognition followed immediately, and the order was rescinded. The U.S. named Frank Carlucci, a young diplomat who had served in the Congo, as its new chargé. For a while Karume seemed mollified, but in early April he asked the U.S. to remove its satellite tracking station permanently "in the interests of the security and defense of Zanzibar." He was incensed over a statement made in New York by William Attwood, the U.S. ambassador to Kenya, that China and East Germany were attempting to turn Zanzibar into a "kind of non-African state." The statement was valid, but its timing was unfortunate. On the same day that Karume ordered the tracking station removed, he accepted the credentials of the new Chinese ambassador, Meng Ying, saying that Zanzibar looked to China "not as a friend but as a real brother."

The question has been debated endlessly in East Africa in the years since 1964; but the prevailing view is that, although the Communist powers were not involved directly in the planning of the Zanzibar revolution, they attempted immediately thereafter—and with considerable success—to exploit it to their own ends. It is generally agreed, furthermore, that the Western countries made a serious mistake by failing to recognize the Karume regime for six weeks after the revolution, while China, the Soviet Union, East Germany, Czechoslovakia and Cuba deluged the Zanzibaris with blessings and support. It is by no means certain, however, that early Western recognition would have affected the outcome significantly. Abeid Karume was an uneducated man whose problems and nightmares ranged from a wild field marshal to the danger of an Arab counter-coup. Inevitably he relied on the young, educated Marxists who had joined his regime, and they quickly molded its policies. Israel, for example, should have become the new government's first and closest friend, because the Israelis had been one of the largest contributors to the Afro-Shirazi party in the years before independence. But when, after the revolution, the Israelis tried to establish relations with the Karume government, they encountered an inexplicable amount of resistance.

Julius Nyerere was deeply angered that the West failed to understand what had happened on Zanzibar. He was particularly furious that the British, having turned the island nation over to an Arab minority government, should seem to be unable to grasp why the African majority had seized power. Later he would dismiss as irrelevant such questions as whether the Afro-Shirazi party was the sole instigator of the coup, or what role John Okello played in the planning; the point was that a black majority, twice denied the right to govern by an electoral process inherited from the colonial power, had taken it by revolutionary means.

"What happened was what the whole world should have known," he said two years later. "But the West declared a Communist takeover! Absurd! We had been talking about this [danger of revolution] for years. These fellows with bows and arrows and pangas took over. But the Western countries said, 'It's Communist!'

"Well, the Communists jumped in. The Zanzibaris had no experience in government. They were ordinary people. Ordinary people! And the Western powers *pulled out!* The Americans were the first to pull out. Why? It was the

Nationalist party that asked them to remove their tracking station. The Afro-Shirazis never had.

"These people had had no experience. Go out and look at them! They had no external support whatever, and they had fear that the British might put the Sultan back. And the Russians, the Chinese and the East Germans were recognizing them. As they say, 'When you are sinking, you try to cling even to a reed.' What did they know or care about the Cold War? They thought, These were good people who were helping them, and bad people who were not. That's all they knew."

But, considering the leftist influences within the new government, would it not have adopted anti-Western policies in any case? "There were left-wing socialists, yes," Nyerere said, "but they were a minority in a minority"— Umma was a minority in the ZNP—"and a splinter from a minority. They would have urged left-wing policies, but it would not have become a Cold War matter. What identified them with the East was the refusal of the Western countries to accept Zanzibar."

On April 22, Nyerere flew to Zanzibar for the first time since the revolution to pay what was described as a one-hour "courtesy visit" on Karume. The following day it was announced at State House in Dar es Salaam that Nyerere and Karume had in fact signed "articles of Union," and that the Republic of Tanganyika and the People's Republic of Zanzibar had agreed to unite.

The news came as such a surprise that nobody knew quite how to interpret it. "Observers regard Union in one of two ways," said an editorial in the *East African Stand-*

173

ard of Nairobi, "either as strengthening Zanzibar's revolutionary regime against extreme elements and containing them offshore, or as an entry of extreme influence to the mainland." Even a few of the supposed participants seemed to have been caught off balance. Zanzibar's External Affairs Minister, Babu, was returning from a trip to Indonesia when the announcement was made; he said in Pakistan, on his way home, that he had no comment. The following day, after arriving in Nairobi, he said he had known about the plan all along and had approved it. At the People's Palace in Zanzibar, Abeid Karume told his followers that Union would not make it necessary for Zanzibar to change its friends, and Julius Nyerere insisted in an address to his National Assembly that the move was inspired by the desire for African unity and had nothing to do with Cold War politics: "There is no other reason. Unity in our continent does not have to come via Moscow or Washington."

Under the interim constitution of the new country, which was to be called the United Republic of Tanganyika and Zanzibar, Nyerere was designated President, Karume First Vice-President and Rashidi Kawawa Second Vice-President. Karume was also named "President" of Zanzibar, although this title was later changed to "head of government." After naming a new Cabinet of twenty-two members, Nyerere held a press conference at which his answers were almost as choppy and defensive as the ones he had given during the week of the army mutiny three months earlier. Where would the new capital be? "Dar es Salaam." Would the Zanzibari forces be disbanded? "They will become part of one army." Would political prisoners be released? "They don't cease to be political prisoners because of the Union." Would confiscated property be returned to former owners? "Why?"

Inevitably, to Nyerere's anger and political embarrassment, the Union was widely interpreted as a triumph for the West. There has been endless speculation about the events that led to the merger, but Nyerere has always insisted that the simplest explanation was the accurate one. According to Nyerere, TANU and the Afro-Shirazi party had always worked closely together and had talked about unity; and one day in March that year, when Karume visited him in Dar es Salaam, Nyerere had said to him, " 'Look, I have made it clear to Prime Minister Kenyatta and to Prime Minister Obote that when they are ready for East African federation, we are ready. I am now saying to you, "When you are ready for federation, we are ready." '

"And," Nyerere continued, "he said, 'What do you mean, when we are ready? We are ready now!'

"This was in March. Union would have been in March. But in March we were holding a series of talks with the other East African countries, and there was just a possibility that we might have federation. So Zanzibar and Tanganyika waited." But on that day in March, Nyerere said, Karume had told him, " 'Call the press—tell them we are ready now.' " And Nyerere had said to him, " 'It must take time.'

"I think genuinely," Nyerere continued, "these are simple, honest leaders of the people. They mean what they say, these true leaders of the people. We had all been saying we wanted to unite, and here was one leader saying, 'We've always said we wanted it when we gained our independence, and now we have it, so let's go ahead.' "

175

* * *

SHORTLY AFTER his conversation with Karume, and at least six weeks before the announcement of Union, Nyerere called in Roland Brown, his attorney general, and told him, "I want you to do some secret work for me." The Zanzibaris were interested in a union with Tanganyika, said Nyerere, and asked Brown to consider what kind of arrangement could be worked out.

Despite the early agreement between Nyerere and Karume, there is evidence of considerable vacillation on the part of the Zanzibaris. Kassim Hanga favored the merger, Babu opposed it, and Karume wavered. Babu's opposition was based, at least in part, on his precarious political position in Zanzibar. A half-caste himself, he held the personal allegiance of only a small number of Zanzibaris; but because of his intelligence and skill, he had made himself invaluable to the Karume government. He knew that TANU and the Afro-Shirazi party were closely aligned, and had no way of knowing what his role would be in a united government. According to one participant, Babu even brought in a lawyer from the mainland to strengthen his argument that, under a Union government, Zanzibar would be swallowed by Tanganyika. He is said to have left for Indonesia believing he had convinced Karume to hold off, at least for the time being.

Nyerere faced an ugly dilemma. As Oscar Kambona once described it to an American journalist, "Our first concern was the growing Communist presence and, second, the danger of the Cold War coming in. The Cold War was in the Congo already—it would have been a straight line across Africa. And there was another problem: he had to

176

show he had his own reasons. The problem was how to isolate Zanzibar from the Eastern countries, yet not be used by the West for its own purposes." Nyerere has never defined the problem in exactly these terms, and might well take exception to Kambona's comment. There is no doubt, however, that his primary motive was to prevent Zanzibar —and Tanganyika—from being drawn into a Big Power confrontation. A friend has recalled that Nyerere said once in high fury, " 'China on the island, and the Americans saying I'm fighting Communism, and it's Vietnam in Africa—and I damned well won't have that.' "

He was deeply worried about the military buildup on the island and the continuing violence, but he was in no position to intervene even if he had wanted to; his own army had been largely disbanded, and he was relying on the Nigerians for his own security. He was also concerned about the safety of the three hundred Tanganyikan policemen who were still on duty in Zanzibar. Some observers in Dar es Salaam have said that Nyerere was ready to remove the policemen, if there were to be no Union, because he didn't want their lives endangered in the event of renewed fighting; and that this prospect, which might well have changed the military balance on the island, is what convinced Karume that he should unite with Tanganyika immediately.

Karume's vacillation is said to have continued until the last moment. He even threatened to stay home from the Dar es Salaam ceremony at which the instruments of Union were to be exchanged, perhaps in anger because the TANU newspaper *The Nationalist* had published the Union announcement prematurely.

177

* * *

FOR A LONG TIME, Nyerere had sharply resented the way in which the British and American press characterized him as "moderate" and "pro-Western." In the post-Union period, when the Western press congratulated him for fighting Communism by seizing the island, Nyerere reacted with rage. Not only did he feel that such tributes had the effect of misinterpreting and perverting his motives; they could also have damaged, if not destroyed, the Union itself by embarrassing the Zanzibaris. It can be argued, of course, that the Zanzibaris were too simple and too preoccupied with their problems to pay much attention to what the overseas press was saying; but it is almost axiomatic in modern African affairs that the exploitable, sooner or later, is exploited by somebody. Nyerere was particularly vulnerable to such charges that year, moreover, because he had called on the British for military assistance. In Cairo at the African heads of state conference in July, Ghana's President Kwame Nkrumah declared that he could not understand why the training of African freedom fighters had been entrusted to an "imperialist agent"—an obvious reference to Tanganyika, where most guerrilla training camps were located. Nyerere angrily replied that, when his country had gone through the "humiliation" of asking help from the former colonial power, "the ambassador of a brotherly African state celebrates and rejoices, and I am forced to request that he be removed." The Tanganyikan government had in fact asked the Ghanaian ambassador to leave for such reasons. Nyerere continued, "I am becoming increasingly convinced that we are divided between those who genuinely want continental government and patiently work for its development, and those who simply use the phrase 'Union government' for the purpose of propaganda. Some people are willing to use their great talent to wreck any chance of unity on our continent, as long as some stupid historian can record that they wanted unity at a time when nobody else did."

In June, *The Economist* of London had declared, in an article entitled "The Perils of Nyerere," that the President had "managed half the work of a python." It continued: "He swallowed Zanzibar all right but he did not crush its fighting force first. The live animal is a long time digesting, and its kicks are being felt hurtfully, and possibly even fatally, deep inside Tanganyika's body politic." Such criticism—an accurate reflection of serious continuing problems within the Union—led to a series of stinging articles in *The Nationalist* against Britain and the U.S. One particularly virulent editorial asserted that "the British put their finger on the trigger to incite the [January] mutiny in order to give them sufficient reason to come back." Britain, it added, "wants to manipulate President Nyerere as if he were a marionette." Soon after that, the National Assembly in Dar es Salaam passed a resolution "deprecating the hostility of the British and American press toward the United Republic." The government, said Rashidi Kawawa, "sadly supported" the resolution.

When asked, two years later, if the anti-Western propaganda campaign had not in fact been a brilliant smoke screen for obscuring whatever pressure Nyerere was trying to apply to Zanzibar that year, a mainland official replied, "It was not a smoke screen. Call it brilliant, if you like, but not a smoke screen. It was an act of insulation."

In August the government invited suggestions for a new name for the United Republic "which gives a sense of

179

unitedness and should be easy to pronounce. The prize for
the accepted proposal will be ten pounds." Two months
later, Nyerere announced the winning title: United Republic of Tanzania. The contest attracted 1,534 entries from
more than forty countries. The favorite names suggested,
besides Tanzania, were Tanzan and Tangibar. Five days
passed before the government, amid general uncertainty,
made its brief further announcement: the correct pro-
nunciation was Tan-za-*ni*-a.

WHAT DISTRESSED the mainland Tanzanians was how little
Zanzibar changed after it united with Tanganyika. Abeid
Karume, driving around the island in a black Austin Prin-
cess, was still referred to as "the President"; the United
Republic was practically never mentioned. Special visas
were still required for travelers from Dar es Salaam, and
there were a few incidents in which Tanganyikan government officials were refused entry to the island. The Zanzibaris continued to conduct their revolution in their own
curious way. In June they nationalized the Zanzibar Electricity Board, as Liberation Army troops surrounded the
offices and power station. Yet, as it happened, the Board
was already a quasi-governmental organization controlled
by a board of six men who, since January, had been appointed by Karume.

All that year, the Union was rumored endlessly to be
on the verge of collapse. At one point Nyerere was said to
have asked the Nigerians to send in a detachment of troops
that would serve as a counter-force to the Zanzibar Liberation Army; but Nyerere has insisted that no such request
was ever made. The three hundred Tanganyikan policemen,
however, were reequipped with submachine guns.

180

The problem was complicated by the Zanzibaris' foreign friends, who were reluctant to sacrifice the diplomatic position they had achieved there. The Tanzanian government requested that all embassies on the island be reduced to consular status as of June 30, but the East Germans failed to remove their embassy for almost a year. The Chinese continued to send military aid directly to Zanzibar, but they announced that they were extending a £10-million interest-free loan to mainland Tanzania, as well as a £5-million loan to Zanzibar.

Even today, more than seven years after the Union, Zanzibar is only partly integrated with Tanganyika. Under the revised interim constitution of 1965, the Union government controls foreign affairs, defense, citizenship, external trade, customs, harbors, civil aviation, posts and telegraphs. The police force is unified but the two branches of the army, now known as the Tanzanian People's Defense Force, are not. The Revolutionary Council still rules by decree; there is no independent judiciary or legislature in Zanzibar, and visitors from the mainland still go through immigration formalities at the Zanzibar airport. TANU and the Afro-Shirazi party have not yet merged. The Zanzibaris voted in the Union's presidential elections of 1965 and 1970, in which Nyerere was reelected unopposed, but there have been no parliamentary or local elections on the island since the revolution. When interviewed in 1968 by the Tanzania *Standard*, Karume said he didn't expect free elections on Zanzibar for fifty years. "Elections are a tool of the imperialists to sabotage the people," he said, referring yet again to the pre-independence elections in which the Afro-Shirazis won the popular vote but failed to win a parliamentary majority. In July 1970, Nyerere

181

was obliged to use the same sort of reasoning in explaining
to his Parliament why the Zanzibaris would not be taking
part in parliamentary elections that year; the islanders
were still afraid that attempts might be made to subvert
the revolutionary regime, he said, and return the masses
to minority control. But he said he hoped that talks on a
new and permanent constitution would be held during the
life of the next Parliament, which will sit until 1975.

From the beginning Nyerere, perhaps unable to do
otherwise, has handled the Zanzibaris with the utmost per-
missiveness. "The Zanzibaris are a proud people," he said
in 1965. "No one has ever intended that they should become
simply the Republic's eighteenth region." On the contrary,
the Zanzibaris have been considerably better represented
in the Union government than they deserved. Zanzibar's
population is 350,000, out of the United Republic's
13,000,000; it is smaller, in fact, than any of the mainland's
seventeen regions. Yet as of 1967, for example, seven of
Nyerere's 22 Cabinet members were Zanzibaris, as were
40 of the 183 members of the Tanzanian Parliament. Unlike his colleagues from the mainland, no Zanzibari had
been elected to Parliament; he held his seat by virtue of his
membership in the Revolutionary Council or his post in the
Zanzibar government. Nyerere has worked consistently to
convince the Zanzibaris that they were benefiting from the
Union. His reasoning, presumably, is that no matter how
slow and painful it may be to achieve complete integration,
it is better to have the Zanzibaris in the Union than outside
it.

Such influence as Nyerere has among the islanders is
based largely on his considerable powers of persuasion.
When Karume's old enemy Othman Shariff came home in

1965 after serving as Tanzania's ambassador to Washington, the Zanzibar government charged him with "prerevolutionary crimes" and locked him up. Nyerere is believed to have arranged for his release to the mainland, where Othman was given a job as a government veterinarian in Mbeya; there he remained for four years before becoming involved in further intrigue. In 1968 the Dar es Salaam government was reported to be discussing retirement terms with the members of the Zanzibar Revolutionary Council—an almost certain prerequisite to free elections and reform—but apparently no agreement was reached.

In countless matters, the Zanzibaris have continued to go their own lawless way, to the consternation of the mainland authorities. "Zanzibar is our cross," one Tanzanian official has been heard to grumble from time to time. In 1966 the Zanzibaris published a law making it illegal for parents to withhold consent for their daughters' marriage. Karume had advocated such laws as a way of overcoming racial differences, but the Arabs and Indians recognized it instantly, and rightly, as an attempt to make their daughters more easily available to powerful African politicians. The Anglican bishop, the Right Reverend Niall Russell, spoke out against the new law, and was promptly expelled from the island.

The controversy was revived in 1970. After four young Persian girls refused to marry the sixty-five-year-old Karume, he ordered the arrest of ten of their male relatives for "hindering the implementation of mixed marriages." He swore he would deport the men, then that he would expel all of the hundred-odd members of the Persian Ithnasheri sect to which the girls and their relatives belonged. And then, after a quiet talk with Nyerere, Karume dropped the charges. Four months later it started all over again. Four Persian girls, apparently different ones, were forced to marry members of the Revolutionary Council, with a fifth member of the council performing the ceremony. Eleven of their male relatives were ordered jailed and flogged by a "people's court" judge who accused them of "sowing the seeds of racism." Mainland women's groups protested angrily, and the *East African Standard* of Nairobi denounced the case as "an appalling throwback to the time of slavery."

One young mainland official tried to explain the situation to a foreign friend: "You must understand it in terms of Zanzibar. Look, Zanzibar was a place of slavery, a symbol of slavery in all Africa. In all that time, if a rich Arab liked an African girl, he took her, that's all. And marriages were arranged by parents, always. But only within each community.

"Now, since the revolution, freedom to the Zanzibaris means the reverse. When an African says to an Arab—or an Indian— 'I like your daughter,' the Arab says, 'Oh, no.' The African says, 'Why not?' The Arab says, 'Well, let's ask her.' The African says, 'What do you mean? It never worked that way before. Why won't she marry me? I'm not a criminal.' "

The mainlander concluded, "You can say to them, 'This is ridiculous, this isn't what freedom means.' But they don't see it that way."

The incident strained relations between Dar es Salaam and the island, and greatly embarrassed Nyerere. His friends were also upset about the damage it caused his moral position in arguing about such African problems as the continuation of the trade embargo on Rhodesia and the British government's plan to resume arms sales to South Africa. "How can we talk about human rights," said one, "when this is going on?"

Unwilling and perhaps unable to settle such Zanzibar problems by force, Nyerere seems to have developed a fatalistic attitude about the Union's ultimate chances of success. "I believe in African unity," he said in late 1969. "But the damned boundaries are not sacred. They were created by the imperialists. The people of Africa are more sacred than those boundaries. I have two bits of a union. Even if the Zanzibaris were not rejected by Tanganyika, if they simply felt the Union was of no use to them, and broke away, and this was the genuine feeling of the Zanzibaris, I could not possibly kill Zanzibaris. If they came in freely, they can leave freely. We did not conquer Zanzibar. And if they remain, this must be of their own free choice.

"This is the only basis on which to build a nation. An empire you keep down by enlarging the army. A nation you keep together by strengthening the internal will to unity."

IN THE YEARS SINCE he was declared an unwanted person in Zanzibar, John Okello has been imprisoned again and again, mostly on immigration charges. In October 1964 he spent ten days in jail in Mwanza, Tanzania, before being deported to Kenya and taken to the Uganda border. Later that year he wandered back to Kenya and was jailed for eighteen months for entering the country illegally. Shortly after his release he returned to Uganda, where, for undisclosed reasons, he was held in preventive detention from July 1967 until September 1968.

In February 1969 he was jailed once more for entering Kenya illegally. The magistrate at Kakamega found Okello guilty of spreading "prohibited publications," and sentenced him to three years in prison. This was a period when the Kenya government was ceremoniously banning Chinese propaganda materials. Okello had no Chinese pamphlets in his possession; but his reputation as a person of magical powers and an exporter of revolutions had preceded him, and the village magistrate was taking no chances. On appeal to the Kisumu High Court, Okello's sentence was reduced to one year. On February 16, 1970, he was released and was flown to Uganda by police aircraft.

IN FEBRUARY 1964, a month after the revolution, Sultan Jamshid moved from London to Southsea, near Portsmouth, with his wife, children, and twenty-five other relatives and aides. Two years later, he was visited in his three-story brick house in Victoria Grove by an American journalist. He seemed surprisingly contented, a shy and amiable young man who was making the best of his new life. A Renault sports car stood in front of his door. He watched television, he said, went sometimes to the pictures, and visited his mother down the street. That summer, he said, he had made a three-month trip to Saudi Arabia and Aden to "see my people," the ones who had fled Zanzibar. He expressed in hardly more than a whisper the ancient hatred of the Arab islanders for the black mainlanders: "They call it revolution, but we say invasion." He had received many reports of life in Zanzibar. "It is not a real union," he said. "The Communists are in control." Recently, he said, he had been visited by some Africans from

186

Kenya who told him that, on a trip to Zanzibar, they had been followed by security men. "I like them to be honest with me," he said. But that was not exactly true. Like political exiles in every age—"I know," the playwright Aeschylus wrote, "how men in exile feed on dreams"—he doted on scraps of hopeful news from home.

(10)

Soon after Tanganyika's union with Zanzibar, Nyerere began to feel the pressure of Western powers that he bring an end to the prevailing chaos on the island and reduce the size of the Chinese and East German presence there. He bridled against such advice, partly because he resented the persistent interest in his country's internal affairs, and partly because he was in no position to enforce his will upon the Zanzibaris. In August, when he let it be known that he was going to accept seven Chinese instructors and four interpreters for his army for six months, a Western diplomat asked him if he realized the risk he was taking. "The maximum risk is that the army will revolt," Nyerere snapped. "My army revolted in January. It was not trained by the Chinese." Expanding on the theme at a press conference, he demanded, "Are the Zanzibaris supposed to sit down like a pack of damn fools and do nothing? They accepted military aid from Russia and China. They had no choice." As for his own army, he said, he had asked several nonaligned countries for instructors and they had turned him down. "What am I supposed to do? The Chinese offer is the nearest thing to what I wanted. What is this Chinese problem?

"This simple request is a little attempt to show that we are nonaligned. But when it comes to actual facts, this country is completely Western, in government, in business, in schools, in everything. The influence of this country is Western. The fact that I, as President, have to explain why I am accepting Chinese aid is itself a big humiliation. This is my explanation and my protest." There were other examples of what the Tanzanians regarded as overbearing pressure, and they continued to react sharply if not always publicly. A few months later, when they were casting around for Western assistance in building a rail line to Zambia, a Western ambassador told Nyerere, "I think you'll find that the railroad to Zambia passes through Zanzibar." The remark sounded to Nyerere like a scarcely veiled threat that he could expect no Western help for the railroad as long as the Communists exerted so much influence on the island.

The first diplomatic dilemma posed by the Union was the problem of what to do about relations with the two Germanys. Since independence, Tanganyika had had extremely cordial relations with West Germany and was counting on Bonn to make a sizable contribution to the new five-year plan that was to be announced in May. In fact, Tanganyika, which constituted most of what had once been German East Africa, had enjoyed a sort of foster child's relationship with the West Germans. On the other hand, East Germany had rushed into Zanzibar after the revolution and established an embassy, its first in Africa. To protect their diplomatic foothold, the East Germans began to build the Zanzibaris a radio transmitter and sent a freighter laden with clothing and other goods; they also promised to rebuild an entire township at Ngambo in Zanzibar Town. Karume assured the East Germans that the islanders would allow nothing to spoil their newly found friendship.

190

Faced with such a curious problem, the Tanzanians expected the West Germans to approve of the Union and to agree to some sort of compromise, such as the presence of an East German consulate in Zanzibar. The United Republic would refrain from recognizing East Germany, the Tanzanians promised, and the net result would be that East Germany would lose its only embassy in Africa. Instead the Bonn government of Chancellor Ludwig Erhard insisted adamantly that such an arrangement would violate the terms of West Germany's Hallstein Doctrine, under which Bonn refused to have diplomatic relations with any nation except the Soviet Union that had relations with East Germany. The matter remained in stalemate until February 1965, when the Tanzanian government announced its decision: while withholding formal recognition, the United Republic would permit the East Germans to open a consulate general in Dar es Salaam in compensation for the closing of their embassy in Zanzibar.

The West German government retaliated with astonishing swiftness. It canceled a military aid program to Tanzania, which had included £4 million in capital aid to be used for the purchase of military aircraft, and withdrew its air and naval training teams virtually overnight. Bonn also announced that the West German Cabinet would, at its next meeting, consider "further moves to put pressure on Tanzania." The West German response represented precisely the sort of clumsy diplomatic bullying of a weak nation by a powerful one that Nyerere most deeply resents. He asked the West Germans to cancel all remaining aid immediately, including £3 million in technical aid that had also been promised. "A hungry dog will accept food in any way you give it to him," he said, "even if you throw

191

it at him. It is different with a human being. You have to be careful with the way you give food to a hungry man. He has his dignity to preserve." He later remarked that some people had "expected the union of Tanganyika and Zanzibar to solve the problem of German reunification, but it did not."

DURING THIS TROUBLED PERIOD, when the mainland Tanzanians were trying to bring peace and order to Zanzibar and were contending with a wider range of diplomatic problems than they had ever faced before, three incidents occurred that severely damaged Tanzania's relations with the United States. In November 1964, Oscar Kambona returned unexpectedly from a vacation in Arusha and called a press conference to announce that the government had "concrete evidence" that "certain Western powers," specifically the U.S. in league with Portugal, were preparing to attack Tanzania. Seemingly enjoying his role as the Tanzanian Paul Revere, Kambona cabled the Organization for African Unity at Addis Ababa: HAVE HONOR TO INFORM YOU THAT THE UNITED REPUBLIC HAS GATHERED SUFFICIENT DOCUMENTARY AND FACTUAL EVIDENCE TO REVEAL THE EXISTENCE OF A PLOT BY CERTAIN WESTERN POWERS TO OVERTHROW THE TANZANIAN GOVERNMENT AND SUBVERT THE NATIONALIST AND LIBERATION MOVEMENTS. Two days later he told a crowd of seven thousand angry Tanzanians at Moshi, "We liked the Americans because they knew how sweet freedom is, and because they pressed the British to give us our freedom. Why are they now trying to undermine our government?"

While anti-Americanism raged across Tanzania, the U.S. embassy in Dar es Salaam waited for almost a week to see the "documentary evidence," which, as it turned out, consisted of three photostats. All three, written in careless French, were reputed to be Western diplomatic messages. One document referred to "special arrangements to overthrow the government of Mr. Julius Nyerere to one still being studied by the Department of State." Another said that the U.S. sought to obtain "assurances from Great Britain that she will not intervene." The third, reputedly addressed to an ambassador, asked for £9,000 for recruiting South Africans for a "putsch." A U.S. diplomat said at the time, "It will be no problem demonstrating that the documents are forgeries. The real question is whether the evidence presented will be accepted."

Nyerere had been spending the week upcountry at Lake Manyara. He was said to have received the documents from his old friend Andrew Tibandebage, who was Tanzania's ambassador to the Congo, and to have given them to Kambona saying, "Deal with this." When Nyerere returned to Dar es Salaam a few days later, Westerners hoped he would make a statement that the documents were false. Instead, at an afternoon rally of about twenty thousand people at the Jangwani playing fields, Nyerere gave a long, emotional speech about world power problems in which he referred again and again to the possibility of a mistake. "It may not be true in this case," he said. If the documents were not genuine, "I would be the first to thank God." The Americans had denied the documents' authenticity, he said, and would be given a chance to prove their claim.

Western diplomats were disappointed that Nyerere had not been more explicit, but tended to place most of the blame on Kambona, who had blandly told them that such public disclosure of unproved allegations represented

193

"the African way of dealing with problems." Some even believed Kambona had used the incident to damage the position of the U.S. in Tanzania and to embarrass Nyerere's own relations with the Western countries.

Both Kambona and Nyerere insisted in later years, however, that Kambona was not responsible. "I was only the announcer," Kambona has said. "He called me from Lake Manyara, and asked me to make them public. Whether they were true or not, we thought this was the best defense against them." Nyerere has essentially agreed. "It's unfair to blame Oscar for that," he has said. "If I hadn't wanted that announced, I wouldn't have given it to him." Yes, of course, Nyerere said, he himself might have used different words or different methods, but basically the responsibility was his.

The documents case was still fresh in the minds of Tanzanians when, in late November, the second incident occurred: Belgian paratroopers borne by U.S. Air Force planes dropped on Stanleyville, in the Congo, to save the lives of a thousand whites who were being held hostage by the Congolese rebels. The airdrop took place while negotiations for the hostages' release were being held in Nairobi between William Attwood, the U.S. ambassador to Kenya, and Thomas Kanza, the Congolese rebel regime's "foreign minister." Of all the statements of protest from African heads of state, none was angrier than Nyerere's: "In an action reminiscent of Pearl Harbor, foreign troops were flown into the Congo at the very moment that negotiations were taking place to secure the safety of all." Oscar Kambona added that the airdrop was "the meanest, most unwarranted and provocative interference by the Western world in the affairs and peace of the African continent."

194

Westerners in general were astonished at the extent of the African reaction against an operation that may well have saved several hundred hostages' lives, and were irritated that the African leaders said little or nothing about the rebels' murder of fifty hostages, including Dr. Paul Carlson, the American missionary.

The key to the reaction against the airlift lies in the Africans' consciousness of their vulnerability. Nyerere had distrusted Moise Tshombe ever since Tshombe led the Katanga secession and at one point had actually suggested to Nyerere the possibility of merging Katanga with Tanganyika. In the years of Congolese fighting, Tshombe had become a symbol of the African who used white support and white mercenaries to kill his brothers and destroy his own country: the black man who hires whites to murder blacks. In Tanganyika during those years, there was no uglier epithet than to call a man a "Tshombe." Nyerere regarded Tshombe's return to Leopoldville as prime minister—the result of the acquiescence if not the connivance of the West —as a betrayal of Africa. "There are three dead men who, if they should come to life today, would ask, '*What* is happening?' They are President Kennedy, Dag Hammarskjöld and Patrice Lumumba." He also believed apparently that the paratroop landing in Stanleyville was aimed not just at rescuing hostages but at ending the Congo rebellion and thus helping the Tshombe regime. It is true that Nyerere and other Africans reacted irrationally to the airdrop; it is also true, however, that, in failing to exert greater pressure against Tshombe's accession to power in Leopoldville, the Western powers failed to understand the depth of the African leaders' hatred of him. When asked why Nyerere had reacted so violently to what was, after all, a humanitarian mission to save lives, a European friend of Nyerere's replied, " 'You'll do all that for a thousand white skins!' That's what they would say. 'And you don't do anything at all about the millions of Africans in South Africa and Rhodesia.' That's the African reaction. Nyerere is not a racialist, but he's a fanatical African."

Nyerere himself tried to explain it to an American visitor in 1966. "One of the best things that could happen to Africa would be for the United States to understand her. This should not be difficult. The United States fought its own revolution in 1776, defining in language that can never be bettered why an otherwise peaceful, sensible people would take up arms and fight. Of the countries born of revolution, the greatest is the United States. Today you have an ethic based on freedom. You judge society by that ethic. You find Alabama intolerable because of your own ethic. I find it very natural that during World War II, Roosevelt should have said to Churchill, 'How can we fight for freedom elsewhere in the world, and yet you stop the Indians from governing themselves?' One accepts that an American would ask, 'How can we justify preserving an empire while we are fighting for freedom elsewhere?' But then something went wrong.

"I think the United States is schizophrenic in this matter. It says, 'You must back up the United States in the anti-Communist struggle.' In some corner of its mind, it accepts that Africans have a right to independence. You relegate Africa's case to some corner; it does not matter very much. If there is a conflict, you back up your allies and not freedom.

"All right. The Congo becomes independent; trouble takes place; there is danger of the Congo getting dismembered. No Communists were involved. What started it off was the mutiny, so the natural effort was to stop the disintegration. On the whole, I think, Kennedy avoided letting it become a Cold War issue; he wanted to work through the U.N. to help Lumumba and the central government.

"All right, then there was a puppet regime, with Adoula. But we didn't quarrel. But eventually the Katanga man was back and Adoula was kicked out! I know the U.S. is not as old in this game as the Europeans, but still: their man was pushed out. I don't believe the U.S. was responsible for bringing Tshombe back—but there he was! The very fellows who had been fighting the U.N. force bring back this fellow—and the U.S. embraces him!

"All right, the United States—a very honorable man —says, 'We joined in the [Stanleyville] operation to rescue the missionaries,' and then the United States is extremely surprised at our reaction! When Africa almost unanimously condemned this! Now I ask, 'Why is the U.S. surprised? Why this failure to understand?' Killing had been going on in the Congo; why did this particular threat of killing disturb them? Mercenaries had been recruited who *enjoyed the killing of Africans*—why doesn't this worry the United States?

"Out of its own ethic, the United States should have been our ally in all this: in stopping the mercenaries, these haters of the human race, who enjoyed killing. Why pick *this*? And then they turn it around and say that we want the missionaries to be exterminated, to be eaten up!

"I've said before, in trying to explain this, try to imagine a Jew who recruits ex-Nazis to go to Israel and assist him in his power struggle. How would the Jews take it? Then suppose he has a powerful ally. And if the Jews

197

react against this man, would his ally be surprised when the Jews react that way?

"The best thing that can happen for us in Africa would be for the United States, this power with a good ethic, to understand us. Our continent is a continent we don't control, and we feel strongly about this."

THE THIRD INCIDENT was the most serious. In January 1965 Nyerere called in the American ambassador, William Leonhart, and told him he believed that two of Leonhart's men were engaged in subversive activities, and were therefore being expelled within twenty-four hours. The two were Robert Gordon, who had been counselor of the embassy in Dar es Salaam for about six months, and Frank Carlucci, the chargé d'affaires in Zanzibar, who had seemed to be performing admirably under difficult circumstances. Nyerere is said to have assured Leonhart, moreover, that he understood that neither the ambassador nor his embassy was involved.

The implication seemed to be that the two men were Central Intelligence Agency employees who were plotting to overthrow the regime in Zanzibar—a plot which the State Department didn't know about but which, when completed, it would approve of. At a subsequent meeting with U.S. diplomats, a member of Nyerere's staff asked, "What about the ammunition they were getting?" The embassy concluded that the source of the accusation lay in the twice-daily telephone conversations that Gordon and Carlucci conducted between Dar es Salaam and Zanzibar. It was also assumed that the conversations had been tape-recorded regularly by intelligence services on one or both sides of the Zanzibar Channel.

The United States government retaliated by expelling the counselor of the two-man Tanzanian embassy in Washington, and by calling Leonhart home for consultations. Tanzania, in consequence, recalled its ambassador, Othman Shariff, and relations remained strained for many months. The Tanzanians were surprised and angered at Washington's action and pointed out that Nyerere—in a curious gesture perhaps intended to help the U.S. save face —had written to President Johnson that the dispute was between Tanzania and "two American individuals . . . who happened to be servants of the American government." Nyerere refused to produce evidence to support the charge against the diplomats and replied: "We are a small country, but we are as much a sovereign state as the U.S. . . . We do not bully, and we do not like being bullied."

What had actually happened, apparently, was a minor classic of U.S. bureaucracy, ludicrous but sad. Carlucci, who had been anxious to boost Abeid Karume's opinion of the U.S., had told the ambassador a few days earlier that he would like to have President Johnson send a message of greetings to Karume on January 12, the first anniversary of the Zanzibar revolution. But which day was Tanzania's national day? Was it Independence Day, December 9; or Saba Saba, July 7; or Revolution Day, January 12; or Union Day, April 26? Leonhart reasoned that the proper national day was December 9, and that the message of greetings should be sent from President to President, Lyndon Johnson to Julius Nyerere. Carlucci persisted: Then how about a message from Vice-President Humphrey to Vice-President Karume? Again Leonhart said no. But he later added that if he was wrong, and other nations sent congratulations, the U.S. would have another chance on the "second twelfth." This meant February 12, which was being celebrated that year as the anniversary of the revolution because January 12 fell during Ramadan. He also said he didn't think anybody "higher than Williams" (Assistant Secretary of State for African Affairs G. Mennen Williams) should sign the message.

A day or two later, Carlucci complained to Gordon on the telephone that he wasn't satisfied with what Leonhart had told him. Gordon replied, "Why don't you go direct? The boss doesn't want any part of it"—meaning: Ask Washington yourself if you want to, but the ambassador doesn't want to get involved. In inveterate bureaucratese, one of the men even used the phrase "Operation Second Twelfth" and the words "have enough ammunition"—meaning: the information necessary for making a case to Washington.

Not surprisingly, the Tanzanian intelligence agents who listened to the conversation failed to comprehend the American jargon. Or perhaps it was the Zanzibari intelligence agents who misunderstood. Or perhaps someone heard the conversation and understood full well its potential for exploitation. In any case, the incident occurred at a time when the level of hysteria was very high. The government was worried about the situation on Zanzibar and about Western reaction to what was happening there. It was also preoccupied with security precautions after the events of the preceding year; visitors noticed copies of *The Invisible Government*, a book about the workings of the CIA, in the offices of several Tanzanian ministers.

Nyerere's friends and colleagues gained the impression that Nyerere genuinely believed the diplomats were plotting, or at least believed it plausible that U.S. agents might be resorting to such methods to overthrow the regime in Zanzibar. "But whether the President understood or not is irrelevant," one Tanzanian has said. "The Zanzibaris did not understand."

IN SUBSEQUENT YEARS, the Vietnam war became an important source of friction. "The U.S. must recover from the delirium of power," Nyerere told a party conference in 1967, although he characteristically matched his criticism of U.S. policy with a tribute to Americans who opposed the war. Not all Tanzanians were so gracious. For several years the TANU-sponsored *Nationalist* had maintained a stridently anti-American line that probably caused more damage to their relations with the U.S. than the Tanzanians realized. One casualty of the ill feeling was the Peace Corps. In 1961 Tanganyika had been the first African country to ask for volunteers, and by 1966 the number of Peace Corpsmen in Tanzania had reached five hundred and eight. But the Corps was criticized steadily by *The Nationalist*; Nyerere himself said the Corps's idealism had disappeared and the organization had been infiltrated by "people whose motives are no good," and in late 1969 the last volunteer went home.

In the early years of its independence, Tanganyika probably inspired more young visitors from America and Western Europe than any other African country. A Ugandan political scientist, Ali Mazrui, published an article in the East African magazine *Transition* in 1967 in which he described a contagious social malady called "Tanzaphilia." He defined the phenomenon as "the romantic spell which Tanzania casts on so many of those who have been closely associated with her," adding: "Many of the most prosaic

Western pragmatists have been known to acquire that dreamy look under the spell of Tanzania." Particularly susceptible, he wrote, were Western liberals who saw in Tanzania—largely because of Nyerere's personality and ideas—a place where they could achieve the political goals on which they had failed at home. Tanzania still has a cult of overseas admirers, but the group's size has been eroded somewhat by the ill feeling and misunderstanding of the last several years.

Americans who live in Tanzania find the antagonism and suspicion difficult to accept. But, as one Tanzanian commented in late 1967, "We are intimidated by the power of the U.S.—the idea that the U.S. could move in on us any time it wanted to, and there would be nothing we could do. There was Stanleyville, and there is Vietnam. Another factor is the growing relationship with China, and the realization that the powerful U.S. doesn't like this and might do something about it. But most of all it is a continuation of 1964, when we felt so helpless."

Relations between the U.S. and Tanzania have gradually improved since 1965, but have never returned to their pre-1964 warmth. Top-level U.S. officials of both the Johnson and Nixon Administrations have tended to visit only those African countries where their receptions were most likely to be friendly, and they rarely stop in Tanzania any more. Nyerere paid a state visit to Canada in 1969 but was not invited to make a stopover in Washington. He visited the United Nations in October 1970 but did not meet Richard Nixon.

NYERERE'S MOST SERIOUS DISPUTE with the West—his break in diplomatic relations with Britain over the Rhodesian declaration of independence—came in December 1965. It had really begun at the Commonwealth Prime Ministers' Conference in June when Nyerere dissociated Tanzania from the portions of the final communiqué that dealt with Rhodesia and Vietnam. "We tried for a long time," Nyerere said, "to get an assurance from the British government that whatever negotiations they were carrying out were aimed at the achievement of independence in Rhodesia on the basis of majority rule. We were unable to receive this assurance." He also took exception to Harold Wilson's proposal that the Commonwealth send a peace mission to Vietnam. "I am merely suggesting," Nyerere said, "that the Commonwealth as such should not appear to be backing Mr. Harold Wilson or the United States on this issue . . . For all I know, China might say it would receive the mission. But I am saying that it is not for us to take action which, going by past performance, appears to be one-sided, and is putting China in the dock." Wilson managed to isolate Nyerere completely; no other member supported his position on either issue.

Nyerere told a friend at the time of the debate, "It's terrible. It makes me seem arrogant. As I started speaking, I knew people in the conference would say, 'Nyerere is taking the position because he wants to establish himself as a radical leader—or because of commitments to China. I could almost *hear* them thinking this."

Nyerere threatened as early as September to withdraw from the Commonwealth if Britain should negotiate independence with the Rhodesian government headed by Ian Smith. At the OAU heads of state conference at Accra in October, in what turned out to be the twilight of Kwame Nkrumah's power, the organization passed a unanimous

203

resolution in which its members threatened to break diplomatic relations with Britain if the British allowed the Rhodesians to declare their independence.

The declaration came on November 11. At first Nyerere counseled caution; Britain, he said, should be given a chance to solve the problem in her own way. On December 6, the OAU foreign ministers voted to "give Britain ten more days to crush the Smith regime," after which they would break relations. Friends have said that Nyerere thought the ultimatum was stupid but concluded, "If we don't do it, nobody will ever take Africa's word again, and, worse, *we* won't believe in our word either."

Surely knowing that nothing would happen to settle the Rhodesian crisis within ten days, Nyerere began immediately to prepare his people for the break in relations on December 15. "My decision could mean hardship," he told a rally at TANU headquarters. "Are you ready to accept it?" Besides the loss of existing British aid, it meant the cancellation of a $20-million loan agreement that was ready to be signed. He also began to reassure British citizens in Tanzania, and warned his people that violence against British residents would not be tolerated. "No British subject need have any fear for his personal safety either from the institutions of the government or from the people of the United Republic." When a group of students set fire to the British high commissioner's car, Nyerere ordered them to go back and apologize.

As support lagged among other OAU members, Nyerere noted that the decision at Accra had been unanimous. "But now," he said, "some African leaders have gone back to their capitals and started to look at their bank balances. This is ridiculous!" When the British complained that the rebellion could not possibly be settled before the deadline imposed by the resolution, Nyerere replied that what was needed was "clear evidence of Britain's intention to take strong action." The demand was for independence "on the basis of majority rule." On December 14, Nyerere delivered his "Honor of Africa" address to the National Assembly, explaining why Tanzania would implement the resolution. The speech was delivered in English because there wasn't time to translate it into polished Swahili. At midnight, Tanzania broke relations. Eight other African countries followed: Guinea, Ghana, Mali, Egypt, Mauritania, Congo Brazzaville, Sudan and Algeria. Twenty-six did not. The British government refused to put down the Rhodesian rebellion by military means, and instead relied unsuccessfully on the imposition of economic sanctions against the Ian Smith regime. Relations between Tanzania and Britain remained broken for thirty-one months.

Oscar Kambona and Labor Minister Michael Kamaliza led demonstrations in Dar es Salaam in support of the decision. Publicly Nyerere said, "If Mr. Wilson has some ambition to be the British Prime Minister who broke the Commonwealth, I can regret it, but I cannot stop him from fulfilling his ambition." And what if Britain should take measures following the deadline? "I will be very pleased if I prove tomorrow to be the greatest fool that Africa has produced." Privately he was dejected by the lack of support and also by the break itself. "They were my friends," he said of the British.

Almost simultaneous with the diplomatic break was the beginning of cooperation between Tanzania and Britain in airlifting emergency supplies of oil to Zambia. The British government had imposed an embargo on oil shipped by its nationals to Rhodesia; the Salisbury regime responded by cutting off the flow of Zambia's oil, which had traditionally passed through Rhodesia from the Mozambican port of Beira. Later the airlift was replaced by a trucking operation between Dar es Salaam and Zambia, and eventually by a 1,000-mile pipeline.

Nyerere agreed in December 1965 to let the Royal Air Force use Tanzanian airfields temporarily, but asked that the British switch to civilian planes as soon as they could. Shortly after that, the British navy sent a frigate laden with oil drums from Aden to Dar es Salaam without securing the permission of the Tanzanian government. Nyerere then asked that no warships be brought to Dar es Salaam. The bluff skipper of the frigate made the correct gesture: he invited the President for lunch. Later, when he was asked by the local press if he had expected the President to accept, he replied, "Why not? Breaking diplomatic relations is no excuse for being rude." Nyerere, who has often shown a great fondness for British character and eccentricity, is said to have laughed heartily at the story.

The diplomatic community in Dar es Salaam tended to respect Nyerere's decision to break relations but viewed it as excessively rigid. "When he has made up his mind," said one Western diplomat, "he sticks to it. It made no sense to break with Britain. It tended to defeat the very thing he was trying to bring about."

Nyerere, however, apparently never regretted the decision. "No," he said a few months later, "we couldn't have lived with ourselves otherwise. We went to Accra, we heads of state. I was there. I could have dissociated myself, I could have said, 'This is absurd.' But I thought it was reasonable, and the matter serious. A few months later, there was a follow-up. I sent my Second Vice-President. They considered what steps might be taken, and they settled on the matter of diplomatic relations. This was something all were capable of. We can't march armies to Rhodesia—we don't *have* the blessed armies. But we could make a strong expression of Africa's feelings on the question of racialism. Fine!

"In private relationships, there are some people we know whose yes means yes and whose no means no. It must be the same here: so that the world can look on this yes as meaning something. Or else they will say, 'Those Africans, you can't rely on them, you never know if their yes means yes.'

"Would it help Tanzania to establish a reputation for undependability? Can young nations afford to be cynical about morals? For old nations, morals become an instrument of power. Can young nations afford this?'"

In September 1965, a few months before the break with Britain, mainland Tanzania had held its first general elections since 1962. Until that time, most Members of Parliament had assumed that they would be renominated by the party and thus would be assured of reelection. Instead the party adopted a new system, under which the National Executive committee selected two candidates for almost every constituency; only six incumbent Members, including Vice-President Rashidi Kawawa and five other Cabinet members, were unopposed. Nyerere similarly was unopposed.

On Zanzibar there were no parliamentary elections; it was still too soon after the revolution, the government explained. But the Zanzibaris, like the mainlanders, had a chance to vote for or against the President. In answer to a question during the campaign, Nyerere told a group of Zanzibaris that it would be dangerous for him to be appointed President for life. "If that happened, you would be right back where you were under the Sultan," he said. "I could even call myself Sultan Nyerere."

He devoted much of his campaign to an explanation of the use of the ballot. "Those who do not wish me to be President for the next five years," he would say, "have simply to put a tick in the space on the ballot paper underneath where it says *hapana* [no]. But if you feel I should continue as President, I hope you will go to the polls and vote for me by putting your tick on the ballot under the word *ndiyo*."

At the beginning of the campaign, the TANU Central Committee selected two symbols, the *jembe* (hoe) and *nyumba* (house), and assigned one to each candidate. The committee assumed that the symbols were of roughly equal value, but political scientists and students who were analyzing the campaign discovered that the symbols themselves quickly became an issue in many constituencies, and that the candidate whose symbol was the *jembe* had a distinct advantage over his opponent.

A British political scientist, Belle Harris, wrote of the campaign in a local magazine, *Mbioni:* "Again and again this kind of phrase occurs in the students' reports: 'All wealth comes from the *jembe*'; 'How many of you have a *jembe* at home?' answered by a roar of '*Ndiyo*'; 'Should we as a nation sleep or wake up and dig?' One Junior Minister carried a hoe around during the campaign . . . Only in one or two constituencies was the symbol of the house used as effectively. For example, in Mbeya the local-born candidate emphasized the common bond of 'our houses are here.' He won."

Another factor in the campaign was the candidate's ability to show that he had not lost the popular touch. Miss Harris wrote: "The students reported that where a candidate adopted the Western 'educative' manner of explaining and justifying government policy, he was considered to be speaking 'above the heads of the people.' "

The scene on election day was much like that of other African countries: as long lines formed at polling places beneath flame trees and baobabs, each voter's thumb was

210

daubed in red indelible ink to prevent him from casting
any more ballots that day.

The size of Nyerere's victory was predictable: 96 percent voted yes, although more than 92,000 of his countrymen cast their ballots against him. The surprise came in
the number of incumbent Members of Parliament who were
defeated. In Rufiji, the proud Bibi Titi Mohamed, the
Junior Minister for Community Development and the
president of the national women's organization, was badly
beaten. Another casualty was Paul Bomani, the Minister
of Finance and one of Nyerere's ablest colleagues. Bomani's
friends pointed out that the voters blamed him for introduc-
ing the new 5 percent development levy on salaries; but it
was also true that the Bomani family was widely resented
in Mwanza for its wealth and specifically for the power it
wielded within the large cotton cooperative, the Victoria
Federation of Cooperative Unions.

All told, two ministers and six junior ministers were
defeated, in addition to three other junior ministers who
had failed to secure the party's nomination for re-election.
Nine backbench M.P.s were also defeated, and another 37
either did not seek re-election or were not renominated. Of
the 107 constituency members of the new Parliament, 86
were freshmen. Among the winners were Derek Bryceson,
the only European in Nyerere's Cabinet, and Amir Jamal,
the only Asian; both were re-elected against African opponents, Bryceson by a majority of almost five to one.

In choosing candidates to fill the ten "nominated"
seats in Parliament, Nyerere took the position that these
appointive posts should not be used to save the careers of
politicians who had been repudiated at the polls; his decision angered Bibi Titi Mohamed, among others. Then, mak-

ing an exception to his own rule, Nyerere named Paul Bomani to a nominated seat and appointed him to the newly created post of Minister of State in the Directorate of Development and Planning; Bomani, he explained, was too valuable a man to lose.

A few months later, Nyerere was asked whether he felt the elections had proved the validity of the country's one-party system. "I think it has vindicated what we have been saying," he said. "By definition, democrats are free people. And the machinery of elections must not be confused with the essentials of democracy. I don't blame Westerners. The only democracies they have known have been multi-party systems, and the only one-party systems they have seen have been non-democratic. But: a multiplicity of parties does not guarantee democracy."

He added, "I can't say we have proved it yet. You don't establish a system with one election. But we have shown we can have *one* free election under our system. My hope now is that we can create the necessary conditions that our experiment can live. And it may lead Westerners to say, 'Well . . . perhaps . . .' "

In a television interview that year, he pursued the point. "To some extent there are safeguards," he said. "But I have sufficient power under the constitution to be a dictator. And frankly I don't believe yet that we can claim the system is safeguarded. The safeguard is not one election, it is a tradition; the true safeguard of democracy is a tradition of democracy."

NYERERE HAS occasionally referred to Dar es Salaam as "Rumorville." This might seem to a casual visitor to be a very odd thing to say about that sleepy little harbor town, fragrant with the smells and spices of the East African coast, whose name in Arabic means "haven of peace."

It is true, however, that a sort of free-floating paranoia sometimes seems to hang suspended in Dar es Salaam's heavy air. Some observers have gone so far as to explain the suspicion and distrust of foreigners as a Tanzanian character trait, a legacy from the age of slavery. In any case, many foreigners seem to have learned to make allowances. A Briton who had lived in Dar es Salaam and served the Tanzanian government for many years once commented wistfully to a visiting American, "You know, we have to allow them to distrust us."

A European psychiatrist who formerly lived in Tanzania attributed the symptoms to a malady that he called "uhuruitis" and described as follows: "Depression, fatigue, almost a return to tribal fears; a considerable increase in anxiety at all levels; a certain amount of secondary guilt that comes from having rejected a father. Another element is the breakup of family ties; the drift from the villages to the towns." The constant bubble of rumor, he felt, was a manifestation of the tension.

Nyerere sometimes complains to friends, "I'm fed up with all this suspicion," and conducts periodic campaigns against it. Once he actually identified a dozen local people who were accused of spreading false rumors and warned them to stop it. At a mass rally on Union Day in 1966, he mentioned some of the prevailing gossip—of dissension within his Cabinet, and of the imminent breakup of the Union. "Three times we had rumors of three different coups," he said. Then he turned and addressed

213

Brigadier Sarakikya, the young army commander, "By the way, Brigadier, what happened to that coup we were supposed to have this morning?"

Discussing the problem one day in 1966, Nyerere said, "Well, I think there are two sources of these rumors. One we can control: the internal source of rumor—mere gossip, born of ignorance or misunderstanding; local mischief. Dar is not big enough to be free of this, and yet not small enough for people to know everybody else and what is happening.

"But there is another source as well, I think. After the army mutiny, I was having a discussion with a foreign diplomat. I was explaining what was happening: 'You know, the town was full of rumors on that Friday.' And he made a remark—I'm a naïve fellow, so to me it was quite significant—he said, 'Have you ever considered establishing your own rumor factory?' Well, I have the feeling there are deliberate rumor factories."

Lady Chesham, who has remained in the Tanzanian Parliament as a national member, remarked tartly in 1966, "There are too many [foreign] wives here who haven't anything to do but write home and tell their friends about how brave they are to be here." She once recalled how, following a private meeting that Nyerere had held with Members of Parliament, a local British journalist had asked her, "Is it true he told you of an attempted coup and named the conspirators?" Lady Chesham replied, "God no! Would he have confided to one hundred and fifty people who had conspired against him? Use your brains, man!" She later added, "The blinking idiot. He's always backing me into corners at sundowners." At the meeting, Nyerere had spoken of Tanzania's role in the world power struggle. "But this has nothing to do with you," he said. "Your politics is the development of Tanzania. You must be on your guard against influences from outside. Pay attention to rumors and, if they are serious, you should report them."

Part of the suspicion, of course, is soundly based. The experience of slavery was followed by a long period of colonialism, during which the Tanganyikans saw Kenya become the center of industry for East Africa and the recipient of a disproportionate share of the colonial power's investment and concern. After independence came the trauma of the army mutiny and the revolution on Zanzibar and the endless series of military coups and civil wars throughout Africa. The Tanzanians also realized that they were taking a measured risk by providing hospitality for at least a dozen refugee organizations or "liberation movements" from South Africa, Southwest Africa, Rhodesia and Mozambique; there is even a group from the French-owned Comoro Islands.

Some of the organizations are little more than store-front offices that serve as gathering places for young men who have fled north to Tanzania and are looking for jobs or scholarships. A few are genuine guerrilla movements, the most active being the Frente de Libertação de Moçambique (the Mozambican Liberation Front, or FRELIMO), which for about six years has been conducting a spasmodic military campaign in northern Mozambique and has virtually controlled two provinces during much of that period. In early 1969 FRELIMO's leader, the American-educated Dr. Eduardo Mondlane, was killed near Dar es Salaam when he tried to open a package that had the appearance of having been sent from somewhere in Europe. Early reports had it that the book-size bomb package had borne an East

German or a Soviet postmark; subsequent rumors added
West Germany, France and even Japan. In any case, Tanzanian authorities concluded that the package had been
slipped directly into the local postal system or even into
FRELIMO's post-office box. The case remains unsolved;
speculation has centered on everybody from the Portuguese, who obviously benefited from a weakening of the
guerrilla movement, to Mondlane's enemies within the
refugee community. Whatever the truth may be, the as-
sassination underscored the vulnerability of African leadership to espionage. It reminded the Tanzanians that South
Africa and Portugal would be greatly advantaged if all
of independent Africa, and particularly Tanzania and
Zambia, were led by men of a different character than
Julius Nyerere and Kenneth Kaunda: men such as Has-
tings Kamuzu Banda of Malawi who would be willing to
live with, trade with, and accept gratuities from the white
regimes of southern Africa.

"AFRICA IS IN A MESS," Nyerere said on his return from an
OAU summit conference in 1966. "There is a devil somewhere in Africa. I am a good superstitious African, and I
believe in devils." At the conference, the delegates had refused, if only temporarily, to renew the budget of the OAU
Liberation Committee; the committee provides funds for
the various guerrilla movements, most of which are based in
Dar es Salaam. "I think the African countries will have to
make up their minds," Nyerere said, "whether they will give
priority to Africa or to their associations with foreign
rulers."

Such outbursts against other African governments are
notable for their rarity. For the most part, Tanzania's dis-

agreements with its neighbors are treated with as much discretion as disputes within the councils of TANU or those between the mainland government and the Zanzibaris. Nothing angers the Tanzanians more than for a foreigner to use Dar es Salaam as a platform from which to denounce another African state or its leader.

The creation of an East African federation composed of Tanzania, Kenya and Uganda has never again seemed as imminent as it did in 1963. In 1967, however, the three countries converted the East African Common Services Organization—an inheritance from the colonial period—into the East African Community, whose headquarters were established at Arusha.

The Community, a common market and administrative union, operates a wide range of services for the three countries. It collects income taxes, customs and excise duties; it operates four independent corporations that run East Africa's airline, railways, harbors, and post and telecommunications; it administers a dozen research organizations. Its branches include an appellate judicial system and a development bank. After intensive bargaining, the three countries agreed to a plan that would give Tanzania and Uganda some assistance in catching up with Kenya's more advanced state of development. Accordingly, the three countries contribute equally to the bank, but the bank's investments and guarantees are then distributed according to a formula that gives preferential treatment to Tanzania and Uganda.

Until early 1971, relations between Tanzania and its Community partners had wavered between the cordial and the correct. The most serious threat to the Community's continued existence was caused by the overthrow of the

217

Uganda President, Milton Obote, in January 1971. Nyerere continued to recognize Obote as President, offered him refuge in Dar es Salaam, and vowed that he would not sit at the same table as Uganda's new military ruler, General Idi Amin Dada. The events in Uganda accelerated Tanzania's tendency to look southward toward Zambia, with whom Tanzania is probably friendlier today than with any other neighbor.

Tanzania's relations with the Congo improved immediately after the removal of Moise Tshombe as premier in 1965. Presumably because he despised Tshombe so intensely, Nyerere was prepared to work more closely with the new President, Joseph Mobutu, even though Mobutu was a military man who had seized power. When the Mobutu government conducted a public hanging of four former Cabinet ministers in 1966, Nyerere said simply, "I can tell you this: it would not have happened here."

The Tanzanians' noisiest quarrel with another African country has been with Malawi, the former Nyasaland. In fact, one measure of the present bitterness is the fact that the Tanzanians stubbornly refer to the lake that separates the two countries by its colonial name, Lake Nyasa, whereas the Malawians have long since changed it to Lake Malawi.

At the heart of the dispute is Dr. Banda, the President of Malawi. Dr. Banda has had a rather odd career. He left his country at the age of thirteen, studied in South Africa, the United States and Britain, and practiced medicine in London and later in Ghana. In 1958, after an absence of almost forty years, he was called back to Nyasaland to lead the country's independence movement. His colleagues were a group of young men who referred to Dr. Banda as "our father"; he in turn called them "my boys."

218

In 1964 Nyasaland attained independence and Dr. Banda's boys became his ministers. Within a few weeks, however, several of them were running for their lives following a dispute with Dr. Banda. Four or five of the former ministers settled in Dar es Salaam; among them was Kanyama Chiume, who had been Oscar Kambona's great friend and fellow teacher at Dodoma years before.

Dr. Banda subsequently accused the Tanzanian government of supporting the rebel ministers, and it may well be that the Malawians received some assistance for a while from one or more Tanzanian leaders, perhaps Kambona. For their part, the Tanzanians have grown increasingly uneasy as Dr. Banda cooperated with the Portuguese and established diplomatic relations with South Africa; they fear that Banda might someday allow the South Africans to use Malawi as a base from which to attack Tanzania and Zambia.

A minor irritant, in addition, has been a dispute about the ownership of Lake Malawi and its shoreline. In his characteristically grandiose style, Banda was once quoted as saying, "Nyerere should be the last person to squeal and squeak. He began it. He provoked me last year by claiming part of our lake. Did he expect me to remain silent? What does he think I am, a jellyfish like himself? I am no jellyfish. In my back there is a bone."

Nyerere is said to believe that Tanzania's relations with Malawi are unlikely to improve very much as long as Banda is in power. In 1966, when the two countries were about to hold discussions over their mutual problems, Banda announced that the talks would deal primarily with Tanzania's surrender of the Malawian ministers who had taken refuge in Dar es Salaam. Nyerere is said to have cabled Banda: "There is no point holding discussions if you don't know what we're talking about."

EVER SINCE the early TANU period, Nyerere had stressed the importance of developing regional confederations as steps toward achieving African unity. He disagreed, however, with Kwame Nkrumah's call for African Union because he believed it unrealistic at that stage and merely self-serving. He also disapproved of the widespread corruption in Ghana; after Nkrumah's overthrow in 1966, Nyerere told friends, "He made the mistake of allowing corruption, and it has overwhelmed him."

Nonetheless, Nyerere was greatly distressed by Nkrumah's overthrow, and viewed it as a defeat for the African cause against Rhodesia and the white south. He was even more upset by the fall of Milton Obote five years later; at the time of the military coup in Uganda, Obote was in Singapore attending the Commonwealth Prime Ministers' Conference, at which he had joined Tanzania and Zambia in threatening to leave the Commonwealth if the British government proceeded with its plan to resume arms sales to South Africa.

In early 1971, following Obote's overthrow, Nyerere announced that Tanzania would train a "people's militia" or home guard to increase the national security. In his speech, he listed some of the events in which such militias might have been useful: the presumed murder of Patrice Lumumba in the Congo in 1961, the fall of Nkrumah in 1966 and of Obote in 1971, and the raid on Guinea in 1970 by a band of hostile forces which, the Guineans charged, were supported by the Portuguese and included some white mercenaries. Nyerere described the attack on Guinea as "a big lesson for us," especially since Tanzania, like Guinea, shared a hostile border with the Portuguese.

A few months after Nkrumah's fall, Nyerere had spoken of the military takeovers that were sweeping across Africa. "The soldiers are in," said Nyerere, "for the purpose of democracy, they say, and it could easily be true. But the method of establishing a government has its own logic. If they come in by the bullet, it will not be easy for them to withdraw from the bullet position."

Asked if he felt there was a way to protect Africa from internal coups, Nyerere replied, "How do you do it? Nkrumah used to talk of a High Command. I disagreed with him on this. Suppose it were like NATO, an alliance of governments organized for self-protection against an external enemy. But how would you use NATO to stop a coup in Britain? How does the outsider go in? I differed with Nkrumah on this because Africa is not going to be attacked from the outside. The answer is unity on the basis of the United States of America; this is the answer to our internal problems."

Only if there was "genuine subversion by an outside power," said Nyerere, would intervention by another African state be justified. "But if there is an internal uprising in Tanzania, what does Africa do? Invade Tanzania? And who invades?"

(12)

Given Nyerere's preoccupation with the problems of developing a backward country, and given also his respect for spartan living and his abhorrence of luxury, his fascination with China was probably inevitable. The events of 1964 and 1965, especially including the union with Zanzibar, caused him to shift to a new political balance further to the left, and the Chinese became the chief foreign beneficiary.

The Peking government had already shown that it was seeking to strengthen its diplomatic presence in East Africa. In the weeks after the revolution, the Chinese had promised the Zanzibaris a £5-million interest-free loan and a shipment of arms. In June, about two months after Union, they offered an additional £10-million to mainland Tanzania. In August, Nyerere signed an agreement for a group of eleven Chinese military technicians, and reacted angrily to Western diplomatic pressure against the move; most of his officers were British-trained, he pointed out, and he had just signed an agreement with West Germany to train an air wing.

In February 1965, Nyerere made an eight-day state visit to China and was struck by the relevance of Chinese problems to those of his own country. He assured his Chinese hosts, "If it were possible for me to lift all the ten million Tanzanians and bring them to China to see what you have done since the liberation, I would do so." Back in Dar

223

es Salaam, he told a press conference, "At times I thought it was unfair that our country should be expecting economic assistance from a country like China, which is being extremely economical, while we are not." He said China's External Affairs Minister, Marshal Chen Yi, told him there were only about ten cars in his ministry, which employed three thousand people. "I passed this information to Oscar [who had been his own External Affairs Minister] immediately," Nyerere said.

In June 1965 he welcomed Chou En-lai to Dar es Salaam, where Chou repeated his famous remark of the previous year that "an excellent revolutionary situation exists in Africa." Kenya and a number of other African governments had objected to this ominous forecast, but Nyerere chose to interpret it as a call for social and economic revolution. "Africa is very much ripe for revolution," he said, "and I can assure you Chou En-lai is not responsible for this. If the revolution is not allowed to take place, Africa will not be Africa."

At a state banquet for Chou, Nyerere described how much the trip to China had meant to him: "The single-mindedness . . . and the conscious and deliberate frugality with which your people and your government are concentrating on development was the thing which most impressed me during my visit to your great country. It was a big lesson for me." As if to underscore his point, Nyerere announced four days later that the government thereafter would serve only beer, soft drinks, tea and coffee at its official receptions, and no more liquor. Except for four-wheel-drive bush vehicles, only automobiles that cost no more than £900 apiece would henceforth be bought for government officials.

Despite the warmth of the reception he gave Chou, Nyerere closed his speech with one of his characteristic warnings about Tanzania's independence: "From no quarter shall we accept direction or neocolonialism, and at no time shall we lower our guard against the subversion of our government or our people. Neither our principles nor our country nor our freedom to determine our own future is for sale."

Neither then nor since have the Chinese made any serious mistakes in their dealings with the Tanzanians, although they soon demonstrated that they did not yet quite understand Nyerere. Shortly after Chou's visit to Dar es Salaam, Nyerere attended the Commonwealth Prime Ministers' Conference in London, the conference at which he dissociated Tanzania from the final communiqué on Vietnam and Rhodesia. At about the same time, President Ahmed Ben Bella, whom Nyerere respected immensely for his support of the liberation struggle against the white regimes in southern Africa, was overthrown in Algeria. The Chinese let it be known that they would recognize the new Algerian regime immediately in order to proceed as planned with the Afro-Asian summit conference in Algiers on June 29. Nyerere is said to have been appalled. "Can't they understand the meaning of friendship?" he asked. "Friendship cannot mean just because a friend is overthrown, you forget him. Now they want me to go to Algeria while Ben Bella is sitting in prison. That my friends can't understand this surprises me, and it surprises them that it surprises me."

He took the position that he wouldn't go to Algiers unless Ben Bella was released, or put on trial and the charges proved. Back in Dar es Salaam, Nyerere was dismayed when the Algerian ambassador, an ardent supporter of Ben Bella, returned from Algiers after the coup and, at the Dar es Salaam airport, denounced Ben Bella as a man who "played off one Algerian against another" to set himself up as dictator. "Everything is in good order and good hands," said the ambassador. Nyerere never received him at State House again.

KENNETH KAUNDA, the President of Zambia, had wanted a railroad north to the Tanganyikan coast long before his country became independent in 1964. Since Zambia had no access to the sea, its copper exports as well as its imports were shipped on rail lines that passed through Rhodesia and the Portuguese territories of Mozambique and Angola. After Rhodesia's unilateral declaration of independence in November 1965, the Zambians became determined to build the northern rail line; they felt, moreover, that if Britain and her allies were unwilling to bring the Rhodesian rebel regime to heel, they could at least build a railroad that would decrease Zambia's dependency on the white south.

As early as 1963, Kaunda had discussed the plan with Nyerere, who sympathized with Kaunda's predicament and, in addition, wanted the railroad as a means of developing southwestern Tanganyika. Kaunda solicited the support of several Western countries—Britain, the U.S., France, Japan, West Germany—without success, but in 1964 the Chinese told him they might be willing to help. The following year, after Chou's visit to Dar es Salaam, the Chinese sent a twelve-man team to make a preliminary survey of the Tanzanian portion of the route.

Western reluctance was based on the cost of the project, which was originally estimated at £60 million and

226

later increased to almost £150 million. The reluctance was fortified by a World Bank report which concluded that a railway was not feasible for the amount of traffic that would be involved, and instead recommended improvements to the highway between the Zambian Copperbelt and Dar es Salaam at a cost of only £11 million. At Kaunda's urging, the British and Canadians then sponsored another survey which, when finished in 1966, estimated the cost of the railway at £126 million, plus another £12 million for port improvements in Dar es Salaam. The Anglo-Canadian report offered the view that the railway could be operated profitably if Zambia committed all or most of its traffic to the route. But by the time the survey was completed, whatever slight Western interest that previously existed had vanished. The U.S. later agreed to rebuild the highway between Iringa and Tunduma, on the Zambian border, at a cost of about $30 million.

"I am determined that this railroad should be built," Nyerere said in July 1965, "and I am prepared to accept money from whomever offers it to see that it is built." Two months later he confirmed that the Chinese had made an offer to build the railroad: "At present we have only one definite offer, and that is from the Chinese." No other offers were ever received. The Tanzanians did not quarrel with the Western arguments that the eleven-hundred-mile rail line was too expensive, but they blamed the West for not placing a very high political priority on what was, after all, the most monumental development project that either the Zambians or the Tanzanians could conceive of. One day in late 1967 a Tanzanian cited to an American friend a London *Sunday Times* article which stated that the American involvement in Vietnam was costing the U.S. £23 million a

227

day. "Our railroad," he said, "could be built for what the Americans are spending in Vietnam *every four days*."

The final agreement was not signed until 1970, following a two-year survey by the Chinese. The accord calls for the Chinese to make a £168-million interest-free loan, which is repayable by Tanzania and Zambia equally in thirty years beginning in 1983. All local costs, including the wages of as many as thirteen thousand Chinese workers, are to be covered by the sale of Chinese goods on credit to state-owned trading corporations in Tanzania and Zambia. Both countries accepted the risk that they might be saddled with some expensive or inferior goods which they might not have bought otherwise.

Among all foreign aid projects completed in Africa, the Tanzam railway will rank just below the Soviet-built Aswan Dam in Egypt and Ghana's Volta River Dam, which was financed primarily by the World Bank, the U.S. and Britain. It will also be the largest foreign aid project ever undertaken anywhere by the Peking government.

Apart from the railroad, the list of other Chinese aid projects to Tanzania was already long. Since Tanganyikan independence, the Chinese had provided $60 million in loans and grants. For the mainland, they built the $7.5 million Friendship textile mill, as well as a farm implement factory, an experimental farm, and a radio transmitter. They also started a Chinese-Tanzanian shipping line with two ships. On Zanzibar they built a rice farm, a cotton farm, a shoe factory, a water-pumping station and a tractor-repair plant. Their influence has increased as that of East Germany has declined; the East Germans made a series of classic foreign aid blunders in Zanzibar, including the supplying of two fishing trawlers which were unsuitable for

228

East African waters because they weren't equipped with refrigeration.

In addition to the technical aid, the Chinese now provide perhaps two hundred instructors for the mainland army and for several of the guerrilla training camps in Tanzania, and about four hundred more for one of the two army battalions on Zanzibar. They have supplied several patrol boats for the Tanzanian marine police, and are currently building a small naval base near Dar es Salaam for which they have promised to provide another six boats.

There are rumors that the Chinese have also offered to build the Tanzanians an air base and to supply them with jet fighters. For five years, Canada played an important role in training Tanzania's army and air wing. When the agreement expired, at the end of 1969, the Tanzanians decided not to renew it. One factor in the decision was Canada's membership in NATO. It is doubtful that the Tanzanians really thought the Canadians would tell the Portuguese their military secrets, but they may have reasoned that in the event of a fight with the Portuguese, the position of the Canadians would be ambiguous, while that of the Chinese would not.

If Nyerere has any misgivings about the size of the growing Chinese presence in Tanzania, he doesn't admit it. "The West," he has said, "which doesn't want to build the railway, doesn't want the Chinese to build it either. So should we go without a railway?" But he added, "We are a stubborn people. The Chinese will learn that if they want to control us they will get into trouble."

EARLY IN 1966, at a time when Tanzania had lost most of the foreign aid it had been receiving from Britain, West

Germany and the U.S., Nyerere was asked if he felt his policies had cost his country any aid unnecessarily.

"The current criticism is that I have tended to be rather over-principled," he said, "and that this has cost us development funds. But this is easier to say than prove. Yes, we have lost some aid—the seven-and-a-half-million-pound loan from the British, for instance. The difficulty, you know, is that a loan is often tied to procurement, and then there is the problem of local costs to go with the loan. But with this loan, the British were paying the local costs, too. It was one of the best we ever received.

"Another example. One country most interested in helping us, because of its history, was [West] Germany. Then we clashed—over German interpretations of Tanzanian unity. I believe this was inevitable. I was not elected to sell the blessed country to the highest bidder.

"The real source of money in the world is the West. The West is wealthy, it has the experience. At one time I was very popular with the Western world, a model of reasonableness during that period. But what development did we get? There is very little philanthropy in the kind of aid required for nation-building. Yes, there is a little. Scandinavia, led by Sweden, is one example. They feel an obligation of wealthy countries, an obligation to assist in development. And Canada too, I think. In Scandinavia it's almost a national feeling. Of course it is present, in varying degrees, in all countries. But it does not dominate decision-making. In the United States, what dominates is: You have got to fight Communism! And particularly: A country must matter, politically, before you can give it aid."

Asked if he felt a country could attract more aid by being nonaligned than aligned to either East or West, he

230

replied, "No. This is not true. It has got to be strategic. For example, the United Arab Republic. India, the same. The problem in giving aid to India is not the millions of needy, but the millions of Chinese [with whom the Indians had fought a few years earlier]. The Indians, after receiving the check [from either the Soviet Union or the U.S.] could easily thank the Chinese!

"We are living in a most unfortunate world. The struggle for power is global. If we were in the Middle Ages, you could ask the Pope to divide it, not between Spain and Portugal but between the U.S. and Russia. But this is changing too; China is around, and she cannot be ignored.

"Africa is Europe's sphere of influence. It was long an appendage of Europe. As far as Africa—the Congo, for example—goes, the world thinks, 'Ah, Communists against the West!' With Ghana, it thinks, 'Chinese and Russians asked to leave!' But this is an over-simplification.

"If it hadn't been for the Cold War, I think the struggle would have been between Europe and the U.S. The struggle would have been America leading the fight for freedom, and Europe saying no, this we can't do. But the Cold War came along. And the U.S. became much more concerned about Russia than about freedom. So it became identified with Europe and with colonialism. And without a single inch of Africa of her own! We say to the U.S., 'You are a revolutionary power!' But no. The U.S. must listen to its allies, and its allies are in Europe. The U.S. still shapes her policies in regard to Africa *through London!* On Nigeria, on Ghana, certainly on East Africa, the U.S. will never listen to us. It will listen to London but not directly to us.

"Well, Europe still wants to keep us as its sphere; and

231

we want to be nobody's sphere. We are not fighting the U.S.; we want to establish a direct relationship. The assumption in the U.S. [in response to news of Tanzania] is: 'They want to be Chinese!' This shorthand is understood! Communists!" He threw up his hands in a gesture of frustration.

The discussion turned to Vietnam and, inevitably, to China and the U.S. "How much are African countries really concerned about Vietnam?" he said. "They are focused mainly on African problems. They are concerned with their own freedom. And what mars their relationship with any country is its attitude toward Africa. I can hardly imagine violent demonstrations over Vietnam in any African capital. Diplomatic talking, yes. Africans may say, 'We do not understand what you are doing.' The maximum you can expect is suspicion.

"I have never felt, myself, that I could play any particular role on Vietnam. There are two aspects to it—the idea part and the hard fact. The idea part is: Have the Americans the right to be there? The practical part is: But they *are* there. So the search for a realistic solution ought to ignore the idea part; it should just recognize the fact that they are there, and find a solution. This can only be done by the big powers. The power of small powers is moral. We can argue morality; we have no other choice.

"I've taken an extremely keen interest [in Vietnam], especially since I got into trouble in London." He was referring, with an ironic shiver, to Harold Wilson's success in isolating him on the question of a Commonwealth peace mission to Southeast Asia the previous year. "At the time I said I didn't understand Vietnam. I disagreed about sending the peace mission—it was wrong, it was a gimmick that wouldn't help much. But Vietnam is a problem of power, basically a problem of power. And in this, small nations suffer. Vietnam is just the line that has been chosen for the struggle. *It could have been Tanzania.*"

The U.S. role in Southeast Asia was based on a fallacy, Nyerere said, of using power to try to contain China. "I don't believe you can contain China. What is the meaning? But I understand power, and therefore I understand the U.S. as a power with global responsibilities and views; I understand that. But what I cannot understand is the policy—started long before Vietnam—based on the idea that one way of assuring world peace is to ostracize China. Use all power—military power, diplomatic power—to treat China as an international leper, make China the untouchable of the modern world! Be suspicious of countries that have dealings with China! This yellow disease! This I do not understand."

Recalling that a leading churchman had questioned his support of the Chinese, Nyerere said, "I was tempted to quote Abraham Lincoln—I believe it was Lincoln—who said, 'God must have loved the common people, otherwise he would not have created so many of them.'" Then, with great feeling: "But these people are our brothers, seven hundred million of them, and they have a right to a share in both the fellowship and also the goods of this planet. But the U.S. says, 'You must spit in the face of China! You must vote every time in the U.N. against China!' This is rubbish, absolute rubbish! As a moral issue I don't understand it. I don't understand those Asian and African countries that, year after year, vote against China—against seven hundred million people. I don't understand it. How do you work for peace that way? The U.S. has a Christian

233

ethic. It's bad enough when hate is preached in a Communist country; but when the song of hate is preached in a Christian country, hate hate hate seven hundred million people . . . !

"I think it's wrong. It's a pity I have to speak as a head of state. If I could speak as a newspaperman, I'd shout it from on top of Kilimanjaro: It's wrong!

"The Chinese [diplomats and technicians] here in Tanzania: their mere presence is a problem. In the beginning, when people asked me about the Chinese here, I would answer, 'They are not causing me trouble.' Now I am being asked, 'Why are they *not* causing trouble? Why are they so *tame* in Tanzania?' I even have a letter an American friend brought me, written to a newspaper, in answer to some bishops and archbishops who feel I'm too friendly to China. So I even have bishops and archbishops worrying about it. I assume the Holy Ghost is less concerned than the bishops, otherwise I'd be facing very serious consequences.

"The Americans are trying to adjust themselves to Russia, thanks to Kennedy. But they have failed to accept China, a proud people, a great people, with a history that goes back for centuries. They are very proud, they speak with one voice, they are no longer just a humiliated giant, they have a pride of achievement. If we are beginning to understand Russia, why not China?

"Kennedy—I have great respect for that man; he was a good man, a great man—one day he had to say to Russia, 'Get out of here,' and the whole world said, 'My God, nuclear war,' and Kennedy took the maximum risk and said, 'Get out of here.' Whatever we may say, it's just possible China is feeling the United States is too close to them—too strong to be so close.

234

"I don't see how the U.S. can in one voice argue the case of the reunification of Germany, and at the same time argue the rejection of China's case. I understand Germany; that's why we did not recognize East Germany. The Chinese themselves tell me it is not the same thing"—he laughed jubilantly—"but it *is* the same thing.

"That's my view on China. We must learn to coexist with China."

Nyerere had often objected to the tendency of the West, and particularly the U.S., to judge Africa in terms of the Cold War. Did he feel there was such a thing as an African Communist? "By definition there shouldn't be an *African* Communist, any more than an African Christian," he answered. "He would be a Communist, wherever you find him. I don't know, there might be such a thing. Intellectual Communists, perhaps, who have been to Europe and have become intellectually convinced Communists. There might be a sprinkling of these. Highly intelligent people, who find it extremely appealing—and are often disillusioned.

"They come back from Europe, and they are confronted with *Africa*. What is the application of Communism to Africa? How do you begin applying the textbook of Communism to Africa? And it is textbook Communism they have learned in London and Paris. But how do you go and preach it in Sukumaland? How? In a peasant country without feudalism, how do you do it? How do you begin?

"An African Communist has a real problem. He may study it in London, but when he comes back to Africa, he finds that it's a tool he cannot apply, and then he realizes that he must become a pragmatist. From a distance, Africa may look like a classical Communist situation. But, in reality, it's a Sukumaland situation."

235

A few years later, pondering the same subject, he wrote: "The Communist theoretical stages are primitive communalism, slavery, feudalism, capitalism and *then* socialism, which follows the destruction of capitalism. China did not quite follow this orthodox path. But even in China they had a highly developed feudalism and some capitalism to destroy. In Africa generally, we have to begin our socialism from tribal communalism and a colonial legacy which did not build much capitalism. Only South Africa has a substantial proletariat on which you could base the application of orthodox Marxism. In Africa generally, in order to apply Marxism we would have to adapt it to a rural economy which is more primitive than that which confronted either the Russian or the Chinese revolutionaries. A good African Communist would be forced to be a revisionist."

(13)

On the third day of January 1967, Nyerere set off on his longest upcountry tour since independence, a four-week journey that took him to eight of mainland Tanzania's seventeen regions and ended with a three-day meeting of the TANU National Executive Committee in Arusha. There he announced the completion of a document that was to be called the Arusha Declaration, the most important of the dozens of major speeches and policy papers he had prepared since independence.

Many of Nyerere's formal speeches are polished and translated, usually from English into Swahili, by his State House staff, which includes Joan Wicken, an English-woman who serves as a personal assistant, and Paul Sozigwa, his press secretary. The six-thousand-word Arusha Declaration was written in Nyerere's unmistakable style, blunt and vivid, and less formal than many of his prepared speeches. It started with an affirmation of the TANU creed of building a democratic socialist state, and outlined the party's policies of socialism and self-reliance. Emphasizing how difficult it was for the government to pay for development out of increased tax revenues, it said: "Knowing all the things which could be done with more milk does not alter the fact that the cow has no more milk." As for aid from overseas, said the Declaration, Tanzania simply could not count on it: "It is stupid to rely on money as the major

237

instrument of development when we know only too well that our country is poor. It is equally stupid, indeed it is even more stupid, for us to imagine that we shall rid ourselves of our poverty through foreign financial assistance rather than our own financial resources . . . Firstly, we shall not get the money. There is no country in the world which is prepared to give us gifts or loans, or establish industries, to the extent that we would be able to achieve all our development targets . . . And even if all the prosperous nations were willing to help the needy countries, the assistance would still not suffice. But in any case the prosperous nations have not accepted a responsibility to fight world poverty." Besides, it continued, "Independence means self-reliance. Independence cannot be real if a nation depends upon gifts and loans from another for its development. How can we depend upon foreign governments and companies for the major part of our development without giving to those governments and countries a great part of our freedom to act as we please? The truth is that we cannot." The only answer, it concluded, was slower growth through self-reliance, and an emphasis on the development of the peasant agricultural economy.

Tacked on to the Declaration as a sort of appendix was a new code of conduct for TANU and government leaders. Among other things, it specified that no leader could hold directorates or shares in any private company, receive two or more salaries, or own any houses that he rented to others.

On the Sunday following his return to Dar es Salaam, Nyerere spoke about the Declaration for two and a half hours to a crowd at the Arnautoglu playing fields. "The important thing," he said, "is that we should not adopt an attitude that nothing can be done until someone else agrees to

give us money. There are many things we can do by ourselves, and we must plan to do them." However, he added,
"it is not being self-reliant to refuse to carry out the directions of a foreign engineer or a foreign manager; it is just
being stupid."

The very next day, to the astonishment of his countrymen, Nyerere announced that the government was national-
izing all banks in Tanzania as the first step in implementing
the Arusha Declaration. He promised full compensation for
nationalized property, and emphasized that private accounts were not affected. "Fellow citizens," he said, "I myself have my money deposited in one of the nationalized
banks. My money is safe. What has been taken over is the
institution and not the customers' deposits." Several of his
Cabinet ministers hugged each other in joy at this triumph
over the imperialists, and soldiers shouted and waved banners in the February heat.

Within the next two or three days, the government announced plans to nationalize a number of insurance companies, import-export firms, mills and sisal estates, and to
purchase a majority interest in seven other firms that made
cement, cigarettes, shoes and beer. There were bitter proph-
ecies from London and Nairobi that the Tanzanian government would be unable to pay the price of the nationalized
properties and would have difficulty running them after the
takeover; both fears, as it turned out, were unfounded. The
value of the properties was first estimated at £100 million,
but appeared by late 1967 to be closer to £15 million or £20
million. The government promoted junior employees and
in a few cases imported specialists to run the companies
until Tanzanians could be trained. At the end of the first
year, Nyerere took the opportunity to praise Tanzania's

239

Indians, who had been exceedingly worried that year about their future in Tanzania and about the new restrictions in Britain's immigration laws. The Indians, said Nyerere, had enabled the nationalization of the banks to work. "These people deserve the gratitude of our country. Yet now"—he used his own Zanaki tribesmen as the butt of the joke, as he often does—"if a Zanaki goes to the bank to borrow money, and is refused a loan because he does not have any security, he comes running to me, saying that the Indians favor each other and that we should make Zanaki managers of the banks. *Wananchi* [countrymen], I beg you to beware of this kind of thinking."

The government later entered into agreements to participate in the ownership of the Italian-built Tiper oil refinery and the rest of the petroleum industry, and in early 1970 announced plans to take over the entire wholesaling system, which was controlled by Asians. The government also nationalized the Tanzania *Standard*, the country's only privately owned English-language daily newspaper. The British editors of the *Standard* had attempted to adopt a sympathetic editorial position in the years after independence; but the sale of the newspaper chain to which the *Standard* belonged to Lonrho, the British conglomerate that had extensive holdings in southern Africa, made the paper more suspect than ever in the Tanzanians' eyes. As an official government paper responsible directly to Nyerere, the *Standard* was supposed to adopt a semi-independent policy; in one of its first issues it published a report that led to the release of twenty-six foreigners who had been jailed without charge. At this stage of Tanzanian history, however, the level of tolerance of published dissent is fairly

240

low; this fact affected the *Standard*'s reporting long before the government took it over.

The Arusha Declaration was followed by two supplementary papers, "Education for Self-Reliance" and "Socialism and Rural Development." The first was a plan for redirecting the country's school system, placing a new emphasis on training the majority of students who will return to the land rather than go on to higher education. The second outlined a three-step process for establishing *ujamaa* cooperative villages. First, said the paper, a group of people should be persuaded to move their houses to a single village, preferably near a water hole, and plant their crops in the vicinity. They should then be persuaded to establish small communal plots, perhaps with ten family groups working together and sharing the proceeds at harvest time. Finally, if the second phase succeeded, the project should be turned into a community farm. The paper emphasized that the process was a gradual one and represented an ideal to be strived for. "We would not automatically become wealthy," it said, "although we could all become a little richer than we are now." A few cooperative farms had existed in Tanzania for a long time, such as the women's farm at Kazima that Nyerere had visited during his Tabora trip in 1966. By the end of 1970, there were said to be as many as one thousand villages throughout the country that were at least calling themselves *ujamaa* cooperatives.

The nationalization program was the only aspect of the Arusha Declaration that was discussed extensively by the press overseas. This was accompanied by a wave of renewed comment that Tanzania was going Communist, and Nyerere's joke that the TANU youth league members

241

were the "green guards" of Tanzania was taken as the latest bit of bizarre evidence that Nyerere, in his "Chinese pajama suit," had fallen under the Maoist shadow.

The most important part of the Declaration from the Tanzanian point of view, however, was the code of conduct it imposed on the political leadership. In June, Bibi Titi Mohamed resigned from the presidency of the national women's organization and from the TANU Central Committee. She was ill, she said, and planned to go "back to the kitchen"; but it was understood in Dar es Salaam that she had had to choose between her public career and her rental property and had, as one observer put it, "opted for capitalism." "Poor Mama Titi," said a Tanzanian woman, "she needs three houses to rest her back in."

Nyerere himself told the National Executive committee in March that he had complied with the new rules. He said his wife had formerly kept a poultry farm at Mji Mwema, near Dar es Salaam, and that she had given it to the Mji Mwema cooperative village. He had sold his old house in the Magomeni section of Dar es Salaam, he said, and was living at Msasani Bay in the new house that he had built with a bank loan. He said he had no other source of income except a small sum from royalties from the first published volume of his speeches and papers, *Freedom and Unity.*

The months following the issuance of the Declaration were a period of political tension, during which government leaders tried to decide how to comply with the code. When a friend asked Nyerere if there couldn't be a transition period, to soften the blow to the leaders affected, Nyerere snapped, "No! It would only give people time for loopholes. We must do it now." The leadership bill, as passed by

Parliament in October, called for Members to submit regular statements of their income and assets and those of their wives to the Speaker; the Speaker, in turn, was directed to submit his statement to the President. The bill gave leaders a year in which to "purify" themselves, and it allowed persons who inherited property three months in which to sell it or give it away, or resign. By mid-September, some thirty M.P.s had already surrendered their monthly parliamentary salaries of £53 6s. in order to retain their seats.

THE DECLARATION was widely interpreted as a product of Nyerere's frustration over the state of the country's development. He had spent a full month upcountry, it was said, visiting with peasants whose lives had barely changed since independence. He was conscious of a slight tendency toward corruption by the privileged—a very modest level of corruption compared to such countries as Nigeria and Ghana and even Kenya, where the greater wealth and higher state of development had caused more money to filter into the hands of leadership. But he was sickened by it, nonetheless, and believed it could destroy the meaning of African freedom.

Nyerere rejected the notion, however, that the Declaration was the direct result of such influences. "If you knew the whole truth," he said a few months later, "it would not be as exciting." In 1962, he noted, he had written a pamphlet on TANU in Swahili which contained many of the same points. "The most important element, the part dealing with self-reliance, is found in the 1962 paper. About development through the work of the people. It must be clear, it said, that the benefits go to the people themselves, and not to their leaders.

243

"Last December [1966], I had a draft of the pamphlet. We had already discontinued giving loans to civil servants to build houses to live in; it turned out that, in some cases, they were renting the houses. We said we were stopping this, and Rashid [Kawawa] said in Parliament that we were stopping it. Also with political people like regional and area commissioners."

He kept pondering over how best to present the problem to the National Executive committee, he said, until he realized: "We can't merely talk about houses, we must talk about leadership in relation to property. The responsibility of leadership in terms of property. The best way was to argue socialism, and to define socialism as a lack of exploitation, and then draw up a list of what this is. So it struck me: instead of a pamphlet I issue out of the blue, this should be the theme of the meeting, and this is how it came about. No"—he grinned—"it wasn't so much out of frustration as inspiration. It was a confirmation of what we ought to be doing. The Declaration says two things: that there is not enough aid for developing countries. But even if there were enough aid to handle all our development, it says no, that would be wrong."

Nyerere was asked if he were not actually making an attack on all the privileged groups in his society at once. "Yes," he said. "This is the intention. If we say we have to develop, it must be very clear to the people that the benefits are going to the people themselves. So you say fine, we'll tackle one group now and another later on. Or you could say, 'We'll just tackle the Indians. Just use the African to help fight the Indian, and the African will help because he can replace the Indian. Tackle your immigrants.' You

could do that. But we would just be postponing the problem. We had set a socialist goal for ourselves, and really we
had no choice. How could we allow exploitation by the indigenous few? So we took them all together—foreign inves-
tors, local capitalists, our own political leaders. In a sense,
we tackled the masses at the same time. We took on everybody.

"How do we engage the people in pursuing objectives
that are not understood? The definition of objectives had
to be total—and uncompromising. Once the decision was
taken that the banks should be in the hands of the government, it's worse for the economy of the country to delay.
Our speed will depend on the realities of the country. But
as a nation we ought to know what we are trying to do."

SUDDENLY—or so it seemed from reading *The Nationalist*
—everybody in Tanzania was caught up in a frenzy of
marching in support of the Arusha Declaration. "Tem-
pered and remolded by the flames of the Spirit of Arusha,"
began a *Nationalist* news story in early September, "nine
gallant youths from Singida have advanced their column on
the longest march of all—through eight regions—in support of the Arusha Declaration, the President and the
party. A long revolutionary column of one hundred and six
people, of all ages, is advancing south toward the capital
where the gallant marchers will make revolutionary con-
tacts with party leaders, and pledge their support for the
Arusha Declaration . . . The gallant marchers will present
Mwalimu with a total of three hundred and thirty shillings
being their contribution of aid for the bereaved parents of
the youth hero, the late Seti Benjamin." Seti Benjamin was

245

a twenty-year-old from Arusha who had collapsed and died at Moshi while marching to Dar es Salaam.

September 26: "A column of seventy-four gallant youths, of an average age between four and six years, has marched into Moshi town from the Kindergarten School at the Police Training School."

September 27: "The column of the gallant youth hero and martyr, Seti Benjamin Mpinga, is now heading south to the capital where they will pledge before *Mwalimu* their unswerving support for the Arusha Declaration."

October 9: "A group of sixteen TANU Youth League members marching thirty-five miles from Ngare Nanyuki to Arusha in support of the Arusha Declaration and the President's move to place under detention traitors of the nation, found themselves joined by a herd of elephants marching peacefully ahead of their column along the way . . . After leading the column for some time, the loyal Tanzanian elephants changed the route . . ."

Suddenly Julius Nyerere was marching too. His trip had started as an ordinary upcountry tour of Mara region, his home territory. In one village he warned townspeople against two dangers—domination of Tanzania by foreign powers, and excessive drinking of *pombe*, the local brew. Then, quite unexpectedly, he and his party walked twelve miles from Butiama, Nyerere's birthplace, to the village of Kiabakari, and the next day they walked twenty-two miles to Bunda. "President Nyerere moved the revolutionary Presidential column further deep into Mwanza region," *The Nationalist* reported a few days later, "covering a distance of fifteen miles from Chamgasa to Nyakaboja where the revolutionary marchers rested." At Nyakaboja,

246

it added, "the entire village was seething with revolutionary enthusiasm emitted by the Spirit of Arusha."

THE PRESIDENT'S PARTY was tired and hot by the time it reached Bunda on the second day. Everybody sat exhausted in the shade of the green-and-white house trailer that Nyerere was using. Somebody asked Bhoke Munanka how the march was going. "Terrible," he groaned. Nyerere, his feet covered with talcum powder, leaned his canvas chair against the trailer, resting. Ackland Mhina, his former secretary, who had recently been named commissioner of Mara region, complained that his legs were chafed. Mhina said he had just learned from Brigadier Sarakikya that a marcher was supposed to reverse his socks every ten miles. " 'You mean I must change my tires every ten miles?' I asked him, and he said yes. I must tell my son. He is leaving on a march of his own in two days' time." The most accomplished marcher in Nyerere's party turned out to be Hashim Mbita, the President's former press secretary, who had been transferred to TANU headquarters and was later to become the party's executive secretary. Mbita had flown from Dar es Salaam to Mwanza the day before, and then took the long bus ride from Mwanza to Butiama. Learning the party had already left, Hashim ran twelve miles to catch up with it.

Late in the afternoon when the sun had faded, Nyerere addressed a rally at Bunda. He had changed from his khaki pants and shirt and cap into a Tanzanian suit. He spoke about the need to use cattle for working the land instead of keeping them as a mere symbol of wealth. "We are sleeping while the Americans are going to the moon!" And he spoke of Africa's shame that it could not control its own affairs.

247

His eyes bulged; he was animated, as usual, and the crowd laughed with him as his voice turned into a staccato mimic. He hadn't wanted to give a speech that day, presumably preferring that the march be allowed to speak for itself. The next day, when the regional commissioner asked him to speak at another stop, he refused. He seemed determined to avoid routine political gestures. Many villagers, consequently, seemed quite bewildered as he passed. In the group of marchers, his head down and covered with a floppy canvas hat, he was unrecognizable.

The country was magnificent, the rim of Lake Victoria gleaming on the horizon. Beside the road were rock outcroppings and anthills as tall as a man. The earth was dry and dusty because the rains were late. "If you want my legs," complained Joseph Namata to nobody in particular, "you can have them." Like Ackland Mhina, Namata was a former member of Nyerere's staff who had recently become a regional commissioner.

That night at Bunda the three beer shops and the teahouse were filled with people, the most exciting occasion since independence. The walls of the Heshima bar had four pictures of Mao Tse-tung on the wall, and one of Nyerere. Had the Chinese ambassador passed through town and given a hundred pounds for a new community center? Had the bar owner received the pictures in the mail and put them on the wall because he had nothing else?

The party was awakened at two and soon was on the road again, everyone groggy, flashlights pointing the way. Nyerere walked on the left, behind Brigadier Sarakikya, who was still as lithe as a runner; at Nyerere's side were two security men. Everyone tried to walk in the tire tracks to avoid the loose gravel. Suddenly two men jumped aside to avoid a snake coiled in the roadway; a soldier kicked it to death expertly.

At last the President called a halt. "Well, fellows, we've done two and a half hours." Hashim Mbita emptied the sand from his shoes. Nyerere noticed Joseph Namata's shoes—brown suede with pointed toes. "Ah, Manhattan," Nyerere said, feigning scorn. "Not so good." Nyerere had been appealing to Tanzanian women that year to discard "illusions of glamor" and the "Manhattan way of life." After crossing a bridge, the group stopped again for tea and bread, and later, hard-boiled eggs. "We should start again now, before our muscles grow stiff," said one of the soldiers, but instead the party tarried for eight hours until the heat was past. The President retired into his trailer; Munanka and Namata drove away, probably to the mission on the road ahead, to get some rest. The others lay on the hoods of Land-Rovers or threw their bedrolls on the concrete floor of the police station house. When a curry lunch was served, Mbita looked for a spoon for a Western visitor; the others, in the tribal African manner, used their fingers. "Take a banana," Hashim said, a gruff good host. "Now! Take more!"

Two of the security men, leaning against a Land-Rover, spoke of a visit to New York. "Do you suppose we'll ever be like that?" one asked. At the remark that Tanzania had changed a great deal in the last five years, they agreed, yes, a bit skeptically; it was changing, yes, but very slowly. Sarakikya spoke of his mountain climbing. He had climbed Kilimanjaro eight times, he said. He had made a vow to climb it every January. But he couldn't get away in 1964 and 1965, he said, when he was very busy.

At five-thirty in the afternoon, Munanka, Namata and

249

the others returned. "The *Wabenzi!*" somebody gibed, using Africa's derisive term for the new "tribe" of affluent politicians who drive Mercedes Benzes. Then the President emerged from his trailer, and the march resumed. This time the villagers had been forewarned; drummers and flag carriers and dozens of kids joined the march. The kids kept crowding in front of the party, and some of the marchers kept pushing them out of the way. It was after dark by the time the party reached the police camp an hour or so ahead of schedule. Then, in the warm evening, everyone sat around in front of the trailer and drank beer and orange Fanta. The President was jovial. He pointed to an older man, barefoot, who had just joined the party, an uneducated man clearly. "This is the fellow," Nyerere said slyly, "who made history by defeating my Minister of Finance." Hashim Mbita, reading a copy of the *Standard* that had just arrived from Dar es Salaam, announced excitedly that Chief Lugusha had been elected TANU chairman for the Tabora Rural district, defeating seven contestants. "Chief Lugusha?" cried Nyerere in incredulous glee. It occurred to an American visitor present that Nyerere must be a fatalist, surely; why else would he take such delight in the bizarre news that the man who had been placed in preventive detention for nine hundred and five days following the 1964 army mutiny had been elected, as if nothing had happened, to a minor party post?

The food was late. "We must eat," said Namata. "We should all be in bed by now," said Sarakikya. Finally, at nine-thirty, a dozen members of the party drove to the comfortable house of two American Maryknoll fathers. The priests greeted the group with elaborate hospitality, painstakingly filling orders for drinks, but the marchers were almost paralyzed with fatigue. Someone complained about how hard it had been to sleep at Bunda the night before with the music playing. "You just make up your mind to sleep," Hashim said, "and you sleep."

They awoke at three, an hour late already. What had happened to the driver? Later, as they marched past the mission at four-thirty, one of the priests was standing waiting, and joined in the march. "Which one is the President?" he asked. They marched for three hours and a half, with no breaks at all, and by the time they finally stopped they had gone fifteen miles. Then they sat down around the trailer, the President's informal court assembled, everyone listening and contributing an occasional quip to the conversation. The young priest lingered in the background until Munanka said, "Ah, here is the poor fellow whom we moved in on last night. Where did you sleep finally?" "In the car," said the priest happily. "Ah," said Nyerere, allowing the invisible barrier to be broken, "so you have been marching too? Ah, good. Good." Then the police served tea with milk and sugar, and hard-boiled eggs.

The marchers continued for eight days, covering one hundred and thirty-eight miles in all, until they reached Mwanza to attend the TANU National Conference. Three miles out of Mwanza, they were met by half the population of the town. As *The Nationalist* described it: "Heralded by peasants' war cries, strains of brass-band tunes, and a din of women's ululation, the President, beaming with revolutionary confidence, steered the Presidential column into the streets of the summit town hedged with crowds of cheering masses . . . *Mwalimu*'s brisk march into the town stunned the masses who on seeing him in sound health were driven wild with admiration and excitement to borders of near

251

frenzy. The entire town was gripped with the revolutionary fervor of the Spirit of Arusha." And so it was. Nyerere's driver, Christopher Kabaka, explaining that he had been ashamed to watch the President walk one hundred and thirty-eight miles in front of him, while he himself was forced to drive his car, gave up his fourteen-day leave in support of the Arusha Declaration. The members of Seti Benjamin's group, having walked four hundred and fifty miles to Dar es Salaam, then traveled on to Mwanza by train, their odyssey at an end.

"I HAD BEEN THINKING of it for several weeks," Nyerere said later, in explaining why he had decided to make the march. "I kept saying to the boys [who marched to Dar es Salaam], 'Don't listen to those people.' " The *Standard* had published an editorial questioning the usefulness of the marching and suggesting that the energy could be better spent by working in the fields. The *Standard* thus became the foil that the TANU sponsors of the marching had been looking for. "After all," Nyerere continued, with a grin, "it's not as if these boys had been building bridges! The marching is a symbol of the acceptance of the challenges ahead of them.

"I thought the only way I could encourage them was to join the youth movement. Also, I felt the time would come when we would have to say, 'Now stop.' But how would you say 'Now stop'? And who would say 'Now stop'? So, after this march, I could say, 'Now stop.' But after the third day of the march, I thought, 'This is very good. Why say stop? If it's good for me, it's good for them.' So they're still marching.

"And also," he said, with a wave to his new press secretary, Paul Sozigwa, "my fellows; I knew them better than I had ever known them before."

But finally, when eight youths from St. Andrews' College reached Arusha, after walking four hundred and thirteen miles from Dar es Salaam, Nyerere told them, "The rains are pouring. Therefore the marches should be abandoned, and instead the people should start their farm work."

(14)

In late 1966, Julius Nyerere was asked how it had happened that there had been no angry fights or schisms within his government during the first five years of independence, no ministers who had fled into exile or been placed behind bars. "It is true," he said. "We have not had violent dismissals or violent resignations. There is an objective reason for this: I've been lucky. I've been one of the luckiest Presidents in Africa. My colleagues are very loyal to me. It is true that people try to imagine cliques working against me; but this is not true.

"You shift responsibilities, of course; I often do that. There are only one or two men who have held the same positions for a long time; there's [Solomon] Eliufoo [the Minister of Education, who later resigned because of illness], who holds his like a sultan. I have dropped a few ministers by giving them other jobs. I appointed two as ambassadors. But why should I shake the damned system? It suits a young country very well.

"It is also true, I think, that it is in my character. Partly, at least. This has weaknesses; you can maintain too many incompetents because you don't want to shake them up. If someone else had been President, I don't know, he might have shaken it up, for the sake of competence. It's possible.

"My colleagues know they are my colleagues. Many are from the party, such as Rashidi, Oscar, Bhoke. These

255

are the political group, the party veterans. Jamal, too, although he didn't actually join the party at the beginning, because of the rules; but he is a virtual founder. Derek Bryceson, somewhat later. So this political group, in a sense, has *been* the party. It has given character to the country. I would need the strongest reason for destroying this unity. And even when it is necessary to remove someone, you do not humiliate him, you give him a job he can do better. In any case, we are building institutions, and habits of government."

Why was it that Oscar Kambona was disliked or distrusted by so many foreigners?

"Oscar is a shy man," Nyerere answered. "In the West you speak of open societies and closed societies. When you have a closed individual, people don't know him too well. When they have gotten to know him, they say, 'Ah, I see; the image is quite wrong.' But it creates a mystery. Secondly, he is not particularly articulate. So, even if you have an opportunity to talk with him, he does not express himself well—maybe even in term of slogans. So outsiders build up a mystery.

"It is never fair, but it is true that my character gives an impression of openness. Well, you can't change this. But it is never fair. Oscar is a man of the people. So is Rashidi, but Rashidi is not a mystery. Rashidi has a detachment; he is not a *personal* sort of person. Oscar feels very strongly. Like all people of feeling, he creates strong attachments. He is a barometer of feeling. Rashidi is an administrator, a doer; he is unemotional. Oscar *feels* for people. When outsiders misjudge Oscar, they are very wrong. They do a disloyalty to Oscar. He is extremely loyal —to the party, to me, to the people. With the others, it is 'the correct thing to do.' With Oscar, it's strong feeling.

"He is very human, very kind. Let me put it this way." A broad grin. "He has some of the faults and qualities of the United States of America. Your country has been accused of having this as one of its faults—I myself have accused it of this. It's a very human fault, but a fault nonetheless. Because you love strongly, you want to be loved strongly. You want to be loved by all! You feel strongly. And when you are accused of something, or misunderstood, you say, '*Me*? Why? We do this and this and this—and we get misunderstood!' A very human thing. And there are others, like Rashidi, who are very British. If you love them, fine. But if not, it won't stop them from doing their work. And they'll certainly shed no tears. No!"

MANY OF OSCAR KAMBONA'S FRIENDS in Dar es Salaam would agree with Nyerere's description. Kambona is a sentimentalist, a man who remembers his old friends and sometimes gets into trouble because of it, a man who was always surrounded by a swarm of hangers-on, job seekers, relatives, cronies; a man who spent a good deal of money, at least by Tanzanian standards, on his friends and extended family.

Almost anyone who talked with Kambona at length during those years would have recognized him as a flawed man, easily wounded, who seemed to have believed from childhood that powerful people whose affection he sought —notably white schoolmasters and later all sorts of foreigners—misunderstood him and disliked him. He once said with self-deprecating humor that he was off to London to let the Commonwealth Office "have a look at this dreadful fellow." The inevitable consequence was that most influential Europeans in Tanganyika in the years before independence did in fact misunderstand and dislike him. He seemed to have an absolute gift for annoying governors by arriving an hour late for dinner parties, and offending sympathetic whites at the beginning of the TANU period by insisting that they must leave party meetings. After independence he was blamed by Europeans for having a hand in almost every act that frightened or angered them or seemed to have racist connotations. Sometimes the blame was ascribed to deviousness, other times to inefficiency, for he was, by all accounts, one of the government's worst administrators. He was blamed for the Preventive Detention Act, and for the early rash of deportations of Europeans. He was accused of Africanizing the police too quickly. He was held partly responsible for the 1964 army mutiny; at the very least he was said to have contributed to a breakdown in army discipline by talking with the enlisted men directly and inviting them to voice their grievances; at the worst he was whispered to have played a mysterious role in the mutiny itself—a rumor for which there is no evidence whatever.

He was blamed for several of the anti-American incidents, notably the 1965 case of the "documents" that alleged a Western conspiracy against his country. Europeans in East Africa tended to like Nyerere and to exonerate him from responsibility for governmental actions they didn't approve of. Even today, many British residents of Kenya who disapprove of Tanzania's socialist policies speak of "Julius" with a grudging affection and a respect for his integrity and some of his actions—his fight against corruption, for example. Kambona always deflected the criticism from Nyerere. As a British journalist once observed, "Nyerere always comes out of it pure; nobody ever blames him. Isn't this the essence of a good politician? You let others do the hatchet work."

There is no proof that Kambona was ever disloyal to Nyerere in the years before 1967, but there is ample reason to believe he was increasingly dissatisfied. Until January 1962, Nyerere had no clearly designated deputy or heir apparent; when he resigned as prime minister, he could have chosen any of at least four of his colleagues—Kambona, Kawawa, Paul Bomani, and perhaps George Kahama, his Home Affairs Minister at the time—to succeed him; he chose Kawawa. Kambona's influence probably reached its peak just before the 1964 mutiny, when he served as minister for both external affairs and defense. In the Cabinet reshuffle that followed, Nyerere gave the defense portfolio to Kawawa, took external affairs himself, and assigned Kambona to regional administration. This, it was said, was a more logical extension of Kambona's duties as secretary-general of TANU, a post that he continued to hold until 1967. Kambona seemed unwilling to accept the fact that, since 1962, Kawawa had been Nyerere's probable successor. At one point in 1964, when Nyerere's colleagues advised him against making a trip that was deemed risky, Kambona spoke with genuine concern about Nyerere's safety, and added, "What would we do without him? Who would take over?" The remark seemed curious, since everyone else assumed Kawawa would take over. (Since the union with Zanzibar, however, the constitution has specified that, in the event of the President's death in office, he would be succeeded by the First Vice-President, Abeid Karume, until a special election can be held.) Another time, when Kambona apparently felt or at least wondered if he were not

259

being shunted aside, he remarked ruefully to a friend that Nyerere "gives you a lot of rope." Occasionally he seemed to betray a jealousy of other people's relationships with the President; after Nyerere's disappearance in the 1964 mutiny, Kambona said to State House aides who had stayed behind, "But you must know where he is. You can get one of his European friends to put him on a boat . . ." Nonetheless, Kambona's colleagues never questioned the fact that he cared passionately about the problems of Africa; he could speak with great feeling about the plight of bright youngsters who would never have the chance to fulfill themselves, and about the freedom struggles in the south.

In 1966 Kambona spent several months in the Netherlands resting and recuperating from what was said to be high blood pressure. By the time he came home to Dar es Salaam, he had lost at least thirty pounds and seemed more relaxed than he had been for years. The following May, Kambona flew to East Germany for a few days; he needed a routine medical checkup, he said. Then, on June 10, he resigned quite suddenly from both his government and party posts because of "circulation troubles." The resignation occurred during a Cabinet reshuffle in which Kambona was being transferred from regional administration to local government and rural development. Tanzanians were particularly surprised that he was leaving not only his new Cabinet post but the secretary-generalship of TANU, which he had held for thirteen years.

In mid-July, the government arrested Eli Anangisye, a former leader of the TANU youth league, who had lost his position in March after leading a youth league attack on the Netherlands Bank in Dar es Salaam following the bank nationalization. As an M.P., he had criticized Tan-

260

zania's acceptance of military assistance from Canada because of Canada's NATO ties with Portugal. A few days after that, the government announced that it had foiled a plot to subvert the government through the armed forces. Two men were detained: Anangisye and Hamisi Salumu, a onetime bodyguard of Kassim Hanga, the Zanzibari—an old friend of Oscar Kambona's—whom Nyerere had dropped the previous month as his Minister of State for Union Affairs.

On the same day, July 22, the Tanzanian Parliament passed a private motion asking Oscar Kambona to state the true reasons for his resignation. Two days later a group of youths marched in protest, asking Nyerere to behead publicly such "traitors" as Anangisye and Salumu. Nyerere charged in a speech that Tanzania had a few "madmen" and a few politicians who were "prostitutes" who valued money more than their personal dignity. The government knew who the "mercenary" politicians were, he said, and would pick them up one by one. After that, three intermediate-level civil servants were placed in detention, and were held until February 1968.

Kambona never appeared in Parliament to clear up the rumors about his resignation. On July 31, it was learned in Dar es Salaam that Kambona and his family had slipped away to Europe; after canceling a reservation to fly to Nairobi by private plane, Kambona had driven from Dar es Salaam to Nairobi, and flown from there to London. Even after the news of Kambona's sudden departure had spread through the capital, someone was still answering the phone at his new Msasani Bay home by saying that Mr. Kambona had merely gone to town.

On August 2, a government communiqué confirmed

that Kambona had left Tanzania secretly without first paying his income tax, and added : "It is known that in Nairobi, Mr. Kambona was seen with a lot of money." It also mentioned a rumor that Kambona had been offered a post by the World Council of Churches. Immediately thereafter, Vice-President Kawawa told a group of National Servicemen that Kambona was observed in Nairobi with "bags full of money," and *The Nationalist*, Kambona's old ally, published an editorial entitled "Secret Exit" : "How does a leader in Tanzania come to have such a lot of money?"

The Tanzanian police might well have arrested Kambona if he had flown to Nairobi by private plane as planned ; whether he took them by surprise when he left by car, or whether he was actually allowed to escape, is still unclear. The government is said to have been split over how to proceed against him ; some members felt he should be arrested for corruption, while others believed he should not be turned into a martyr but should be permitted to get away.

The defection of Kambona, who had long been one of the three or four best-known politicians in the country, produced an atmosphere of stress. It came during the period, moreover, when the leadership was trying to adjust to the rigid requirements of the Arusha Declaration. Several diplomatic observers in Dar es Salaam believed that, to some extent, the feverish wave of marching in support of the Declaration was sponsored by the TANU organization in order to demonstrate to the full leadership that the people were behind the President.

More than a week after his arrival in London, Kambona declared that he was the victim of a plot to overthrow the President. In a jumble of charges of plots and mischief-making he claimed that there was "no friction at all between the President and myself. The President's enemies know full well that to get rid of him they must first get rid of me." An undercover power struggle had broken out in Tanzania, he charged, led by a small but influential group that opposed the Arusha Declaration and had found loopholes in the law by which to transfer their property to their children and families. This group, said Kambona, controlled "the intelligence service, the police, army and other key positions," and had been trying to frame him and assassinate him. As for the peculiar way in which he had left East Africa, Kambona explained that he had wanted to drive through Moshi enroute to Nairobi so that he could say goodbye to his wife's family. "As soon as my health is restored," he said, "I shall go home. I have no intention of deserting my constituents."

Some of Kambona's friends thought that, by his curious statement, he was hoping Nyerere would invite him to return. Instead Nyerere, very angry, told a group of visitors from Morogoro, Kambona's constituency, that Kambona should be stripped of his seat in Parliament. Nyerere called on Kambona to come home, resign his seat and seek re-election, and promised that he would be renominated by the National Executive. "He deceived Tanzania and Africa as a whole," Nyerere said. "I trusted him and all of you trusted him too. When he came to me to say that he wanted to resign because of failing health, I trusted him, because it is true that his health is not good." Now Kambona was saying in London, said Nyerere, that "he and Kassim Hanga were the founders of the Union. He said in London that there will be a revolution in Tanzania within three months." Apparently, said Nyerere, Kambona hated Rashidi Kawawa because "in 1962 I made Mr. Kawawa prime minister instead of him."

263

The argument continued for several months; in a sense, in fact, it has never ended. Kambona offered to come home and resign if Nyerere would resign; then he threatened to hold a press conference at which he would "lift the lid off politics in Tanzania." *The Nationalist* answered him: "Say what you have to say, or be branded a coward and a traitor to Tanzania and to Africa." The TANU youth league called for his expulsion from the party for "traitorous" activity, charging that he was being used by "capitalists and colonialists both in and outside the country."

In September, both Kassim Hanga and Denis Phombeah, another friend of Kambona's, left Tanzania for London. Hanga had recently been dropped as Vice-President of Zanzibar as well as minister for Union affairs in Nyerere's Cabinet; Phombeah had been removed as commissioner of commerce and marketing and subsequently from a post in the foreign ministry. Three months later, Hanga returned to Dar es Salaam and almost immediately was placed in preventive detention, as were two of Oscar Kambona's brothers, Otini and Mattiya. *Ulimwengu*, a Swahili paper that Otini Kambona edited, was closed down.

In January 1968, making his full-scale attack at last, Kambona declared that Nyerere was "making himself a dictator," and condemned the recent arrest of Hanga as "a bleak chapter for Tanzania." Kambona claimed that the Tanzanians had given assurances to Sékou Touré, the President of Guinea, that Hanga would not be arrested. So how, asked Kambona, could he himself go home?

On January 12 in Dar es Salaam, Rashidi Kawawa disclosed to the National Assembly that Kambona had deposited a total of £44,340 in cash in his local bank account between June 1965 and December 1966, including a telegraph remittance for £29,050 that he had received from London on December 6, 1966. In addition, said Kawawa, Kambona owned five houses—three in Dar es Salaam, one in Songea and one in Morogoro—whose total value was estimated at £24,280. In Kambona's behalf, Kawawa noted that, in addition to a government salary, Kambona had been awarded £2,500 in 1964 following a successful libel action against a London newspaper.

A day or two later a very tense scene took place before twenty thousand people at a Zanzibar Day rally in Dar es Salaam. Nyerere denounced Kambona as "a thief and a prostitute": "He stole from Africa to build himself and his brothers houses and attempted to buy the people as well, whom he mistook to be fellow prostitutes." Then, said Nyerere, Kambona had called him a dictator because "we put in detention his fellow liar, whom I have brought here today for a purpose." Ordering that Kassim Hanga be brought before the crowd, Nyerere said to him, "I don't know what you told Sékou Touré." To the crowd he said, "After his return, I did not intend to detain him. But he started saying he had been called back by the army in Zanzibar, which was a lie." To Hanga: "That's why I detained you."

After his return from London, Hanga had told a Zanzibari friend in Dar es Salaam that the Zanzibar authorities were locking up his friends and relatives on the island. Even more imprudently, he had implied to someone else, who was in fact a police agent, that he was waiting in Dar es Salaam for a move by the military authorities on Zanzibar against Abeid Karume. In December 1968 Hanga was released from detention on Nyerere's order.

Two months earlier, Kambona and eight others had been expelled from TANU by the party's National Executive committee. A few days later, Kambona was fined £25 in London for illegal possession of a firearm.

IN NOVEMBER 1967, more than three months after Kambona had fled to London, Nyerere was reminded of how he had described Kambona in conversation a year earlier. "Yes, I remember," he said. "And did I tell you what a professor of mine once said? 'A dictator is like all of us. A person with a strong desire to be loved. And where he goes wrong is, he says, "I love being loved, so love me—or else!" '

"Well, I can tell you what I understand about my friend. Last year Oscar had very bad health. That's absolutely genuine. His heart was bad. He had gone to Addis Ababa, and they had a silly row over whether to accept the Ghana delegation [to an OAU conference]. And afterward he came to me and said, 'My doctor says I should go for treatment.' I said, 'Of course, go. Go to Holland immediately.' I gave him a letter to Prince Bernhard's doctor, who had treated two of my colleagues.

"Well, he was away quite a few months. When he came back, he was much better. He had lost a lot of weight. This year—in April, I think—he said his doctor had said he should get a medical checkup. I said, 'Yes, please go.' So he went—this time to East Germany, for a 'second opinion.' In a few weeks he wrote and said, 'I'm worried, I think I may have to resign.' Sometime after this, a Dutch friend of mine said, 'I think Oscar will resign, and he has asked me to inquire about a job with the World Council of Churches.' He said, 'I think you will find him a very changed man.' "

Kambona returned in time for the meeting of the National Executive committee in Iringa, Nyerere continued, where Kambona spoke frankly of his ill health and confided,

"One day I may ask you to let me go." "So," noted Nyerere, "this was the third reference to his health." In early June, Nyerere announced a Cabinet reshuffle. "And on the eighth, twenty minutes before the ministers were due to take the oath, he came to me and said, 'Look, *Mwalimu*, if you had told me about this, I would have said I should resign.' I argued with him upstairs; I said, 'Let's reach no conclusion. You come in the evening and we will discuss it.' We came down together. He said, 'I must go this time.' He gets these feelings of despondency. I told him, 'I can't stop you, but have you considered the timing?' "—the fact that the resignation would coincide with the Cabinet reshuffle. "He said, 'Look, *Mwalimu*, I'm always misunderstood. If I resign now, I'll be misunderstood. If I wait, I'll be misunderstood.' Well, this sounded quite all right to me. But he said he would wait before resigning the secretary-generalship.

"And," Nyerere continued, "trouble began almost immediately. Hashim [Mbita] told me, 'But he has also resigned as secretary-general!' I thought, 'Well, he will explain later.' Then Ben Mkapa, of *The Nationalist*, said, 'But what is the real story?' I said, 'He resigned for his health, as he said.' 'But,' Mkapa said, 'he *came* [to the press conference] *with Hanga!*' " Nyerere threw up his hands in confusion.

"The following Saturday—we hold a Central Committee meeting every Saturday—I had expected him to come and explain. I told them the real reason was his health, but many didn't accept this. That evening, an elder of TANU came to see me. I said, 'He resigned because of his health. If you don't believe me, go and ask him.' The elder said, 'I've just come from his house. He says he resigned because of Hanga.' I said, 'Good heavens!' I said, 'But this is rubbish! An intelligent person doesn't resign because of another person, he resigns on principle!' "

During the negotiations that followed, Nyerere told intermediaries, "I'm not taking back Hanga. *I* form this government." Finally Kambona appeared before the Central Committee. "He said some things that shocked me a little bit," Nyerere said. "I felt he was mentally tired. He said, 'I'm frightened, I have my brother staying with me to protect me.' I told him, 'Rest, take leave.' He came to my house. He said yes, he would go to Morogoro. Well! That's not my idea of a rest—Morogoro was his constituency!

"In the meantime," continued Nyerere, referring to the five men who were put in preventive detention, "we rounded up these clots, really they were clots. And he panicked and left the country. We had asked for his diplomatic passport. Hanga had submitted his. I think this may be the thing that did it; I think he thought we would stop him from leaving the country."

He spoke again of Oscar in an earlier time. "His sense of insecurity was always sufficient to me to explain his every foible. I could explain everything because of this.

"He loves the myths. We took Oscar on in early 1955, and he left for London in 1956." Why? "As a result of insecurity—because he was not loved by every member of the Central Committee. And he stayed in London until 1959. Finally Oscar told me, 'All right, I'll come back. But what about those fellows in the Central Committee who never write to me?' I said, 'Look, Oscar, I can't promise that every member of the Central Committee is going to love you.' And he returned to find that the party had been built by others—and by confident people. We did all sorts of things to rehabilitate him."

Reflecting on the number of important events in which Kambona had played an ambiguous role, Nyerere insisted that he himself, and not Kambona, was responsible for the American "documents" case of 1965. And yet, said Nyerere, yes, it was true that he was looking back on earlier events in the light of what he had learned in recent months. "If there is something I don't understand," he said, "I begin to read history backwards." And had he reconsidered the events of the 1964 army mutiny? "No, I haven't read it back that far. Maybe someday, but not yet."

THE CONSPIRACIES AND CHARGES of conspiracy continued. In August 1969, Kassim Hanga was arrested once more, along with Othman Shariff, who had remained as regional veterinary officer in Mbeya since 1965. The Zanzibaris accused fourteen men of plotting to overthrow the Karume government; among these fourteen were Hanga, Shariff, and two others who were arrested on the mainland and turned over to the Zanzibar government by Tanzanian authorities. Weeks passed. In November, Karume announced that, following a secret trial, four of the alleged plotters had been executed, nine remained in prison and one had been acquitted. In a gesture that was both slovenly and cruel, he failed to specify which four had been executed. As of early 1971, the deaths of Hanga and Shariff had not yet been confirmed.

Karume's announcement meant that Nyerere had unwittingly condemned as many as four men to death without a proper trial by surrendering them to the Zanzibar authorities. When asked why he had agreed to let them go, he said later, "For cross-examination. I wanted to be satisfied that there was a case. How could I say to Karume,

'Since you think you have a case, you come to the mainland to talk to them'?" Nyerere's decision, moreover, was made at a time when petty plotting was harassing the government in Dar es Salaam as well as Zanzibar; it was a serious mistake nonetheless.

In October 1969, Bibi Titi Mohamed, the former head of the national women's organization, and Michael Kamaliza, the former Labor Minister and former Secretary-General of the National Union of Tanganyika Workers, were placed in preventive detention, along with four army officers, for activities "not conducive to good law and order." A day later, a former news editor of *The Nationalist*, Gray Mattaka, was arrested at the Nairobi airport and turned over to Tanzanian authorities; he was said to have been acting as an emissary for Oscar Kambona. In the ensuing treason trial, Mrs. Mohamed, Mattaka and two other defendants were convicted of plotting to overthrow the government and assassinate the President, and were sentenced to life imprisonment. Kamaliza and an army officer received ten-year terms.

The existence of a wider conspiracy was never proved, but the government believed Oscar Kambona had played a part in both the Bibi Titi–Kamaliza case on the mainland and the Hanga-Shariff affair on the island. Kambona himself remained in London, his current sources of income unknown. A witness in the mainland trial testified that Kambona had shown him a cache of $500,000 in London and had said he could "get more where that came from" by communicating with a friend in the United States Information Service in London. However bizarre and convoluted African politics may become when tinted with international intrigue, many Tanzanians were skeptical—far more skeptical than they would have been in 1965. Some reasoned that the Americans, like the British, had had ample opportunity to assess Kambona's character and job prospects and would be unlikely to subsidize him, even if they were working actively against Nyerere. Could Kambona, on the other hand, be receiving support from other foreign sources, perhaps in the Eastern bloc? Or had he merely been uncharacteristically thrifty while serving in the Tanzanian government and on the OAU Liberation Committee? The problem in this, as in so many other matters, is that Nyerere can never be quite sure whom he can trust.

271

(15)

MAN-EATER AT SINGIDA IS GENUINE LION. A police spokesman at Singida yesterday denied reports that the famed killer lionmen were operating again following the deaths of six children in the Mtipa division this year. 'It is not the lionmen, but a man-eater that has killed the children. A game scout, assisted by villagers, is hunting it.'

The lionmen of Singida terrorized the region some years ago. Witchdoctors enslaved people who, dressed in lion skins, killed a number of people in the area. —The Standard, *March 1966*

An M.P. asked in the National Assembly yesterday if there was a fish which had the form of a woman.

The Minister for Lands, Settlement and Water Development, Mr. Maswanya, told the member, Mr. Saileni (Kilosa West) that mermaids do not exist.

Replying on behalf of the Minister for Agriculture, Forests and Wild Life, Mr. Maswanya added that sea cows, mostly seen around Mafia and Kilwa, were most probably mistaken for mermaids. Sea cows preferred to live near river mouths and fed on sea weed, and were hunted for their meat and fat. In Tanzania they were preserved by law.

Stories of mermaids were heard as far back as the

273

ancient times, and they were probably spread by sailors who wanted to impress others.
—The Standard, *October 1966*

THE CONTRAST between the primitive and the modern is something that the visitor to Tanzania never quite comes to terms with. On the one hand, for at least fifteen years Tanzania has had the best organized political party in eastern Africa; yet many Tanzanians still feel a far deeper sense of identification with their tribe than with their country. Tanzania is a land in which a foreign tourist can travel virtually anywhere—execept, at present, to the military zones in the south opposite the border with Mozambique—without encountering danger or hostility; curiosity and suspicion, perhaps, but almost never hostility. It can therefore come as quite a jolt to be reminded, as on an evening flight between Dar es Salaam and Nairobi, that Tanzania by night remains to this day a world of blackness broken only by the piercing orange dots of an occasional village fire. Julius Nyerere travels among his people almost constantly, sometimes for weeks at a time without a rest; he has probably spoken directly to as large a percentage of his countrymen as any head of state on earth. Yet, when he visited the isolated village of Mbulu three or four years ago, he was greeted with this astonishing question from an incredulous tribal elder: "Are you the *Mwalimu?* We thought the *Mwalimu* was a white man."

IN DECEMBER 1967 the government announced the results of a new census, the first since 1957. The census revealed that the population had reached 12,125,000, had increased by almost 35 percent in the previous decade, and would

274

double by the year 1992. More important, the census showed that the population was higher by 1,700,000 than the latest estimate published only three months earlier by the Government Statistical Department; the population, it turned out, was increasing at a rate of two and seven-tenths of one percent rather than the two and two-tenths of one percent that the government had estimated. This dismaying information showed that the country's economic progress since independence had been even more modest than the Tanzanians had realized. In 1964, based on a population estimate of 10,500,000, the government had calculated the per capita income at about $54. In actuality, the population at that time was approaching 12,000,000, so the true per capita income was considerably lower.

In his 1969 speech to the TANU National Executive committee, Nyerere recalled his government's progress in expanding secondary education: 7,100 children would enter secondary school that year, as compared with some 5,200 in 1964 at the beginning of the previous five-year plan. But in consequence, he added, the expansion of the primary school system had necessarily been neglected. "Indeed the census has revealed," he told the committee, "that the chances of a seven-year-old Tanzanian going to school are worse now than we thought they were when we drew up the first plan. At that time we used to say that about fifty percent of our children went to school. The much larger population of the country, which was revealed in the census figures, showed us that the actual percentage in 1964 was nearer forty-six percent, and even now, at the end of the plan period, only about forty-seven percent of our children can find a primary school place."

Moreover, said Nyerere, a large number of primary

school children were leaving school after only four years, and would probably forget most of what they had learned; so the government had decided to remove the Standard IV examination and increase the number of classes at Standards V, VI and VII to enable virtually every child who entered primary school to get a full seven years' primary education.

The delegates cheered, but Nyerere quickly told them the price of this decision: the further postponement of one of the country's most cherished goals. "The effect of giving priority to eliminating the Standard Four examination," he said, "is that by the end of the second five-year plan we will still only have places for about fifty-two percent of our eligible children in Standard One. But no child who enters primary school this year or afterwards will have to take that examination; they will go straight to Standard Seven. It will, however, now be 1989 before we are able to introduce universal primary education in Tanzania."

Later in the same speech, he turned to some of his favorite criticisms of the Tanzanian diet. "Those who have seen the Chinese working on the railway survey," he said, "or the Americans building the road to Zambia, will have noticed how our people get tired very quickly in comparison with the Chinese and the Americans. The reason is not that our people are lazy. It is that they do not get enough meat, eggs, fish and milk, or other protein foods even to feed their bodies properly. But, although this is well-known, if you suggest to our citizens that they should keep chickens, they will ask, 'Where shall we sell them?' Or: 'Where shall we sell the eggs?' These are very stupid questions ... And what of fruit? We act as if fruit is only good for Europeans or for children ..."

276

* * *

IN 1968, FOR THE FIRST TIME, the Tanzanian Parliament refused to pass a bill that the Nyerere government had sponsored. The bill was a proposal to grant gratuities—which could be used as retirement income—for ministers, regional commissioners and area commissioners. Nyerere, for whom the law already provided a pension, had recently been shocked by the illness of Solomon Eliufoo, his long-time Minister of Education, who had been paralyzed by a stroke; and this may have induced him to recommend the gratuities bill at that time. In any event, the proposal was angrily denounced by M.P.s as contrary to the spirit of the Arusha Declaration, and was soundly defeated.

When asked about it the following year, Nyerere said he had decided not to press the matter. "Parliament had a point. In the atmosphere of the Arusha Declaration, perhaps my timing was wrong. I had to bow to Parliament. But this matter can't be elevated to a principle. A person can work at developing the state for five or ten years; and when the time comes, he just goes. I don't see how we can justify this. The manager of the National Development Corporation can have a pension or a gratuity when he goes, but not a minister." Besides, he added, "it's not a principle in Tanzania, because *I* have a pension. I'm not a king, I'm paid in recognition of services. So how do you distinguish between me and the ministers?"

On that same day in late 1969, Nyerere commented on the government's proposals for a new marriage bill—a measure that was already being described in Nairobi and overseas as a "two wives for every Christian" bill. "As of now—to use an American expression—we recognize Christian marriages, Moslem marriages, tribal marriages, Hindu

277

marriages. We have always accepted that Moslems can have four wives, and tribalists can have ten or twenty. Tribal polygamy, Christian monogamy, both are recognized by the law as it is.

"Now we are saying, We are a secular state. Certain laws can be regarded as laws of the state, or of God, or the church. 'Thou shalt not kill' is also a law of the state, and we would take a man who violates it to court. But some church laws are not laws of the state. 'Thou shalt not eat meat on Fridays,' for example. Moslems don't take pork. But the state doesn't get involved in this. In Tanzania, marriage falls into this category. Islam says, 'You may have no more than four wives.' Christians can have only one wife. If a Moslem takes a fifth wife, we don't prosecute him. If a Christian takes two wives, we prosecute him. Why? The British introduced the system."

Under the existing laws, Nyerere continued, "if I [as a Christian] take a second wife, I can be prosecuted. How do we explain this? We accept that Moslems can have four wives, and tribalists can have ten or twenty. The police constable who arrests me may be a polygamist himself. The prosecutor may be a polygamist, as well as the magistrate who sentences me to four years at hard labor. This is ridiculous."

Under the new law, he explained, "we are abolishing the law of bigamy. Then the position will be exactly the same for everybody. Legally, a man may not take another wife; but we won't prosecute him if he does. It will be between himself and his wife and his God. We are not legislating morality. When two marry, it will be a monogamous marriage. But we are saying they can choose—they can agree—to change their status to polygamy."

278

The bill also provided that henceforth the traditional bride-price could be paid on a sort of installment plan. "We are saying," Nyerere explained, "that bride-price should not delay marriage. If it is not paid, this will not invalidate the marriage. It can be paid later. We hope the custom of bride-price will die. But no, we are not making it illegal." Implying that the tradition was still deeply rooted in tribal tradition, he added with a shiver, "After all, we have elections next year."

The elections of 1970 proved to be a reprise of the 1965 voting. Nyerere, again unopposed, was overwhelmingly re-elected—this time by 97 percent of the vote—to another five-year term. Two ministers, two junior ministers and a dozen backbenchers were defeated. Once again, parliamentary elections on Zanzibar were postponed.

In early 1971, in a series of emergency actions associated with the shock that followed the overthrow of Milton Obote in Uganda, the Tanzanian Parliament hastily passed a law that empowered the government to take over all rental property, both residential and commercial, that was valued at more than $14,500. The act required that compensation be paid only to owners of buildings which were less than ten years old, apparently on the theory that owners of older buildings had already received an adequate return on their investments. The measure was inspired by socialist motives —to end the "exploitation by landlords"; but since most of the property involved was owned by Asians, it had the effect of further reducing the wealth of the Asian community.

PROBABLY NYERERE's most controversial initiative in African affairs was his support of the Biafran rebel regime against the Nigerian government. Tanzania was the first African country to grant diplomatic recognition to Biafra; three others followed. Nyerere's position surprised many of his friends because it seemed to mark a break with the majority of orthodox African nationalists; it also seemed inconsistent with his customary support of the concept of national unity, whether it had been the unity of the Congo, Germany or Vietnam. In November 1969, a few months before the collapse of the Biafran rebellion, Nyerere explained why he had felt it necessary to side with the Ibo tribesmen against Nigeria.

"It was the Ibos who said, 'We can't have independence for Eastern Nigeria alone,' when they had been virtually offered it by the British in 1956. Now, the Ibos are not a bunch of damned fools. They're not socialists, but they are dynamic, intelligent and hard-working. They decided to cooperate with federation. They said, 'We can't have a Nigeria without the north.' The north, meanwhile, worked hard to control the west; the area that was raped was the west.

"The first coup was directed at the central government. Abubakar [Balewa] was a very good man, but it was a corrupt government. And when the West used to put up Nigeria as an example of African democracy, I was sick. *Every job had a price.*

"The first coup was an Ibo coup. I don't like this, but it happened. They killed, but very selectively; I think [General Yakubu] Gowon says twelve were killed. The second coup was anti-Ibo. Ibos were virtually expelled from the Federation. Thirty thousand were massacred, and two million became refugees from Nigeria. A Tanzanian landing at Lagos was asked, 'Are you an Ibo?' But the Ibos continued to search for a formula for a united Nigeria. Even after massacre and expulsion from the rest of Nigeria, they were still working for a united Nigeria. Even if no one else could see it, Africa should have seen it. Africa should have said to Nigeria, 'Look, what are you asking?'

"Africa didn't. Because the idea had been drummed into us that every African state has its own Biafra. This is stupid nonsense. It confuses the weakness of African governments with the weakness of African states, which is a very different thing; governments have fallen, but the states have remained. There is a desire to be together. I know there is a desire in Tanzania to create an East African nation. Are the Sukuma determined to establish a Sukuma nation? No. Or my little tribe of forty thousand, is it determined? No. I have said it before [to Africa]: You are learning the wrong lesson from Nigeria.

"After all, nations do break up. Senegal and Mali broke up. One of the touching moments of the 1963 OAU conference was when [Presidents Leopold] Senghor and Modibo Keita embraced. They can still become one; but they didn't kill one another."

It was then that he added his view of his own troubled Union: "If the Zanzibaris felt the Union was of no use to them, and broke away, and this was the genuine feeling of the Zanzibaris, I could not possibly kill Zanzibaris. If they came in freely, they can leave freely, we did not conquer Zanzibar. And if they remain, this must be borne of their own free choice."

AT THE TIME of Tanganyika's independence, Nyerere used to say to friends, "If only I can have three years"; "If I can have just five years." In 1969 he told a reporter he was torn between staying in office to carry out his own ideas and retiring in order to encourage new leadership. In 1970, during a visit to one of the hundreds of new *ujamaa* co-operative villages, he promised the local farmers that he would retire to such a settlement someday to live in peace and to write his memoirs.

Part of the burden that Nyerere carries—and he shares it with the continent's other leaders—is that he has seen too many of Africa's best men killed. Among the ones he knew and respected were Sylvanus Olympio of Togo and Sir Abubakar Balewa of Nigeria. Another was Tom Mboya, Kenya's brilliant young Minister of Planning and Development, who was shot to death in a Nairobi street in 1969 under circumstances that have never been fully explained; Nyerere trusted him and counted on his wisdom and co-operation in every round of conferences concerning the East African Community. Still another was Eduardo Mondlane, the president of FRELIMO, the Mozambican Liberation Front, who was killed in Dar es Salaam in early 1969. All four men were assassinated, either by their countries' enemies or their own. To be an African leader in this era is to be reminded again and again of one's vulnerability.

Those who believe that Nyerere would genuinely like to retire point out that he once resigned as prime minister without warning because he wanted to rebuild the party. It is difficult to imagine, however, that he would choose to retire at this stage of Tanzania's history. His presence is essential to the survival of the Union; the Zanzibaris are not always swayed by his powers of persuasion, but they would certainly be less susceptible to anybody else's.

As the 1970 elections indicated, Nyerere's political strength does not seem to have been greatly affected, if at

all, by the defection of Kambona or by the 1970 treason
trial. As of early 1971, Kambona was still in London, apparently living either on his savings or on revenues from
unknown sources, obsessively mailing Christmas cards to
Members of the Tanzanian Parliament and sending occasional letters of condolence to persons who have been dismissed by the Tanzanian government.

On Zanzibar, a general air of lawlessness prevailed.
The four forced marriages of Persian girls to Revolutionary Council members remained in effect, but no additional
ones had taken place following the widespread protests from
mainland Tanzania and overseas. The executions of Kassim Hanga and Othman Shariff were still unconfirmed but,
as a European who knew both men said in late 1970, "I
haven't talked to anybody who believes they are alive." In
May 1971, in still another case, the Zanzibaris condemned
nineteen more men to death for alleged plotting.

When an assistant or an institution falters, Nyerere's
solution is to step up his own dialogue with the people; as
if, by traveling more and more, he can inspire more and
more *ujamaa* communities and self-help projects, higher
and higher cotton and tobacco yields, can fire the people's
enthusiasm all by himself—and to a great extent he has
done just that. His aim, often expressed, is to block somehow the rapid rise of the elite—the ambitious politicians,
the university graduates returning from overseas, the prosperous men of the towns—and to address his government
to the primary task of advancing the lives of the peasant
majority.

About this rigidly idealistic scheme there is a suggestion of futility. It is hard to imagine that the fight
against the creation of an elite will not be lost; that there

283

will not be, in the end, a privileged class of university graduates who earn twenty or thirty times as much as peasant farmers. Presumably Nyerere disagrees; in any case he perseveres. Years ago, he gave an eloquent talk to the schoolchildren of Tabora in which he said again and again, "We must run while they walk": Africa must run as fast as it can to catch up with the modern world. He knew full well—and his Arusha Declaration underscored this fact—that the race was anything but a fair contest, was indeed already lost: the developed world was running faster and faster, while the developing world was falling further and further behind. No matter, Nyerere says, in a thousand variations; we must move on as best we can.

TANZANIANS SOMETIMES COMPLAIN that they are badly misreported by the overseas press, and often they are right. Only one Western news organization, Reuters, maintains a staff correspondent in Dar es Salaam; the others cover Tanzania from Nairobi, Kenya, if not from Europe. The Tanzanians are sensitive to the fact that, as a rule, the Nairobi-based correspondents visit their country only once or twice a year; they also suspect that the correspondents are overly influenced by the Kenyans and particularly by the British community of Kenya, which tends to regard Tanzania as socialist, pro-Chinese, hotheaded and somehow a bit threatening.

The problem is complicated by the situation on Zanzibar. Western readers find it hard to comprehend that when, for instance, Abeid Karume declares that there shall be no elections on Zanzibar for fifty years, his statement has no relation to the policies of the Union government to which he theoretically owes allegiance. There is, however, another news problem, perhaps common to every neglected country in the world but particularly severe in the case of Tanzania. What is important about Tanzania is the imaginative and often experimental way in which Nyerere's government is trying to solve African problems—a difficult subject to explain in a newspaper or television report.

On the other hand, a land where human beings pretend to be lionmen and M.P.s at Question Time ask whether mermaids exist is obviously full of oddities that make extraordinary stories. Sometimes a minister or a regional commissioner or some lesser official will launch a campaign, often on his own initiative—and suddenly, from reading the overseas papers, it seems as if the whole of Tanzania is engaged in a frenzy of fighting mini-skirts, hair straighteners, bleaches and other threats to "Tanzania's culture and the aims of the Arusha Declaration"; or forcing the noble Masai to discard their blankets and ochre and nakedness in favor of khaki trousers and shirts.

A more legitimate but greatly exaggerated story dealt with the 1967 deportation drive by Home Affairs Minister Lawi Sijaona against the country's Indian aliens, which coincided with similar but more serious anti-Asian campaigns in Kenya and Uganda. Some three hundred Asian residents were ordered to leave the country, but most of the deportation orders were later canceled. Often Nyerere contributes to the ambiguity by remaining aloof—as in the case of the youth league's campaign against mini-skirts—until the phenomenon plays itself out.

A further reason for misunderstanding is that, even at close range, Tanzanian politics remain ultimately incomprehensible to outsiders. Decisions are made in the secrecy of party councils; disagreements become publicly known

285

months or even years after the fact. One reason for the secrecy may be racial pride: to keep family quarrels obscured from a hostile world. Certainly there is a racial undertone to all sorts of undertakings. A European acquaintance once suggested to Nyerere that he should switch the job assignments of two British employees of the Tanzanian government. Nyerere stared in mocking disbelief. "A *white face* for a *white face?*" he demanded jubilantly, rolling his eyes in wonder. "Ahhh, my friend, how little you understand African politics."

AMERICAN TOURISM IN EAST AFRICA is on the increase, but not one tourist in fifty is as interested in Africa's people as in its wildlife. Indeed, the American public seems to accord to Tanzania about as much attention as it gives to any other subject that must be both defined and pronounced. A Tanzanian businessmen once remarked that when he visits the U.S., he is frequently asked, "*Where?* Is that one of those places that changed its name?"

The indifference may be based in part on a disenchantment with Africa since 1960: the spawning of so many truculent and unviable little states; the ravaging wars of the Congo and Nigeria. But it has occurred at a time when the position of the U.S. is approaching a point of crisis in Africa, or at least in those countries of Africa that are not prepared to come to terms with the white south. In its relations with these countries, the U.S. has several handicaps: its substantial private investment in South Africa; its NATO connection with Portugal and its close ties with the other present and former colonial powers; its own race problem; and—increasingly, in the late sixties—its disastrous adventure in Vietnam. If there is any hopeful sign at all, it may be the prospect that the American black community may someday exercise the sort of influence on U.S. policy in Africa that American Jews exert at present on Middle East policy; but that day is by no means imminent.

The British relationship with Tanzania underwent another crisis in late 1970 when the Conservative government of Prime Minister Edward Heath appeared to have decided to resume arms sales to South Africa. Along with Zambia and Uganda, Tanzania threatened to leave the Commonwealth if the sales took place. After talking with Heath in London, Nyerere described the British attitude as "almost a psychological desire to defy; it's the nearest thing you can think of to the Suez mood." Back in Dar es Salaam, he gibed at the British by attributing to them the sort of thin-skinned protests often associated with young African states: " 'Why can't we make decisions for ourselves? Are we not independent like anyone else? Do we have to be pushed around by little countries like Tanzania?' " At the Commonwealth Prime Ministers' Conference in Singapore in January 1971, the question of arms sales was referred to a special eight-nation committee for further study, thereby postponing but hardly settling the Commonwealth dispute.

The Chinese, on the other hand, have steadily strengthened their position in Tanzania since 1965. The primary reason for their huge aid commitment to Tanzania and Zambia is still uncertain. Some Western observers have suggested that, for one thing, the Chinese would like to acquire down-range facilities for the testing of intercontinental ballistic missiles launched from the Asian mainland. Many of Nyerere's Western friends believe, however, that if he has demonstrated anything at all during Tanzania's first decade of independence, it is that neither his country's nonalignment policy nor anything else is for sale, not even for the price of a railroad; and that the Chinese must, to some extent, realize this.

Some Western diplomats have pointed out that if a military build-up in Tanzania should lead eventually to a serious stage of fighting with the Portuguese, backed by the South Africans, Tanzania could find itself dangerously dependent upon the Chinese, and on whatever terms the Chinese might choose to offer.

However that may be, it seems clear that the Chinese are in the process of making a long-range commitment to Africa. The 1965 policy article of Lin Piao, the Vice-Chairman of the Chinese Communist party and Mao Tse-tung's heir apparent, envisioned the encirclement of the "cities of the world" by the "countryside of the world," and thus of the advanced countries by the non-advanced. On such a scale, the Africans have a natural affinity with the Chinese. Through the Tanzam railway, the Chinese are seeking to demonstrate not only the quality of their technology but their willingness to build a large development project that the rich Western countries refused to undertake. Presumably the Chinese are also calculating that the Western nations will continue to withdraw their aid and abdicate their influence; that the white countries will draw together when the crisis comes in southern Africa, as it surely will; and that the countless individual relationships that bind the men and institutions of Tanzania and its neighbors with those of Britain and, to a lesser extent, America will not survive beyond the next twenty or thirty years.

Such a view presupposes that the Tanzam railway will be completed successfully and that the Chinese will manage

288

at last to solve their own economic problems at home. And indeed, if the Western nations continue to deal half-heartedly and unresponsively with the problems of African development, there may be a terrible inevitability about such a calculation.

AT THE END OF A LONG VISIT to Dar es Salaam, an American visitor once asked Nyerere what sort of country he would want Tanzania to be in twenty years' time. Both he and his press secretary of that period, George Rockey, burst out laughing; in terms of the crisis of the moment, whatever it may have been, the question seemed impossibly remote. Nevertheless, as usual, he tried to answer. "Twenty years from now I hope there won't be a Tanzania," he said. "If there is not an *Africa*, then at least I hope there will be an East Africa. But if we have failed to use African nationalism to destroy our nationalism; if we have failed to take another step toward Pan-Africanism during that period; we should at least have a Tanzania that is very committed to Pan-Africanism itself. And by that time we should have a society of which the people are very proud; we should really have built a classless society. So, if there should still be a Tanzania twenty years from now, I hope it will be a classless society very committed to an African goal."

Several years later, toward the end of 1969, he was asked the same question, and this time he answered it somewhat differently. "I still believe history has assigned Tanzania to us," he said. "This is our piece, a piece we do for Africa. The future of the African is in Africa. We could get so bogged down in Tanzania that we lose sight of Africa. But even now in Africa, we are already more identified with Africa than with Tanzania. Our problems are African problems. This is more true than on any other continent; African problems are really very African. We can only join this march of humanity as Africans; we have no other choice.

"Recently I visited Canada and Sweden. Well, the more knowledgeable people I met knew I was from Tanzania. But really, to them I was just an African. And rightly so. The real revolution we have to work out is African."

(16)

A FEW WEEKS AFTER his Tabora trip in 1966, Julius Nyerere paid a five-day visit to Kilimanjaro region, in the
northeast of Tanzania. During the earlier trip he had often
praised the hard-working Chagga who had gotten rich by
growing coffee on the slopes of Mount Kilimanjaro, and he
had urged the people of Tabora to emulate them. Now, in
Chaggaland, he took a different tack. "Ah, the Chagga are
verrry conservative," he said, jubilantly chiding Miss Lucy
Lameck, who represented the region in Parliament and was
a junior minister in his government. "The Chagga want us
to expand the mountain," he continued, "and expanding
the mountain is very expensive." "They *have* been conservative, *Mwalimu*," Miss Lameck replied defensively, "but
they are changing." Nyerere's point, which was reasonable
but perhaps not realistic, was that the Chagga should begin
to move from their over-populated mountain to less thickly
settled places in Tanzania. "I leave you with two ideas," he
said at one stop. "Kilimanjaro region has a big population—five hundred thousand, the size of Gabon—and it is
growing by ten thousand a year. If we want to maintain
this population, we must increase the yields per acre. Secondly, Tanzania is a big country. Everybody can move. The
Rufiji basin, for instance, is as large as Great Britain, and
very fertile. Our country is different from most others: the
land belongs to all the people. Any Tanzanian can live anywhere in Tanzania."

291

One morning as his procession drove through the cool, lush, incredibly green countryside, with the great mountain looming above, the Chagga turned out by the tens of thousands to cheer him and toss flowers. "Well, you have seen our population explosion," Nyerere told a visitor, laughing. "I never saw so many Chagga babies in my life." When he stopped at a mission station, the people gave him two sheep, one for himself and one for his wife. "*Mwalimu,* you are the shepherd," said one, "and we give you the sheep." As Nyerere was about to return to his car, a young man stepped forward and, like a cheerleader in a frenzy, stood directly in front of the President and began to shout, "Secondary school! Secondary school! If you will allow us, sir, we shall build a secondary school!"

This, it soon became clear, was the main concern of all the Chagga. "You see," Ackland Mhina, the President's secretary, explained to a foreign visitor, "the problem of this region is the problem of progress. In the Central region, an area secretary would have to convince a parent to send a child to school. But here the parent has already sent his children to school, and wants higher schooling for them."

Over and over, at every meeting, a local TANU official would lead the crowd in a litany of Tanzanian politics.

Chairman: *Uhuru!*
Crowd: *Uhuru!*
Chairman: *Uhuru na* Nyerere!
Crowd: *Uhuru na* Nyerere!
Chairman: *Uhuru na* TANU!
Crowd: *Uhuru na* TANU!

And so on. As each visitor from Dar es Salaam was introduced, he would greet the crowd by shouting, "*Uhuru na* Nyerere" or "*Uhuru na kazi,*" freedom and work, the

292

TANU motto. At such meetings, Nyerere made it clear that the villagers could not hope for any more secondary schools in the near future. "It is a dream," he would say, "to think that all children who have attained Standard Seven can expect to have a secondary education. We could build more schools if we could produce more, but we can't produce more if we all stay in Kilimanjaro."

Then he would tell the people about his stop at Vudee village two days earlier. Vudee lies in the Usambara mountains, and for three years the villagers of Vudee had been engaged in the arduous and painfully slow task of chipping a road to their village out of rock. "They get firewood," Ackland Mhina explained. "They light a fire, and when the rock becomes hot, they pour buckets of cold water, and this makes the rock break." Nyerere urged the Chagga to work as hard as the people of Vudee; at Vudee he had asked the villagers to work as hard as the Chinese and had promised to send one of them, a Mr. Marigani, to China to see how hard the Chinese worked to improve their lives.

In the evening, at the presidential lodge in Moshi, Nyerere remarked, "What they need here is piped water and electricity. Right now many could afford to buy electricity if it were available." When asked how long it would take to provide it, he replied, "Maybe eternity," with that ironic shiver of his. "We have no money." Grinning, he added, "If it wasn't for Vietnam, maybe I could ask for a Marshall plan."

THE FOLLOWING MORNING Nyerere answered questions at two separate meetings at the Kawenzi secondary school. He sat perched on a sort of throne chair, leaning his chin on his ebony stick. The first meeting was for adults and, like

293

the one at Tabora a few weeks earlier, it dealt with purely practical matters. "Why did the government put a duty on copper spray?" a farmer asked. Nyerere said he didn't know but would look into it.

An hour later Nyerere spoke to the students of the Kawenzi school, and the meeting was very lively. "Shouldn't the people of Rhodesia try the passive-resistance techniques of Gandhi?" a girl asked. Nyerere said he doubted it. "Whether these techniques will work or not depends on the situation. Suppose my father was a doctor, and he refused to treat a patient, and in protest I refused to eat. Then it might work. On the second or third day, my father might agree to treat the patient. But in Rhodesia, [Ian] Smith might be happy to have the African population reduced."

"Sir," a boy asked, "it sometimes happens that you recognize new governments and you don't tell us whether you have recognized them. For example, the Congo. We do not know your stand on the Congo, and yet I understand you have visited there recently."

"What further proof do you want," Nyerere said, "that I recognize the Congolese government?"

"Why is it that in Britain there are no African Members of Parliament," asked another, "while in Tanzania we have Europeans in Parliament? Why shouldn't we do away with the white members and give their seats to the people of Tanzania?" The question drew a burst of laughter because —as Mhina explained later—it implied that Tanzania should use Britain as a model of democracy. Nyerere answered angrily, "One of the reasons for rejecting the British system is their discrimination, and one of the rules of TANU is that all men are our brothers, regardless of color. That is what we have been fighting for."

One boy asked, "What happens to us, with our education, when we go back to our home areas?" Nyerere replied sharply, "What do you expect is going to happen to you? In Tanzania, ninety-six percent of the people live on the land and farm it. Therefore, ninety-six percent must go to the land where the people are, and four percent can go to the cities. In America it is almost exactly the opposite, so in America most graduates can expect to go to the cities."

AT THE PRESIDENTIAL LODGE that night, Nyerere was visited by a United Nations agricultural expert, a heavy-set Swede, who invited him to visit the U.N.'s ten-thousand-acre experimental farm that might someday accommodate ten thousand cotton growers. "Fine," Nyerere said. "I am a very big cotton man. When can I see it? Tomorrow?" He turned to his secretary. "No? Tomorrow is too full? When must I be back in Dar es Salaam? When am I going to Nachingwea?" Turning back to his visitor, Nyerere said, "No. Look, brother. Friday. Tomorrow they will rush us too much."

On Friday morning, a few hours after he had planned to fly back to Dar es Salaam, Nyerere was met at the cotton farm by the U.N. man, who introduced him to an aide. "Did you meet Mohamed Abdul, from the UAR?" "I met Mohamed," Nyerere said. "Mohamed, we should trade. Half a million of our people for half a million of yours who know about irrigating. That would do it, eh?"

As he walked through the irrigation scheme, Nyerere seemed preoccupied and said little. At one point, when someone mentioned the shortness of time, he murmured, almost to himself, "Plenty of time. Time is no problem. Money is the problem." At the end of the tour, the U.N. man told him, "When you come back in October, it will all be green. Thank you for encouraging us, sir."

"I'll be back, I'll be back," Nyerere said. "I don't know who is encouraging who."